Writer's Choice

GRAMMAR
WORKBOOK

8

McGraw-Hill

New York, New York   Columbus, Ohio   Woodland Hills, California   Peoria, Illinois

Glencoe/McGraw-Hill

A Division of The **McGraw·Hill** *Companies*

Imprint 2000

Printed in the United States of America.

Send all inquiries to:
Glencoe/McGraw-Hill
8787 Orion Place
Columbus, Ohio 43240-4027

ISBN 0-02-635149-8 (Student Edition)
Writer's Choice Grammar Workbook 8

11 12 13 14   024   03 02 01 00

Contents

*H*andbook of Definitions and Rules

SUBJECTS AND PREDICATES

1. The **simple subject** is the key noun or pronoun that tells what the sentence is about. A **compound subject** is made up of two or more simple subjects that are joined by a conjunction and have the same verb.
   The **lantern** glows.   **Moths** and **bugs** fly nearby.

2. The **simple predicate** is the verb or verb phrase that expresses the essential thought about the subject of the sentence. A **compound predicate** is made up of two or more verbs or verb phrases that are joined by a conjunction and have the same subject.
   Rachel **jogged** down the hill.
   Pete **stretched** and **exercised** for an hour.

3. The **complete subject** consists of the simple subject and all the words that modify it.
   Golden curly hair framed the child's face.
   The soft glow of sunset made her happy.

4. The **complete predicate** consists of the simple predicate and all the words that modify it or complete its meaning.
   Lindy **ate a delicious muffin for breakfast.**
   The apple muffin **also contained raisins.**

5. Usually the subject comes before the predicate in a sentence. In inverted sentences, all or part of the predicate precedes the subject.
   (You) Wait for me at the corner. (request)
   Through the toys **raced** the **children.** (inverted)
   Is the **teacher** feeling better? (question)
   There **are seats** in the first row.

PARTS OF SPEECH

Nouns

1. A **singular noun** is a word that names one person, place, thing, or idea.
   aunt   meadow   pencil   friendship

   A **plural noun** names more than one person, place, thing, or idea.
   aunts   meadows   pencils   friendships

2. To help you determine whether a word in a sentence is a noun, try adding it to the following sentences. Nouns will fit in at least one of these sentences:
   He said something about _____.   I know something about a(n) _____.
   He said something about **aunts.**   I know something about a **meadow.**

3. A **common noun** names a general class of people, places, things, or ideas.
   sailor   city   holiday   music

   A **proper noun** names a particular person, place, thing, event, or idea. Proper nouns are always capitalized.
   Captain **A**hab   **R**ome   **M**emorial **D**ay   *Treasure Island*

4. A **concrete noun** names an object that occupies space or that can be recognized by any of the senses.

    leaf   melody   desk   aroma

    An **abstract noun** names an idea, a quality, or a characteristic.

    loyalty   honesty   democracy   friendship

5. A **collective noun** names a group. When the collective noun refers to the group as a whole, it is singular. When it refers to the individual group members, the collective noun is plural.

    The **family** eats dinner together every night. (singular)
    The **council** vote as they wish on the pay increase. (plural)

6. A **possessive noun** shows possession, ownership, or the relationship between two nouns.

    Monica's book   the **rabbit's** ears   the **hamster's** cage

Verbs

1. A **verb** is a word that expresses action or a state of being and is necessary to make a statement. A verb will fit one or more of these sentences:

    He _____.   We _____.   She _____ it.
    He **knows.**   We **walk.**   She **sees** it.

2. An **action verb** tells what someone or something does. The two types of action verbs are transitive and intransitive. A **transitive verb** is followed by a word or words—called the direct object—that answer the question *what?* or *whom?* An **intransitive verb** is not followed by a word that answers *what?* or *whom?*

    Transitive: The tourists **saw** the ruins.   The janitor **washed** the window.
    Intransitive: Owls **hooted** during the night.   The children **played** noisily.

3. An **indirect object** receives what the direct object names.

    Marcy sent **her brother** a present.

4. A **linking verb** links, or joins, the subject of a sentence with an adjective or a noun.

    The trucks **were** red. (adjective)
    She **became** an excellent swimmer. (noun)

5. A **verb phrase** consists of a main verb and all its auxiliary, or helping, verbs.

    We **had been told** of his arrival.
    They **are listening** to a symphony.

6. Verbs have four **principal parts** or forms: base, past, present participle, and past participle.

    Base: I **talk.**   Present Participle: I am **talking.**
    Past: I **talked.**   Past Participle: I have **talked.**

    Regular verbs form the past and past participle by adding *-ed* to the base.

7. **Irregular verbs** form the past and past participle in other ways.

PRINCIPAL PARTS OF IRREGULAR VERBS

Base Form	Past Form	Past Participle	Base Form	Past Form	Past Participle
be	was, were	been	lead	led	led
beat	beat	beaten	lend	lent	lent
become	became	become	let	let	let
begin	began	begun	lie	lay	lain
bite	bit	bitten *or* bit	lose	lost	lost
blow	blew	blown	put	put	put
break	broke	broken	ride	rode	ridden
bring	brought	brought	ring	rang	rung
catch	caught	caught	rise	rose	risen
choose	chose	chosen	run	ran	run
come	came	come	say	said	said
do	did	done	see	saw	seen
draw	drew	drawn	set	set	set
drink	drank	drunk	shrink	shrank *or* shrunk	shrunk *or* shrunken
drive	drove	driven			
eat	ate	eaten	sing	sang	sung
fall	fell	fallen	sit	sat	sat
feel	felt	felt	speak	spoke	spoken
find	found	found	spring	sprang *or* sprung	sprung
fly	flew	flown			
freeze	froze	frozen	steal	stole	stolen
get	got	got *or* gotten	swim	swam	swum
give	gave	given	take	took	taken
go	went	gone	tear	tore	torn
grow	grew	grown	tell	told	told
hang	hung	hung	think	thought	thought
hang	hanged	hanged	throw	threw	thrown
have	had	had	wear	wore	worn
know	knew	known	win	won	won
lay	laid	laid	write	wrote	written

8. The principal parts are used to form six verb tenses. The **tense** of a verb expresses time.

Simple Tenses
Present Tense: She **speaks.** (present or habitual action)
Past Tense: She **spoke.** (action completed in the past)
Future Tense: She **will speak.** (action to be done in the future)

Perfect Tenses
Present Perfect Tense: She **has spoken.** (action just done or still in effect)
Past Perfect Tense: She **had spoken.** (action completed before some other past action)
Future Perfect Tense: She **will have spoken.** (action to be completed before some future time)

9. **Progressive forms** of verbs are made up of a form of *be* and a present participle and express a continuing action. **Emphatic forms** are made up of a form of *do* and a base form and add emphasis or ask questions.
   Progressive: Marla **is babysitting.**   The toddlers **have been napping** for an hour.
   Emphatic: They **do prefer** beef to pork.
                 We **did ask** for a quiet table.

10. The **voice** of a verb shows whether the subject performs the action or receives the action of the verb. A sentence is in the **active voice** when the subject performs the action. A sentence is in the **passive voice** when the subject receives the action of the verb.
    The robin **ate** the worm. (active)
    The worm **was eaten** by the robin. (passive)

Pronouns

1. A **pronoun** takes the place of a noun, a group of words acting as a noun, or another pronoun.

2. A **personal pronoun** refers to a specific person or thing. **First-person** personal pronouns refer to the speaker, **second-person** pronouns refer to the one spoken to, and **third-person** pronouns refer to the one spoken about.

	Singular	Plural
First Person	I, me, my, mine	we, us, our, ours
Second Person	you, your, yours	you, your, yours
Third Person	he, she, it, him, her, his, hers, its	they, them, their, theirs

3. A **reflexive pronoun** refers to the subject of the sentence. An **intensive pronoun** adds emphasis to a noun or another pronoun. A **demonstrative pronoun** points out specific persons, places, things, or ideas.
   Reflexive: **Nikki** prepares **himself** for the day-long hike.
   Intensive: **Nikki himself** prepares for the day-long hike.
   Demonstrative: **That** was a good movie! **These** are the files you wanted.

4. An **interrogative pronoun** is used to form questions. A **relative pronoun** is used to introduce a subordinate clause. An **indefinite pronoun** refers to persons, places, or things in a more general way than a personal pronoun does.
   Interrogative: **Whose** are these?   **Which** did you prefer?
   Relative: The bread **that** we tasted was whole wheat.
   Indefinite: **Someone** has already told them. **Everyone** agrees on the answer.

5. Use the subject form of a personal pronoun when it is used as a subject or when it follows a linking verb.
   He writes stories.   Are **they** ready?   It is **I**. (after linking verb)

6. Use the object form of a personal pronoun when it is an object.
   Mrs. Cleary called **us**. (direct object)   Stephen offered **us** a ride. (indirect object)
   Sara will go with **us**. (object of preposition)

7. Use a **possessive pronoun** to replace a possessive noun. Never use an apostrophe in a possessive personal pronoun.
   Their science experiment is just like **ours**.

8. When a pronoun is followed by an appositive, use the subject pronoun if the appositive is the subject. Use the object pronoun if the appositive is an object. To test whether the pronoun is correct, read the sentence without the appositive.
We eighth-graders would like to thank you.
The success of **us** geometry students is due to Ms. Marcia.

9. In incomplete comparisons, choose the pronoun that you would use if the missing words were fully expressed.
Harris can play scales faster than **I** (can).
It is worth more to you than (it is to) **me**.

10. In questions use *who* for subjects and *whom* for objects.
Who wants another story?
Whom will the class choose as treasurer?

In subordinate clauses use *who* and *whoever* as subjects and after linking verbs, and use *whom* and *whomever* as objects.
These souvenirs are for **whoever** wants to pay the price.
The manager will train **whomever** the president hires.

11. An **antecedent** is the word or group of words to which a pronoun refers or that a pronoun replaces. All pronouns must agree with their antecedents in number, gender, and person.
Marco's **sister** spent **her** vacation in San Diego.
The huge old **trees** held **their** own against the storm.

12. Make sure that the antecedent of a pronoun is clearly stated.
UNCLEAR: Mrs. Cardonal baked cookies with her daughters, hoping to sell **them** at the bake sale.
CLEAR: Mrs. Cardonal baked cookies with her daughters, hoping to sell **the cookies** at the bake sale.
UNCLEAR: If you don't tie the balloon to the stroller, **it** will blow away.
CLEAR: If you don't tie the balloon to the stroller, **the balloon** will blow away.

Adjectives

1. An **adjective** modifies, or describes, a noun or pronoun by providing more information or giving a specific detail.
The **smooth** surface of the lake gleamed.
Frosty trees glistened in the sun.

2. Most adjectives will fit this sentence:
The _____ one seems very _____.
The **handmade** one seems very **colorful**.

3. **Articles** are the adjectives *a, an,* and *the.* Articles do not meet the preceding test for adjectives.

4. A **proper adjective** is formed from a proper noun and begins with a capital letter.
Tricia admired the **Scottish** sweaters.
Our **Mexican** vacation was memorable.

5. The comparative form of an adjective compares two things or people. The superlative form compares more than two things or people. Form the comparative by adding -er or combining with *more* or *less*. Form the superlative by adding -est or combining with *most* or *least*.

POSITIVE	COMPARATIVE	SUPERLATIVE
slow	slower	slowest
charming	more charming	most charming

6. Some adjectives have irregular comparative forms.

POSITIVE:	good, well	bad	far	many, much	little
COMPARATIVE:	better	worse	farther	more	less
SUPERLATIVE:	best	worst	farthest	most	least

Adverbs

1. An **adverb** modifies a verb, an adjective, or another adverb. Adverbs tell *how, where, when,* or *to what extent*.
   The cat walked **quietly.** (how)
   She **seldom** misses a deadline. (when)
   The player moved **forward.** (where)
   The band was **almost** late. (to what extent)

2. Many adverbs fit these sentences:
   She thinks _____. She thinks _____ fast. She _____ thinks fast.
   She thinks **quickly.** She thinks **unusually** fast. She **seldom** thinks fast.

3. The comparative form of an adverb compares two actions. The superlative form compares more than two actions. For shorter adverbs add -er or -est to form the comparative or superlative. For most adverbs, add *more* or *most* or *less* or *least* to form the comparative or superlative.
   We walked **faster** than before.
   They listened **most carefully** to the final speaker.

4. Avoid **double negatives**, which are two negative words in the same clause.
   INCORRECT: I have not seen no stray cats.
   CORRECT: I have not seen any stray cats.

Prepositions, Conjunctions, and Interjections

1. A **preposition** shows the relationship of a noun or a pronoun to some other word. A **compound preposition** is made up of more than one word.
   The trees **near** our house provide plenty **of** shade.
   The schools were closed **because of** snow.

2. Common prepositions include these: *about, above, according to, across, after, against, along, among, around, as, at, because of, before, behind, below, beneath, beside, besides, between, beyond, but, by, concerning, down, during, except, for, from, in, inside, in spite of, into, like, near, of, off, on, out, outside, over, past, round, since, through, till, to, toward, under, underneath, until, up, upon, with, within, without.*

3. A **conjunction** is a word that joins single words or groups of words. A **coordinating conjunction** joins words or groups of words that have equal grammatical weight. **Correlative conjunctions** work in pairs to join words and groups of words of equal weight. A **subordinating conjunction** joins two clauses in such a way as to make one grammatically dependent on the other.

I want to visit the art gallery **and** the museum. (coordinating)
Both left **and** right turns were impossible in the traffic. (correlative)
We go to the park **whenever** Mom lets us. (subordinating)

COMMON CONJUCTIONS

Coordinating:	and	but	for	nor	or	so	yet

Correlative:	both...and	neither...nor	whether...or
	either...or	not only...but also	

Subordinating:	after	as though	since	when
	although	because	so that	whenever
	as	before	than	where
	as if	even though	though	wherever
	as long as	if	unless	whether
	as soon as	in order that	until	while

4. A **conjunctive adverb** clarifies a relationship.
Frank loved the old maple tree; **nevertheless,** he disliked raking its leaves.

5. An **interjection** is an unrelated word or phrase that expresses emotion or strong feeling.
Look, there are two cardinals at the feeder.   **Good grief!** Are you kidding?

CLAUSES AND COMPLEX SENTENCES

1. A **clause** is a group of words that has a subject and a predicate and is used as a sentence or a part of a sentence. There are two types of clauses: main and subordinate. A **main clause** has a subject and a predicate and can stand alone as a sentence. A **subordinate clause** has a subject and a predicate, but it cannot stand alone as a sentence.
                         main   sub.
She became a veterinarian because she loves animals.

2. There are three types of subordinate clauses: adjective, adverb, and noun.

   a. An **adjective clause** is a subordinate clause that modifies a noun or pronoun.
   The wrens **that built a nest in the backyard** are now raising their young.

   b. An **adverb clause** is a subordinate clause that often modifies the verb in the main clause of the sentence. It tells *when, where, how, why,* or *under what conditions.*
   Before they got out, the goats broke the fence in several places.

   c. A **noun clause** is a subordinate clause used as a noun.
   Whatever we do will have to please everyone. (subject)
   The prize goes to **whoever can keep the squirrels away from the feeder.** (object of preposition)

3. Main and subordinate clauses can form several types of sentences. A **simple sentence** has only one main clause and no subordinate clauses. A **compound sentence** has two or more main clauses. A **complex sentence** has at least one main clause and one or more subordinate clauses.

                              main

Simple: The apples fell off the tree.

                   main   main

Compound: The dancers bowed, and the audience clapped.

                        sub.   main

Complex: Because they turn to face the sun, these flowers are called sunflowers.

4. A sentence that makes a statement is classified as a **declarative sentence.**
My dad's favorite horses are buckskins.

An **imperative sentence** gives a command or makes a request.
Please close the door on your way out.

An **interrogative sentence** asks a question.
When will the mail carrier arrive?

An **exclamatory sentence** expresses strong emotion.
Watch out!
What a view that is!

Phrases

1. A **phrase** is a group of words that acts in a sentence as a single part of speech.

2. A **prepositional phrase** is a group of words that begins with a preposition and ends with a noun or pronoun, which is called the **object of the preposition**. A prepositional phrase can act as an adjective or an adverb.
The house **on the hill** is white. (modifies the noun *house*)
Everyone **in the house** heard the storm. (modifies the pronoun *everyone*)
The geese flew **toward warmer weather.** (modifies the verb *flew*)

3. An **appositive** is a noun or pronoun that is placed next to another noun or pronoun to identify it or give more information about it. An **appositive phrase** is an appositive plus its modifiers.
Our sister **Myra** is home from college. Her college, **Purdue University,** is in Indiana.

4. A **verbal** is a verb form that functions in a sentence as a noun, an adjective, or an adverb. A **verbal phrase** is a verbal and other words that complete its meaning.

   a. A **participle** is a verbal that functions as an adjective. Present participles end in *-ing*. Past participles usually end in *-ed*.
   The **squeaking** floor board gave me away.   The **twisted** tree was ancient.

   b. A **participial phrase** contains a participle and other words that complete its meaning.
   Moving quickly across the room, the baby crawled toward her mother.

c. A **gerund** is a verbal that ends in *-ing*. It is used in the same way a noun is used.
Sailing is a traditional vacation activity for the Andersons.

d. A **gerund phrase** is a gerund plus any complements or modifiers.
Walking to school is common for many school children.

e. An **infinitive** is a verbal formed from the word *to* and the base form of a verb. It is often used as a noun. Because an infinitive acts as a noun, it may be the subject of a sentence or the direct object of an action verb.
To sing can be uplifting. (infinitive as subject)
Babies first learn **to babble**. (infinitive as direct object)

f. An **infinitive phrase** contains an infinitive plus any complements or modifiers.
The flight attendants prepared **to feed the hungry passengers**.

SUBJECT-VERB AGREEMENT

1. A verb must agree with its subject in person and number.
   The kangaroo **jumps**. (singular)   The kangaroos **jump**. (plural)
   She **is leaping**. (singular)   They **are leaping**. (plural)

2. In **inverted sentences** the subject follows the verb. The sentence may begin with a prepositional phrase, the word *there* or *here*, or a form of *do*.
   Into the pond **dove** the *children*.
   Does a *bird* **have** a sense of smell?
   There **is** a *squeak* in that third stair.

3. Do not mistake a word in a prepositional phrase for the subject.
   The **glass** in the window **is** streaked. (The singular verb *is* agrees with the subject, *glass*.)

4. A title is always singular, even if nouns in the title are plural.
   ***Instant World Facts* is** a helpful reference book.

5. Subjects combined with *and* or *both* need a plural verb unless the parts are of a whole unit. When compound subjects are joined with *or* or *nor*, the verb agrees with the subject listed last.
   Canterbury and Coventry have famous cathedrals.
   A **bagel and cream cheese is** a filling snack.
   Either two short **stories** or a **novel is** acceptable for your book report.

6. A verb must agree in number with an indefinite pronoun subject. Indefinite pronouns that are always singular: *anybody, anyone, anything, each, either, everybody, everyone, everything, neither, nobody, no one, nothing, one, somebody, someone,* and *something*
   Always plural: *both, few, many, others,* and *several*
   Either singular or plural: *all, any, most, none,* and *some*

   Most of the snow **has** melted.   **All** of the children **have** eaten.

USAGE GLOSSARY

a lot, alot Always write this expression, meaning "very much" or "a large amount," as two words.

The neighbors pitched in, and the job went **a lot** faster.

accept, except *Accept*, a verb, means "to receive" or "to agree to." *Except* may be a preposition or a verb. As a preposition it means "other than." As a verb it means "to leave out, to make an exception."

I **accept** your plan.   We ate everything **except** the crust.

all ready, already *All ready* means "completely prepared." *Already* means "before" or "by this time."

They were **all ready** to leave, but the bus had **already** departed.

all together, altogether The two words *all together* mean "in a group." The single word *altogether* is an adverb meaning "completely" or "on the whole."

The teachers met **all together** after school.

They were **altogether** prepared for a heated discussion.

beside, besides *Beside* means "next to." *Besides* means "in addition to."

The sink is **beside** the refrigerator.

Besides the kitchen, the den is my favorite room.

between, among Use *between* to refer to or to compare two separate nouns. Use *among* to show a relationship in a group.

The joke was **between** Hilary and Megan.

The conversation **among** the teacher, the principal, and the janitor was friendly.

bring, take Use *bring* to show movement from a distant place to a closer one. Use *take* to show movement from a nearby place to a more distant one.

You may **bring** your model here.

Please **take** a brochure with you when you go.

can, may *Can* indicates the ability to do something. *May* indicates permission to do something.

Constance **can** walk to school.

She **may** ride the bus if she wishes.

choose, chose *Choose* means "to select." *Chose* is the past participle form, meaning "selected."

I **choose** the blue folder.

Celia **chose** the purple folder.

fewer, less Use *fewer* with nouns that can be counted. Use *less* with nouns that cannot be counted.

There were **fewer** sunny days this year.

I see **less** fog today than I expected.

formally, formerly *Formally* is the adverb form of formal. *Formerly* is an adverb meaning "in times past."
They **formally** agreed to the exchange.
Lydia **formerly** lived in Spain, but now she lives in New York City.

in, into Use *in* to mean "inside" or "within" and *into* to indicate movement or direction from outside to a point within.
The birds nest **in** the trees.
A bird flew **into** our window yesterday.

its, it's *Its* is the possessive form of the pronoun *it*. Possessive pronouns never have apostrophes. *It's* is the contraction of *it is.*
The dog lives in **its** own house.   Who is to say whether **it's** happy or not.

lay, lie *Lay* means "to put" or "to place," and it takes a direct object. *Lie* means "to recline" or "to be positioned," and it never takes an object.
We **lay** the uniforms on the shelves each day.
The players **lie** on the floor to do their sit-ups.

learn, teach *Learn* means "to receive knowledge." *Teach* means "to give knowledge."
Children can **learn** foreign languages at an early age.
Mr. Minton will **teach** French to us next year.

leave, let *Leave* means "to go away." *Let* means "to allow" or "to permit."
I will **leave** after fourth period.
Dad will **let** me go swimming today.

loose, lose Use *loose* to mean "not firmly attached" and *lose* to mean "to misplace" or "to fail to win."
The bike chain was very **loose.**
I did not want to **lose** my balance.

many, much Use *many* with nouns that can be counted. Use *much* with nouns that cannot be counted.
Many ants were crawling near the anthill.
There was **much** discussion about what to do.

precede, proceed *Precede* means "to go or come before." *Proceed* means "to continue."
Lunch will **precede** the afternoon session.
Marly can **proceed** with her travel plans.

quiet, quite *Quiet* means "calm" or "motionless." *Quite* means "completely" or "entirely."
The sleeping kitten was **quiet.**
The other kittens were **quite** playful.

raise, rise *Raise* means "to cause to move upward," and it always takes an object. *Rise* means "to get up"; it is intransitive and never takes an object.
Please **raise** your hand if you would like to help.
I left the bread in a warm spot to **rise.**

sit, set *Sit* means "to place oneself in a sitting position." It rarely takes an object. *Set* means "to place" or "to put" and usually takes an object. *Set* can also be used to describe the sun going down.

Please **sit** in your assigned seats.   **Set** those dishes down.
The sun **set** at 6:14.

than, then *Than* is a conjunction that is used to introduce the second element in a comparison; it also shows exception. *Then* is an adverb meaning "at that time."
Wisconsin produces more milk **than** any other state.
First get comfortable, **then** look the pitcher right in the eye.

their, they're *Their* is the possessive form of the personal pronoun *they*. *They're* is the contraction of *they are.*
The Westons returned to **their** favorite vacation spot.
They're determined to go next year as well.

theirs, there's *Theirs* means "that or those belonging to them." *There's* is the contraction of *there is.*
Theirs is one of the latest models.
There's another pitcher of lemonade in the refrigerator.

to, too, two *To* is a preposition meaning "in the direction of." *Too* means "also" or "excessively." *Two* is the number that falls between one and three.
You may go **to** the library.
It is **too** cold for skating.
There are only **two** days of vacation left.

where at Do not use *at* in a sentence after *where.*
Where were you yesterday afternoon? (*not* Where were you at yesterday afternoon?)

who's, whose *Who's* is the contraction of *who is. Whose* is the possessive form of *who.*
Who's willing to help me clean up?
Do you know **whose** books these are?

your, you're *Your* is the possessive form of *you. You're* is the contraction of *you are.*
Please arrange **your** schedule so that you can be on time.
If **you're** late, you may miss something important.

CAPITALIZATION

1. Capitalize the first word of every sentence, including direct quotations and sentences in parentheses unless they are contained within another sentence.
   In *Poor Richard's Almanack,* Benjamin Franklin advises, "**W**ish not so much to live long as to live well." (**T**his appeared in the almanac published in 1738.)

2. Capitalize the first word in the salutation and closing of a letter. Capitalize the title and name of the person addressed.
   Dear Professor Nichols:
   Sincerely yours,

3. Always capitalize the pronoun *I* no matter where it appears in the sentence.
   Since **I** knew you were coming, **I** baked a cake.

4. Capitalize the following proper nouns:

   a. Names of individuals, the initials that stand for their names, and titles preceding a name or used instead of a name
   Governor **C**ordoba   **A. C. S**hen
   Aunt **M**argaret   **D**r. **H. C. H**arada
   General **D**iaz

   b. Names and abbreviations of academic degrees, and *Jr.* and *Sr.*
   Richard **B**oe, **Ph.D.**
   Sammy **D**avis **Jr.**

   c. Names of cities, countries, states, continents, bodies of water, sections of the United States, and compass points when they refer to a specific section of the United States
   Boston   **D**ade **C**ounty   **N**orth **C**arolina   **A**ustralia
   Amazon **R**iver   the **S**outh

   d. Names of streets, highways, organizations, institutions, firms, monuments, bridges, buildings, other structures, and celestial bodies
   Route 51   **C**ircle **K S**ociety   **T**omb of the **U**nknown **S**oldier
   Golden **G**ate **B**ridge   **C**oventry **C**athedral   **N**orth **S**tar

   e. Trade names and names of documents, awards, and laws
   No-**S**neez tissues   the **F**ourteenth **A**mendment
   Golden **G**lobe **A**ward   the **M**onroe **D**octrine

   f. Names of most historical events, eras, holidays, days of the week, and months
   Boston **T**ea **P**arty   **B**ronze **A**ge   **L**abor **D**ay   **F**riday   **J**uly

   g. First, last, and all important words in titles of literary works, works of art, and musical compositions
   "**I A**sk **M**y **M**other to **S**ing" (poem)   *Giants in the Earth* (book)
   Venus de **M**ilo (statue)   "**A**merica, the **B**eautiful" (composition)

   h. Names of ethnic groups, national groups, political parties and their members, and languages
   Hispanics   **C**hinese   **I**rish   **I**talian   **R**epublican party

5. Capitalize proper adjectives (adjectives formed from proper nouns).
   English saddle horse   **T**hai restaurant   **M**idwestern plains

PUNCTUATION, ABBREVIATIONS, AND NUMBERS

1. Use a period at the end of a declarative sentence and at the end of a polite command.
   Mrs. Miranda plays tennis every Tuesday.
   Write your name in the space provided.

2. Use a question mark at the end of an interrogative sentence.
   When will the new books arrive?

3. Use an exclamation point to show strong feeling and indicate a forceful command.

Oh, no!　　　It was a terrific concert!　　　Don't go outside without your gloves on!

4. Use a comma in the following situations:

  a. To separate three or more words, phrases, or clauses in a series
    A tent, sleeping bag, and sturdy shoes are essential wilderness camping equipment.

  b. To set off two or more prepositional phrases
    After the sound of the bell, we realized it was a false alarm.

  c. After an introductory participle and an introductory participial phrase
    Marveling at the sight, we waited to see another shooting star.

  d. After conjunctive adverbs
    Snow is falling; however, it is turning to sleet.

  e. To set off an appositive if it is not essential to the meaning of the sentence
    Mr. Yoshino, the head of the department, resigned yesterday.

  f. To set off words or phrases of direct address
    Micha, have you called your brother yet?
    It's good to see you, Mrs. Han.

  g. Between the main clauses of compound sentences
    Whiskers liked to watch the goldfish, and she sometimes dipped her paw in the bowl.

  h. After an introductory adverb clause and to set off a nonessential adjective clause
    Whenever we get careless, we always make mistakes.
    Spelling errors, which are common, can now be corrected by computer.

  i. To separate parts of an address or a date
    1601 Burma Drive, Waterbury, Connecticut
    She was born on February 2, 1985, and she now lives in Bangor, Maine.

  j. After the salutation and close of a friendly letter and after the close of a business letter
    Dear Dad,　　　Cordially,　　　Yours,

5. Use a semicolon in the following situations:

  a. To join main clauses not joined by a coordinating conjunction
    The house looks dark; perhaps we should have called first.

  b. To separate two main clauses joined by a coordinating conjunction when such clauses already contain several commas
    After a week of rain, the farmers around Ames, Iowa, waited hopefully; but the rain, unfortunately, had come too late.

  c. To separate main clauses joined by a conjunctive adverb or by *for example* or *that is*
    Jen was determined to win the race; nonetheless, she knew that it took more than determination to succeed.

6. Use a colon to introduce a list of items that ends a sentence.
   Bring the following tools: hammer, speed square, and drill.

7. Use a colon to separate the hour and the minute in time measurements and after business letter salutations.
   12:42 A.M.   Dear Sir: Dear Ms. O'Connor:

8. Use quotation marks to enclose a direct quotation. When a quotation is interrupted, use two sets of quotation marks. Use single quotation marks for a quotation within a quotation.
   "Are you sure," asked my mother, "that you had your keys when you left home?"
   "Chief Seattle's speech begins, 'My words are like the stars that never change,'" stated the history teacher.

9. Always place commas and periods inside closing quotations marks. Place colons and semicolons outside closing quotation marks. Place question marks and exclamation points inside closing quotation marks only when those marks are part of the quotation.
   "Giraffes," said Ms. Wharton, "spend long hours each day foraging."
   You must read "The Story of an Hour"; it is a wonderful short story.
   He called out, "Is anyone home?"
   Are you sure she said, "Go home without me"?

10. Use quotation marks to indicate titles of short stories, poems, essays, songs, and magazine or newspaper articles.
    "The Thrill of the Grass" (short story)
    "My Country 'Tis of Thee" (song)

11. Italicize (underline) titles of books, plays, films, television series, paintings and sculptures, and names of newspapers and magazines.
    Up from Slavery (book)
    Free Willy (film)
    The Spirit of '76 (painting)
    Chicago Tribune (newspaper)
    Weekend Woodworker (magazine)

12. Add an apostrophe and -*s* to form the possessive of singular indefinite pronouns, singular nouns, and plural nouns not ending in -*s*. Add only an apostrophe to plural nouns ending in -*s* to make them possessive.
    everyone's best friend
    the rabbit's ears
    the children's toys
    the farmers' fields

13. Use an apostrophe in place of omitted letters or numerals. Use an apostrophe and -*s* to form the plural of letters, numerals, and symbols.
    is + not = isn't
    will + not = won't
    1776 is '76
    Cross your *t*'s and dot your *i*'s.

14. Use a hyphen to divide words at the end of a line.
    esti-mate   mone-tary   experi-mentation

15. Use a hyphen in a compound adjective that precedes a noun. Use a hyphen in compound numbers and fractions used as adjectives.
    a blue-green parrot
    a salt-and-pepper beard
    twenty-nine
    one-third cup of flour

16. Use a hyphen after any prefix joined to a proper noun or a proper adjective. Use a hyphen after the prefixes *all-*, *ex-*, and *self-* joined to a noun or adjective, the prefix *anti-* joined to a word beginning with *i-*, and the prefix *vice-* except in the case of *vice president.*
    all-knowing   ex-spouse   self-confidence
    anti-inflammatory   vice-principal

17. Use dashes to signal a break or change in thought.
    I received a letter from Aunt Carla—you have never met her—saying she is coming to visit.

18. Use parentheses to set off supplemental material. Punctuate within the parentheses only if the punctuation is part of the parenthetical expression.
    Place one gallon (3.8 liters) of water in a plastic container.

19. Abbreviate a person's title and professional or academic degrees.
    Ms. K. Soga, **Ph.D.**
    Dr. Quentin

20. Use the abbreviations *A.M.* and *P.M.* and *B.C.* and *A.D.*
    9:45 A.M.   1000 B.C.   A.D. 1455

21. Abbreviate numerical measurements in scientific writing but not in ordinary prose.
    The newborn snakes measured 3.4 **in.** long.
    Pour 45 **ml** warm water into the beaker.

22. Spell out cardinal and ordinal numbers that can be written in one or two words or that appear at the beginning of a sentence.
    Two hundred twenty runners crossed the finish line.
    Observers counted **forty-nine** sandhill cranes.

23. Express all related numbers in a sentence as numerals if any one should be expressed as a numeral.
    There were **127** volunteers, but only **9** showed up because of the bad weather.

Copyright © by Glencoe/McGraw-Hill

24. Spell out ordinal numbers.
Nina won **third** place in the spelling bee.

25. Use words for decades, for amounts of money that can be written in one or two words, and for the approximate time of day or when A.M. or P.M. is not used.
the **nineties**   **ten** dollars   **sixty** cents   half past **five**

26. Use numerals for dates; for decimals; for house, apartment, and room numbers; for street or avenue numbers; for telephone numbers; for page numbers; for percentages; for sums of money involving both dollars and cents; and to emphasize the exact time of day or when A.M. or P.M. is used.
June **5, 1971**   Apartment **4G**   **$207.89**
0.0045   **1520 14**th Street   **8:20** A.M.

VOCABULARY AND SPELLING

1. Clues to the meaning of an unfamiliar word can be found in its context. Context clues include definitions, the meaning stated; example, the meaning explained through one familiar case; comparison, similarity to a familiar word; contrast, opposite of a familiar word; and cause and effect, a reason and its results.

2. The meaning of a word can be obtained from its base word, its prefix, or its suffix.
telegram **tele** = distant   dentate **dent** = tooth
subarctic **sub** = below   marvelous **-ous** = full of

3. The *i* comes before the *e*, except when both letters follow a *c* or when both letters are pronounced together as an $\bar{a}$ sound. However, many exceptions exist to this rule.
y**ie**ld (*i* before *e*)   rec**ei**ve (*ei* after *c*)   w**ei**gh ($\bar{a}$ sound)   h**ei**ght (exception)

4. An unstressed vowel is a vowel sound that is not emphasized when the word is pronounced. Determine how to spell this sound by comparing it to a known word.
inform**a**nt (compare to *information*)   hosp**i**tal (compare to *hospitality*)

5. When joining a prefix that ends in the same letter as the word, keep both consonants.
illegible   **diss**ervice

6. When adding a suffix to a word ending in a consonant + *y*, change the *y* to *i* unless the prefix begins with an *i*. If the word ends in a vowel + *y*, keep the *y*.
tr**ied**   play**ed**   spra**ying**

7. Double the final consonant before adding a suffix that begins with a vowel to a word that ends in a single consonant preceded by a single vowel if the accent is on the root's last syllable.
pop**ping**   transfer**red**   unforget**table**

8. When adding a suffix that begins with a consonant to a word that ends in silent *e*, generally keep the *e*. If the suffix begins with a vowel or *y*, generally drop the *e*. If the suffix begins with *a* or *o* and the word ends in *ce* or *ge*, keep the *e*. If the suffix begins with a vowel and the word ends in *ee* or *oe*, keep the *e*.
state**ly**   nois**y**   courage**ous**   agree**able**

9. When adding -*ly* to a word that ends in a single *l*, keep the *l*. If it ends in a double *l*, drop one *l*. If it ends in a consonant + *le*, drop the *le*.

   meal, meal**ly**   full, ful**ly**   incredible, incredib**ly**

10. When forming compound words, maintain the spelling of both words.

    backpack   honeybee

11. Most nouns form their plurals by adding -*s*. However, nouns that end in -*ch*, -*s*, -*sh*, -*x*, or -*z* form plurals by adding -*es*. If the noun ends in a consonant + *y*, change *y* to *i* and add -*es*. If the noun ends in -*lf*, change *f* to *v* and add -*es*. If the noun ends in -*fe*, change *f* to *v* and add -*s*.

    mark**s**   leach**es**   rash**es**   fox**es**
    fl**ies**   el**ves**   li**ves**

12. To form the plural of proper names and one-word compound nouns, follow the general rules for plurals. To form the plural of hyphenated compound nouns or compound nouns of more than one word, make the most important word plural.

    Wilson**s**   Diaz**es**   housekeeper**s**
    sister**s**-in-law   editor**s**-in-chief

13. Some nouns have the same singular and plural forms.

    deer   moose

Composition

Writing Themes and Paragraphs

1. Use **prewriting** to find ideas to write about. One form of prewriting, **freewriting**, starts with a subject or topic and branches off into related ideas. Another way to find a topic is to ask and answer questions about your starting subject, helping you to gain a deeper understanding of your chosen topic. Also part of the prewriting stage is determining who your readers or **audience** will be and deciding your **purpose** for writing. Your purpose—writing to persuade, to explain, to describe something, or to narrate—is partially shaped by who your audience will be.

2. To complete your first **draft**, organize your prewriting into an introduction, body, and conclusion. Concentrate on unity and coherence of the overall piece. Experiment with different paragraph orders: **chronological order** places events in the order in which they happened; **spatial order** places objects in the order in which they appear; and **compare/contrast order** shows similarities and differences in objects or events.

3. **Revise** your composition if necessary. Read through your draft, looking for places to improve content and structure. Remember that varying your sentence patterns and lengths will make your writing easier and more enjoyable to read.

4. In the editing stage, check your grammar, spelling, and punctuation. Focus on expressing your ideas clearly and concisely.

5. Finally, prepare your writing for presentation. Sharing your composition, or ideas, with others may take many forms: printed, oral, or graphic.

Outlining

1. The two common forms of outlines are sentence outlines and topic outlines. Choose one type of outline and keep it uniform throughout.

2. A period follows the number or letter of each division. Each point in a sentence outline ends with a period; the points in a topic outline do not.

3. Each point begins with a capital letter.

4. A point may have no fewer than two subpoints.

SENTENCE OUTLINE
I. This is the main point.
  A. This is a subpoint of *I.*
    1. This is a detail of *A.*
      a. This is a detail of *1.*
      b. This is a detail of *1.*
    2. This is a detail of *A.*
  B. This is a subpoint of *I.*
II. This is another main point.

TOPIC OUTLINE
I. Main point
  A. Subpoint of *I*
    1. Detail of *A*
      a. Detail of *1*
      b. Detail of *1*
    2. Detail of *A*
  B. Subpoint of *I*
II. Main point

Writing Letters

1. Personal letters are usually handwritten in indented form (first line of paragraphs, each line of the heading and inside address, and the signature are indented). Business letters are usually typewritten in block or semiblock form. Block form contains no indents; semiblock form indents only the first line of each paragraph.

2. The five parts of a personal letter are the heading (the writer's address and the date), salutation (greeting), body (message), complimentary close (such as "Yours truly,"), and signature (the writer's name). Business letters have the same parts and also include an inside address (the recipient's address).

PERSONAL LETTER

BUSINESS LETTER

Heading _____

Salutation

Body

Complimentary Close _____
Signature———————

Heading _____

Inside Address

Salutation

Body

Complimentary Close _____
Signature———————

3. Reveal your personality and imagination in colorful personal letters. Keep business letters brief, clear, and courteous.

4. **Personal letters** include letters to friends and family members. **Thank-you notes** and **invitations** are personal letters that may be either formal or informal in style.

5. Use a **letter of request**, a type of business letter, to ask for information or to place an order. Be concise, yet give all the details necessary for your request to be fulfilled. Keep the tone of your letter courteous, and be generous in allotting time for a response.

6. Use an **opinion letter** to take a firm stand on an issue. Make the letter clear, firm, rational, and purposeful. Be aware of your audience, their attitude, how informed they are, and their possible reactions to your opinion. Support your statements of opinion with facts.

Troubleshooter

· ·

Sentence Fragments

PROBLEM 1

Fragment that lacks a subject

frag	Martha asked about dinner. (Hoped it was lasagna.)
frag	I jogged around the park twice. (Was hot and tired afterward.)
frag	Li Cheng raced to the bus stop. (Arrived just in the nick of time.)

SOLUTION

Martha asked about dinner. She hoped it was lasagna.
I jogged around the park twice. I was hot and tired afterward.
Li Cheng raced to the bus stop. He arrived just in the nick of time.

Make a complete sentence by adding a subject to the fragment.

PROBLEM 2

Fragment that lacks a predicate

frag	The carpenter worked hard all morning. (His assistant after lunch.)
frag	Ant farms are fascinating. (The ants around in constant motion.)
frag	Our class went on a field trip. (Mammoth Cave.)

SOLUTION

The carpenter worked hard all morning. His assistant helped after lunch.

Ant farms are fascinating. The ants crawl around in constant motion.

Our class went on a field trip. Mammoth Cave was our destination.

Make a complete sentence by adding a predicate.

PROBLEM 3

Fragment that lacks both a subject and a predicate

frag   I heard the laughter of the children. (In the nursery.)

frag   (After the spring rain.) The whole house smelled fresh and clean.

frag   The noisy chatter of the squirrels awakened us early. (In the morning.)

SOLUTION

I heard the laughter of the children in the nursery.

After the spring rain, the whole house smelled fresh and clean.

The noisy chatter of the squirrels awakened us early in the morning.

Combine the fragment with another sentence.

More help in avoiding sentence fragments is available in Lesson 3.

Run-on Sentences

PROBLEM 1

Two main clauses separated only by a comma

run-on (Extra crackers are available, they are next to the salad bar.)

run-on (Hurdles are Sam's specialty, he likes them best.)

SOLUTION A

Extra crackers are available. They are next to the salad bar.

Make two sentences by separating the first clause from the second with end punctuation, such as a period or a question mark, and starting the second sentence with a capital letter.

SOLUTION B

Hurdles are Sam's specialty; he likes them best.

Place a semicolon between the main clauses of the sentence.

PROBLEM 2

Two main clauses with no punctuation between them

run-on (The law student studied hard she passed her exam.)

run-on (Kamil looked for the leash he found it in the closet.)

SOLUTION A

The law student studied hard. She passed her exam.

Make two sentences out of the run-on sentence.

SOLUTION B

Kamil looked for the leash, and he found it in the closet.

Add a comma and a coordinating conjunction between the main clauses.

PROBLEM 3

Two main clauses without a comma before the coordinating conjunction

run-on   You can rollerskate like a pro but you cannot ice skate.

run-on   Julian gazed at the moon and he marveled at its brightness.

SOLUTION

You can rollerskate like a pro, but you cannot ice skate.
Julian gazed at the moon, and he marveled at its brightness.

Add a comma before the coordinating conjunction.

More help in avoiding run-on sentences is available in Lesson 6.

Lack of Subject-Verb Agreement

PROBLEM 1

A subject separated from the verb by an intervening prepositional phrase

agr	The stories in the newspaper (was) well written.
agr	The house in the suburbs (were) just what she wanted.

SOLUTION

The stories in the newspaper were well written.
The house in the suburbs was just what she wanted.

Make sure that the verb agrees with the subject of the sentence, not with the object of a preposition. The object of a preposition is never the subject.

PROBLEM 2

A sentence that begins with here *or* there

agr	Here (go) the duck with her ducklings.
agr	There (is) the pencils you were looking for.
agr	Here (is) the snapshots from our vacation to the Grand Canyon.

> **SOLUTION**
>
> **Here goes the duck with her ducklings.**
>
> **There are the pencils you were looking for.**
>
> **Here are the snapshots from our vacation to the Grand Canyon.**
>
> In sentences that begin with *here* or *there,* look for the subject after the verb. Make sure that the verb agrees with the subject.

PROBLEM 3

An indefinite pronoun as the subject

> agr   Each of the animals (have) a unique way of walking.
>
> agr   Many of the movies (was) black and white.
>
> agr   Most of the leaves (is) turning colors.

> **SOLUTION**
>
> **Each of the animals has a unique way of walking.**
>
> **Many of the movies were black and white.**
>
> **Most of the leaves are turning colors.**
>
> Some indefinite pronouns are singular, some are plural, and some can be either singular or plural. Determine whether the indefinite pronoun is singular or plural, and make the verb agree.

PROBLEM 4

A compound subject that is joined by and

agr	The students and the teacher (adores) the classroom hamster.
agr	The expert and best source of information (are) Dr. Marlin.

SOLUTION A

The students and the teacher adore the classroom hamster.

Use a plural verb if the parts of the compound subject do not belong to one unit or if they refer to different people or things.

SOLUTION B

The expert and best source of information is Dr. Marlin.

Use a singular verb if the parts of the compound subject belong to one unit or if they refer to the same person or thing.

PROBLEM 5

A compound subject that is joined by or or nor

agr	Either Hester or Sue (are) supposed to pick us up.
agr	Neither pepper nor spices (improves) the flavor of this sauce.
agr	Either Caroline or Robin (volunteer) at the local food pantry.
agr	Neither the coach nor the screaming fans (agrees) with the referee's call.

SOLUTION

Either Hester or Sue is supposed to pick us up.

Neither pepper nor spices improve the flavor of this sauce.

Either Caroline or Robin volunteers at the local food pantry.

Neither the coach nor the screaming fans agree with the referee's call.

Make the verb agree with the subject that is closer to it.

More help with subject-verb agreement is available in Lessons 53–57.

Copyright © by Glencoe/McGraw-Hill

Incorrect Verb Tense or Form

PROBLEM 1

An incorrect or missing verb ending

tense	We (talk) yesterday for more than an hour.
tense	They (sail) last month for Barbados.
tense	Sally and James (land) at the airport yesterday.

SOLUTION

We talked yesterday for more than an hour.

They sailed last month for Barbados.

Sally and James landed at the airport yesterday.

To form the past tense and the past participle, add *-ed* to a regular verb.

PROBLEM 2

An improperly formed irregular verb

tense	Our hair (clinged) to us in the humid weather.
tense	Trent (drinked) all the orange juice.
tense	The evening breeze (blowed) the clouds away.

> **SOLUTION**
>
> **Our hair clung to us in the humid weather.**
> **Trent drank all the orange juice.**
> **The evening breeze blew the clouds away.**
>
> Irregular verbs vary in their past and past participle forms. Look up the ones you are not sure of. Consider memorizing them if you feel it is necessary.

PROBLEM 3

Confusion between a verb's past form and its past participle

> tense   Helen has took first place in the marathon.

> **SOLUTION**
>
> **Helen has taken first place in the marathon.**
>
> Use the past participle form of an irregular verb, and not its past form, when you use the auxiliary verb *have.*

More help with correct verb forms is available in Lessons 18–24.

Incorrect Use of Pronouns

PROBLEM 1

A pronoun that refers to more than one antecedent

pro   The wind and the rain came suddenly, but (it) did not last.

pro   Henry ran with Philip, but (he) was faster.

pro   When Sarah visits Corinne, (she) is glad for the company.

SOLUTION

The wind and the rain came suddenly, but the rain did not last.

Henry ran with Philip, but Philip was faster.

When Sarah visits Corinne, Corinne is glad for the company.

Substitute a noun for the pronoun to make your sentence clearer.

PROBLEM 2

Personal pronouns as subjects

pro   (Him) and Mary unfurled the tall, white sail.

pro   Nina and (them) bought theater tickets yesterday.

pro   Karen and (me) heard the good news on the television.

> **SOLUTION**
>
> **He and Mary unfurled the tall, white sail.**
>
> **Nina and they bought theater tickets yesterday.**
>
> **Karen and I heard the good news on the television.**
>
> Use a subject pronoun as the subject part of a sentence.

PROBLEM 3

Personal pronouns as objects

> *pro*   The horse galloped across the field to Anne and (I.)
>
> *pro*   The new signs confused Clark and (they.)
>
> *pro*   Grant wrote (she) a letter of apology.

> **SOLUTION**
>
> **The horse galloped across the field to Anne and me.**
>
> **The new signs confused Clark and them.**
>
> **Grant wrote her a letter of apology.**
>
> An object pronoun is the object of a verb or preposition.

Need More Help?

More help with correct use of pronouns is available in Lessons 25–30.

Incorrect Use of Adjectives

PROBLEM 1

Incorrect use of good, better, best

adj	Is a horse (more good) than a pony?
adj	Literature is my (most good) subject.

> ### SOLUTION
>
> **Is a horse better than a pony?**
> **Literature is my best subject.**
>
> The words *better* and *best* are the comparative and superlative forms of the word *good.* Do not use the words *more* or *most* before the irregular forms of comparative and superlative adjectives.

PROBLEM 2

Incorrect use of bad, worse, worst

adj	That game was the (baddest) game our team ever played.

> ### SOLUTION
>
> **That game was the worst game our team ever played.**
>
> Do not use the words *more* or *most* before the irregular forms of comparative and superlative adjectives.

PROBLEM 3

Incorrect use of comparative adjectives

adj   This bike is (more faster) than my old bike.

SOLUTION

This bike is faster than my old bike.

Do not use *-er* and *more* together.

PROBLEM 4

Incorrect use of superlative adjectives

adj   Kara said it was the (most biggest) lawn she ever had to mow.

SOLUTION

Kara said it was the biggest lawn she ever had to mow.

Do not use *-est* and *most* together.

More help with the correct use of adjectives is available in Lessons 31–34.

Troubleshooter

Incorrect Use of Commas

PROBLEM 1

Missing commas in a series of three or more items

com	We saw ducks geese and seagulls at the park.
com	Jake ate dinner watched a movie and visited friends.

SOLUTION

We saw ducks, geese, and seagulls at the park.
Jake ate dinner, watched a movie, and visited friends.

If there are three or more items in a series, use a comma after each item except the last one.

PROBLEM 2

Missing commas with direct quotations

com	"The party" said José "starts at seven o'clock."
com	"My new book" Roger exclaimed "is still on the bus!"

SOLUTION

"The party," said José, "starts at seven o'clock."

"My new book," Roger exclaimed, "is still on the bus!"

If a quotation is interrupted, the first part ends with a comma followed by quotation marks. The interrupting words are also followed by a comma.

PROBLEM 3

Missing commas with nonessential appositives

com   Maria our new friend is from Chicago.

com   The old lane a tree-lined gravel path is a great place to walk on a
       hot afternoon.

SOLUTION

Maria, our new friend, is from Chicago.

**The old lane, a tree-lined gravel path, is a great place to walk on a
hot afternoon.**

Decide whether the appositive is truly essential to the meaning of the sentence. If it is not essential, set it off with commas.

PROBLEM 4

Missing commas with nonessential adjective clauses

> com   Karen who started early finished with her work before noon.

SOLUTION

Karen, who started early, finished with her work before noon.

Decide whether the clause is truly essential to the meaning of the sentence. If it is not essential, then set it off with commas.

PROBLEM 5

Missing commas with introductory adverb clauses

> com   When the wind rises too high the boats lower their sails.

SOLUTION

When the wind rises too high, the boats lower their sails.

Place a comma after an introductory adverbial clause.

More help with commas is available in Lessons 78–81.

Incorrect Use of Apostrophes

PROBLEM 1

Singular possessive nouns

apos	(Pablos) new bicycle is in (Charles) yard.
apos	(Bills) video collection is really great.
apos	That (horses) saddle has real silver on it.

SOLUTION

Pablo's new bicycle is in Charles's yard.

Bill's video collection is really great.

That horse's saddle has real silver on it.

Place an apostrophe before a final *-s* to form the possessive of a singular noun, even one that ends in *-s*.

PROBLEM 2

Plural possessive nouns that end in -s

apos	The (girls) team won the tournament.
apos	The (boats) sails are very colorful against the blue sky.
apos	The model (cars) boxes are in my room.

SOLUTION

The girls' team won the tournament.

The boats' sails are very colorful against the blue sky.

The model cars' boxes are in my room.

Use an apostrophe by itself to form the possessive of a plural noun that ends in *-s*.

PROBLEM 3

Plural possessive nouns that do not end in -s

apos   The (deers) best habitat is a deep, unpopulated woodland.

apos   The (childrens) clothes are on the third floor.

SOLUTION

The deer's best habitat is a deep, unpopulated woodland.

The children's clothes are on the third floor.

When a plural noun does not end in *-s,* use an apostrophe and an *-s* to form the possessive of the noun.

PROBLEM 4

Possessive personal pronouns

apos   The poster is (her's,) but the magazine is (their's.)

> ### SOLUTION
>
> **The poster is hers, but the magazine is theirs.**
>
> Do not use apostrophes with possessive personal pronouns.

PROBLEM 5

Confusion between its *and* it's

> apos   The old tree was the last to lose (it's) leaves.
>
> apos   (Its) the best CD I have ever heard them put out.

> ### SOLUTION
>
> **The old tree was the last to lose its leaves.**
> **It's the best CD I have ever heard them put out.**
>
> Use an apostrophe to form the contraction of *it is.* The possessive of the personal pronoun *it* does not take an apostrophe.

More help with apostrophes and possessives is available in Lesson 84.

Troubleshooter

PROBLEM 1

Words that refer to ethnic groups, nationalities, and languages

cap   Many (irish) citizens speak both (english) and (gaelic.)

SOLUTION

Many Irish citizens speak both English and Gaelic.

Capitalize proper nouns and adjectives referring to ethnic groups, nationalities, and languages.

PROBLEM 2

The first word of a direct quotation

cap   Yuri said, "(the) rain off the bay always blows this way."

SOLUTION

Yuri said, "The rain off the bay always blows this way."

Capitalize the first word of a direct quotation if it is a complete sentence. A direct quotation is the speaker's exact words.

More help with capitalization is available in Lessons 73–76.

Name _____

Name _____

Unit 1: ɔu

Lesson 1

Kinds of Se

A group of wor
begin with a ca
a period. An in

Florida summe
Are summers i

▶ **Exercise 1 Writ**
int. **(interrogative)**

___int.___   Can yo

_____   **1.** I'm goi

_____   **2.** Is the p est

_____   **3.** My gra

_____   **4.** Mitche

_____   **5.** Margar

_____   **6.** Claire,

_____   **7.** Are yo

_____   **8.** You ar

_____   **9.** How lo

_____ **10.** Our so

_____ **11.** The bu

_____ **12.** The wi

_____ **13.** Have y

_____ **14.** Which

_____ **15.** The title o

Grammar

_____ **16.** Go to sleep

_____ **17.** Walk through the flower bed carefully

_____ **18.** Speak louder

_____ **19.** I have never felt so frightened

_____ **20.** Play that song again

_____ **21.** Be home by ten o'clock

_____ **22.** Wait for me at the corner

_____ **23.** Put more paint on the other side

_____ **24.** Don't cross the street against the light

_____ **25.** Wait for an hour before you go swimming

_____ **26.** That's my favorite song

_____ **27.** Put on some mosquito repellant

_____ **28.** Walk quickly to the nearest exit

_____ **29.** This movie is funny

_____ **30.** I never even saw the ball

_____ **31.** Answer the phone politely

_____ **32.** I aced the test

_____ **33.** Please come to our party

_____ **34.** You did a great job

_____ **35.** I lost my keys

_____ **36.** Be sure to remember your umbrella

_____ **37.** Be careful going down the stairs

_____ **38.** Bring a Number 2 pencil to class

_____ **39.** Watch how I do this

_____ **40.** This food is delicious

Lesson 3
Sentence Fragments

Every sentence must have a subject and a predicate to express a complete thought. The **subject** part of a sentence names who or what the sentence is about. The **predicate** part tells what the subject does or has. It can also describe what the subject is or is like.

SUBJECT   PREDICATE
My friend Joel   will play in the volleyball tournament.

A **sentence fragment** is a group of words that lacks a subject, a predicate, or both. A fragment does not express a complete thought.

Will play in the volleyball tournament. (lacks a subject)
My friend Joel. (lacks a predicate)
Without a doubt. (lacks both a subject and a predicate)
Without a doubt, my friend Joel will play in the volleyball tournament.
(expresses a complete thought)

▶ **Exercise 1** Write *sentence* in the blank before each word group that expresses a complete thought. Write *fragment* next to each word group that does not express a complete thought.

_____fragment_____   Wore her warmest sweater.

_____   **1.** The survivors of the earthquake showed great courage.

_____   **2.** Caused problems everywhere.

_____   **3.** Every Sunday their family went hiking.

_____   **4.** Even the rain couldn't dampen their spirits.

_____   **5.** Rode calmly and quietly in the backseat.

_____   **6.** Rose in the air like a bird.

_____   **7.** Of his meal untouched.

_____   **8.** Hundreds of firefighters fought the forest fires last summer.

_____   **9.** The thought escaped him.

_____   **10.** As fragile as glass.

_____   **11.** In the park for our picnic.

Grammar

_____ **12.** Our newspaper arrived late on Tuesday.

_____ **13.** Janette, who's coming at four.

_____ **14.** Simply everywhere.

_____ **15.** Postponed for the second time.

_____ **16.** Ted climbed to the top of the stadium.

_____ **17.** They played their very best.

_____ **18.** In every nook and cranny.

_____ **19.** Available at five o'clock.

_____ **20.** She was preparing her résumé.

▶ **Exercise 2 Write a complete sentence by adding a subject, a predicate, or both to each sentence fragment. Punctuate your sentences correctly.**

Grinned and cackled. __The ugly troll grinned and cackled._____

1. Marla and Kimberly. _____

2. On the shelves. _____

3. Dusted the books. _____

4. Maple and elm trees. _____

5. Greeted Eloisa. _____

6. At the library. _____

7. John Kimura the dentist. _____

8. Looked at Isabel. _____

9. Flat, sandy fields. _____

10. The mystery of space. _____

11. In the closet. _____

12. Busy traffic. _____

13. Carmen and her sister. _____

14. Followed the directions. _____

15. Saw the falling star. _____

16. Around the bend. _____

Lesson 4
Subjects and Predicates: Simple and Complete

Both a subject and a predicate may consist of more than one word. The **complete subject** includes all of the words in the subject part of a sentence. The **complete predicate** includes all of the words in the predicate part of a sentence.

COMPLETE SUBJECT   COMPLETE PREDICATE
My younger brother   likes alphabet soup for lunch.

The **simple subject** is the main word or group of words in the complete subject. The **simple predicate** is the main word or group of words in the complete predicate. The simple predicate is always a **verb**, a word or words that express an action or a state of being.

SIMPLE SUBJECT   SIMPLE PREDICATE
My younger **brother**   **likes** alphabet soup for lunch.

▶ **Exercise 1** **Draw a vertical line between the complete subject and the complete predicate.**

People | call Australia the continent "down under."

1. Australia is one of the most spectacular countries in the world.

2. The country is both the smallest continent and the largest island.

3. This small continent lies in the Southern Hemisphere.

4. The coastline of Australia is irregular.

5. It measures 12,210 miles.

6. The island state of Tasmania once formed the southeastern corner of the mainland.

7. The Great Barrier Reef continues along the eastern coast for 1,250 miles.

8. Four species of coral reef compose the chain of reefs and islands.

9. Australia's western regions form a great plateau.

10. The climate ranges from temperate to tropical.

11. Forty percent of Australia has only two seasons: hot and wet or warm and dry.

12. The average rainfall ranges from five to fifteen inches.

13. Australia's natural lakes fill with water only after heavy rains.

Grammar

14. The country's major lakes are salt water.

15. Most of the land is desert.

16. Australia's four deserts include the Simpson, the Gibson, the Great Sandy, and the Great Victoria.

17. Few rivers exist in the western part of this country.

18. Aqueducts and tunnels channel water from the Snowy Mountains for irrigation and hydroelectric power in the southeast.

19. The Australian Alps rise to 7,310 feet in the Eastern Highlands.

20. Ayers Rock in central Australia is a tourist attraction.

▶ **Exercise 2 Draw one line under the simple subject and two lines under the simple predicate.**

Australia has many unique plants and animals.

1. Forests cover the east coast of Tasmania.

2. The forests consist mainly of pine trees.

3. The dingo is a doglike animal.

4. It hunts sheep.

5. Dingoes prey on kangaroos as well.

6. Many people find wallabies interesting.

7. They are small members of the kangaroo family.

8. Wallabies belong to the marsupial order.

9. Female wallabies carry their young in a pouch.

10. Two species of crocodiles dwell in Australia.

11. The Queensland lungfish has no gills.

12. A lungfish breathes with a single lung.

13. Six hundred fifty species of birds live in Australia.

14. One hundred species of venomous snakes lurk on the ground.

15. The ocean offers seventy species of sharks.

16. Sharks pose no threat to people in most cases.

Lesson 5
Subjects and Predicates: Compound

A sentence may have more than one simple subject or simple predicate.

A **compound subject** is two or more simple subjects that have the same predicate. The subjects are joined by *and, or, either...or, neither...nor,* or *but.*

Oregon and **Washington** lie in the Pacific Northwest. (compound subject)

A **compound predicate** is two or more simple predicates, or verbs, that have the same subject. The verbs are connected by *and, or, either...or, neither...nor,* or *but.*

Many people neither **enjoy** nor **appreciate** modern art. (compound predicate)

Grammar

▶ **Exercise 1** Each of these sentences has either a compound subject, a compound predicate, or both. Draw one line under the simple subjects in each compound subject. Draw two lines under the simple predicates in each compound predicate.

Water <u>streamed</u> across the street and <u>ran</u> into the gutter.

1. Apples and pears grow on trees.

2. Workers pick apples and package them for sale.

3. Joi and her sisters sang for the congregation.

4. Wes or Raquel showed the office to the guests.

5. We ate and slept on the bus.

6. The ceiling and the walls are the same color.

7. Both Arizona and New Mexico have hot deserts.

8. Thoughtful neighbors and friends of the family sent sympathy cards.

9. Either red or blue clashes with this color.

10. Copper and iron have many uses.

11. In 1947, French president Charles de Gaulle and his party strengthened the central government of France.

12. Many Europeans both understand and use the English language.

13. Crocodiles and alligators swim in the water but hunt on land.

Grammar

14. Boll weevils seek the scent of cotton and destroy the plants.

15. A city council or other government body discusses the proposed law and votes on it.

16. Both tennis and badminton require rackets.

17. Puppies and kittens play and sleep most of the day.

18. Scientists perform research with care and conduct experiments with even more care.

19. Crabs and lobsters crawl along the ocean floor.

20. Farmers grow crops in the summer and harvest them in the fall.

21. Marie and Pierre Curie won the 1903 Nobel Prize in physics.

22. Exercise and diet are the keys to good health.

23. Fred Astaire and Ginger Rogers danced, acted, and sang in many movies.

24. Dams hold back water and prevent flooding.

25. The papers, books, and pencils lie in a neat pile on the desk.

26. Students study in the classroom and exercise in the gymnasium.

27. A calculator or computer adds, subtracts, multiplies, and divides rapidly.

28. One large box or several small cartons hold many books.

29. Trains and trucks carry large amounts of food and goods.

30. Tomás and his family swam and hiked last weekend.

31. Water freezes at 32°F and boils at 212°F.

32. The soccer team ran and kicked its way to victory.

33. Hurricanes or other strong winds uproot trees.

34. The carpenters measured and cut the wood for our new barn.

35. Cars and trucks burn diesel fuel.

36. The president and her cabinet posed for photographs.

37. The freshman class raised money and donated presents to charity.

38. Lorraine read the book and wrote her report in one week.

39. Prisms and other glass objects separate light into its component colors.

40. The Congo River begins in Zaire, flows 2,718 miles, and empties into the Atlantic Ocean.

Lesson 6
Simple and Compound Sentences

A **simple sentence** has one subject and one predicate. The subject and the predicate in a simple sentence may be simple or compound.

SUBJECT	PREDICATE
Oscar	fed the dog.
Oscar and Cathy	fed and groomed the dog.

A **compound sentence** contains two or more simple sentences joined by a comma and a coordinating conjunction (*or, nor, and, either...or, neither...nor, but*) or by a semicolon.

Oscar fed the dog, **and** he groomed him.
Oscar's dog likes to run; Cathy's dog prefers to sleep.

Two or more simple sentences joined incorrectly result in a **run-on sentence**. Correct a run-on sentence by writing separate sentences, by adding a comma and a conjunction, or by adding a semicolon.

Patti practiced every day for the recital she played flawlessly. (run-on)
Patti practiced every day for the recital. She played flawlessly. (separated)
Patti practiced every day for the recital, and she played flawlessly. (joined by a comma and a conjunction)
Patti practiced every day for the recital; she played flawlessly. (joined by a semicolon)

▶ **Exercise 1** Write *S* in the blank before each simple sentence, *C* before each compound sentence, and *R* before each run-on sentence.

___C___   The trumpets blared, and the king entered the room.

_____ **1.** Ketchup makes french fries taste better.

_____ **2.** I walked and walked for days.

_____ **3.** Hydrogen has weight, but you can't weigh it on an ordinary scale.

_____ **4.** Air is taken into the lungs oxygen is absorbed into the bloodstream.

_____ **5.** You can buy your ticket in advance, or you can buy it at the door.

_____ **6.** Radar detects objects in darkness and bad weather.

_____ **7.** Humans can't see well in the dark, nor can they hear sounds more than about one kilometer away.

_____ **8.** I read it, but I didn't understand it.

_____ **9.** Korean foods and Thai foods can be very spicy.

_____ **10.** You can ask questions, but you may not find the answers.

_____ **11.** The choir sang and clapped for the audience.

_____ **12.** Neither fog nor hail stops the letter carrier.

_____ **13.** Max found the light bulb he couldn't find a ladder.

_____ **14.** The first modern computer was built in 1946; it processed 5,000 calculations per minute.

_____ **15.** The South American condor is smaller and heavier than the California condor.

▶ **Exercise 2** **Draw one line under each simple subject and two lines under each simple predicate. Circle each coordinating conjunction.**

Stuart dialed the phone, (and) he waited for someone to answer.

1. The athletes ran for a long time, and they breathed hard.

2. I went there last year, but I cancelled my reservation this year.

3. She called me, but she wrote more often.

4. I studied hard, and I passed the test.

5. Did you find it, or do you need my help?

6. The skies were cloudy, but I saw no rain.

7. He just sat there; nobody talked to him.

8. Most plants require plenty of sunlight, but some plants thrive in low light.

9. Colorado is a beautiful state, and it has nice weather.

10. The game was close, but we won it in the last minute.

11. I can ride a bike, and I can also fix it.

12. Chimpanzees live in the rain forests of Africa; they eat berries, fruit, and some meat.

13. Pluto is the smallest planet in the solar system, and it is farthest from the sun.

14. Rice tastes good, but I prefer potatoes.

15. Tanya saw the birds, and she heard their calls.

☑ Unit 1 **Review**

▶ **Exercise 1** Draw a vertical line between each complete subject and complete predicate. If a sentence is compound, circle the coordinating conjunction.

Evelyn|heard the birds, (but) she|couldn't see them.

1. An American, Theodore Maiman, developed the laser in 1960.

2. The Canadian flag bears a red maple leaf.

3. The flags of Italy and Hungary share the same colors, but the stripes differ.

4. Scott Joplin received a special Pulitzer citation in 1976.

5. Amphibians and reptiles are cold-blooded animals.

6. Chicago and Atlanta have big, busy airports, but Chicago's airport is busier.

7. Babe Zaharias won three U.S. Women's Open golf titles, and Betsy Rawls claimed the title four times.

8. Vostok, Antarctica, holds the record for the lowest temperature on the earth's surface.

9. A galaxy is a system of stars, dust, and gas.

10. Sharon walked out the door, and everyone waved good-bye.

11. The Senate has 100 members, and the House of Representatives consists of 435 members.

12. Islam is the major religion of northern Africa and the Middle East.

13. Both Presidents Harrison and Tyler began their terms in 1841.

14. The respiratory system provides the body with oxygen and rids it of carbon dioxide.

15. The plate tectonic theory explains certain changes in the earth's crust.

16. Nina wore a blue shirt, and both she and Robin wore blue jeans.

17. The carpenters painted and wallpapered the bedroom and the hallway.

18. Billie Jean King holds four U.S. tennis championship titles and won at Wimbledon six times.

19. Umberto Nobile, an Italian, flew over the North Pole in an airship in 1926.

20. Warm air expands and rises, and cool air descends.

Cumulative Review: Unit 1

▶ **Exercise 1** Write *declarative, interrogative, exclamatory,* or *imperative* in the blank to identify the kind of sentence. Add the correct punctuation mark. Write *fragment* if the word group is not a complete thought.

_____imperative_____ Bring me a glass of water, please.

_____ 1. On Tuesday morning the choir leaves for its European tour

_____ 2. Our area of the state has received twelve inches of snow

_____ 3. Which person concealed the evidence

_____ 4. What a mess that puppy made

_____ 5. On a day everyone could be there

_____ 6. Sit over here away from the door

_____ 7. Brianna was promoted to editor of the school newspaper

_____ 8. Have you ever tried fly-fishing

_____ 9. This ride is making me dizzy

_____ 10. Meet us outside the restaurant at 11:30 A.M

▶ **Exercise 2** Write *S* in the blank before each simple sentence and *C* before each compound sentence. Draw one line under each simple subject and two lines under each simple predicate.

___S___ The nail had punctured the right front tire.

_____ 1. The tallow was used in candles and soap.

_____ 2. Are these blueprints all right, or will you need others?

_____ 3. Pikes Peak is in Colorado; it is 14,110 feet above sea level.

_____ 4. Outdoor sports are great, but only in the summer.

_____ 5. Cardinals nest in our yard every spring.

_____ 6. Ballet interests Emily; she is seeing *The Nutcracker* this weekend.

_____ 7. People lease cars from Uncle Ferdinand.

_____ 8. We decided on the Italian food, and Margo ordered Mexican food.

Unit 2: Nouns

Lesson 7
Nouns: Proper and Common

A **noun** names a person, place, thing, or idea. When a word names a specific person, place, thing, or idea, it is a **proper noun**. The first word and all other important words in proper nouns are capitalized. When a word names any person, place, thing, or idea, it is a **common noun**. Common nouns are not capitalized.

	PERSON	PLACE	THING	IDEA
Proper Noun:	Sinia Yakov	Canada	Bill of Rights	Islam
Common Noun:	man	country	document	religion

▶ **Exercise 1** Underline each common noun and circle each proper noun. Draw three lines under each proper noun that should be capitalized.

Dr. martin luther king Jr. was the highly respected african american who led the civil rights movement during the 1950s and 1960s.

1. A baby named martin luther king jr. was born in atlanta, Georgia.

2. His family lived in a two-story house on Auburn avenue.

3. His father, martin Luther King sr., was a minister and the son of a sharecropper.

4. His mother, Alberta williams king, was a teacher.

5. King skipped two grades at booker T. Washington high school.

6. Still a teenager, king graduated from morehouse College.

7. King first thought of becoming a doctor or a lawyer but finally decided to go into the ministry.

8. While still at morehouse, king was ordained in the church of his father.

9. King was elected co-pastor at the church upon his graduation from college.

Grammar

10. The hardworking young man went on to graduate school at crozer theological

    Seminary in chester, Pennsylvania.

11. King was very intelligent and an avid reader.

12. King studied the ideas of people such as martin luther, mohandas Gandhi, jesus of

    nazareth, aristotle, plato, and adam smith.

13. King earned the degree of bachelor of divinity at crozer.

14. King won a fellowship to go to the university of his choice for his doctorate.

15. King chose to go to boston university.

16. King also took courses in philosophy at Harvard.

17. While at boston university, king met an intelligent and beautiful woman named

    coretta scott.

18. Coretta scott was a soprano, studying voice at the new england conservatory of music.

19. King and scott married a few years after their first encounter.

20. Coretta and Martin Luther King jr. had four children: yolanda denise, Martin luther III,

    dexter, and Bernice albertine.

21. While still working on his doctoral degree, king received a letter from a church in

    montgomery, Alabama.

22. The letter stated that the church would be happy to have king preach.

23. The church was located on dexter avenue and was called the dexter avenue baptist

    church.

24. The church was close to the impressive alabama state capitol, where the legislature meets.

25. Ironically, Jefferson davis had been sworn in as the new president of the Confederacy

    on the steps of that same building.

Lesson 8
Nouns: Concrete and Abstract

Grammar

Concrete nouns name things that can be experienced with any of the five senses—touch, sight, hearing, smell, and taste. **Abstract nouns** name ideas, qualities, or feelings that cannot be experienced with any of the five senses.

Abstract Nouns:	sadness	truth	freedom	intelligence	justice
Concrete Nouns:	frown	book	rain	library	music

▶ **Exercise 1** Underline each concrete noun once and each abstract noun twice.

My dad tells me cleanliness is important.

1. A commercial pilot must have a lot of flying experience.

2. My uncle, aunt, and cousin live in a large trailer.

3. The judge reminded the witness to tell the truth.

4. The inventor had an idea that would help the auto industry improve safety.

5. The playful beagle liked to chase its tail.

6. The hardworking farmer was disappointed with the weather.

7. The walls and ceiling of the room were black with age and dirt.

8. Clouds covered the sun and sky.

9. Many people voted in the elections last fall.

10. The veterinarian spent time and energy examining horses.

11. My cat gets great pleasure on the windowsill on a sunny day.

12. During the holiday season, the malls are bursting with people.

13. The museum held paintings and sculptures of great beauty.

14. The girl's bravery during the disaster did not go unnoticed.

15. As huge waves crashed onto the shore, the beachcombers fled in fear.

16. The college students lived in a quiet dormitory.

17. The florist made a bouquet of roses for their anniversary.

18. The teacher at the preschool showed much patience.

Grammar

19. Small children like to play with blocks.

20. The tennis player hit the ball with accuracy and determination.

21. At the traffic light, the driver pressed the brake.

22. The long-legged spider spun a web under the stairs in the basement.

23. The newspaper had a big article about the economy.

24. The black crow sat on the fence and stared at the scarecrow.

25. Using coupons is a good way for shoppers to cut costs.

26. The triathlete collapsed with exhaustion after reaching the finish line.

27. While taking the test, the student frowned in concentration.

28. Tourists watched in fascination as the volcano oozed lava.

29. The leek is a type of onion that blooms in the spring.

30. The bird in the tree held the interest of the cat.

31. The painter looked at the canvas in satisfaction.

32. After listening to the patient, the psychologist fell deep into thought.

33. Late into the evening, the chemist worked in the laboratory.

34. The children took great care to be gentle when holding the hamster.

35. The bodybuilder lifted the heavy barbell with ease.

36. Unable to find the toy, the baby cried in frustration.

37. The athlete possessed raw talent and ability.

38. A conference to deal with hunger and starvation was held in a hotel.

39. A well-balanced diet helps to maintain good health.

40. Scientists have found that many industrial processes are not good for the

environment.

▶ **Writing Link** **Write a paragraph that describes your city or town and what you like or dislike about it. Use both concrete and abstract nouns.**

_____

_____

_____

Lesson 9
Nouns: Compounds, Plurals, and Possessives

Grammar

Compound nouns are nouns that are made up of two or more words. Compound nouns can be one word, like the word *football,* or more than one word, like *rocking chair.* Other compound nouns have two or more words that are joined by hyphens, such as *hand-me-down.*

To form the plural of most compound nouns written as one word, add *-s* or *-es.* To form the plural of compound nouns that are hyphenated or written as more than one word, make the most important part of the noun plural.

ONE WORD
snowmobile**s**, baseball**s**, grandfather**s**

HYPHENATED
father**s**-in-law   baby-sitter**s**   runner**s**-up

MORE THAN ONE WORD
home run**s**   music box**es**   quarter horse**s**   surgeon**s** general

A **possessive noun** names who or what has something. Possessive nouns can be common or proper nouns, singular or plural, compound or not. To form the possessive of all singular nouns and of plural nouns not ending in *-s,* add an apostrophe and *-s.* To form the possessive of plural nouns already ending in *-s,* add only an apostrophe.

boy**'s**   boss**'s**   Luis**'s**   women**'s**   puppies**'**

▶ **Exercise 1** Write in the blank the plural form of each compound noun.

jelly bean   __jelly beans_____

1. fund-raiser _____

2. attorney-at-law _____

3. sister-in-law _____

4. nutcracker _____

5. stomachache _____

6. funny bone _____

7. sweatshirt _____

8. motor home _____

9. sergeant at arms _____

10. beehive _____

11. color guard _____

12. steam iron _____

13. farmhand _____

14. workshop _____

15. stepfather _____   **18.** minute hand _____

16. mailbox _____   **19.** drawstring _____

17. bill of health _____   **20.** field trip _____

▶ **Exercise 2 Complete each sentence by writing the correct possessive form of the noun in parentheses.**

_____Marietta's_____ hands felt cold and clammy. (Marietta)

1. The young sailor sounded the _____ horn. (ship)

2. The _____ performance during the big game was not good enough to win. (players)

3. _____ test scores improved dramatically. (Dennis)

4. The _____ teeth were sharp as razors. (bobcat)

5. The _____ vacation was relaxing and fun. (Ramoses)

6. I can do a lot of my homework on my _____ computer. (parents)

7. The _____ loud and persistent chirping caused Cole to wake up. (birds)

8. The teacher enjoyed the sound of the _____ laughter. (children)

9. During autumn, the _____ colors change. (leaves)

10. The _____ weight is more than one ton. (Liberty Bell)

11. The _____ movement began to gain momentum. (women)

12. After the touchdown, the _____ cheering was deafening. (fans)

13. The hook caught in the _____ mouth. (fish)

14. In the sunlight, the _____ leaves grew wildly. (plant)

15. The _____ soup was piping hot and delicious. (cook)

16. _____ largest city is Chicago. (Illinois)

17. The _____ route never changed. (bus)

18. _____ reign was one of the longest in Great Britain's history.

(Queen Victoria)

Lesson 10
Nouns: Collective

A **collective noun** names a group that is made up of individuals.

The **family** struggled through the **crowd** to see the **band.**

COLLECTIVE NOUNS

class	family	herd	audience	orchestra	panel
staff	team	swarm	jury	flock	

Collective nouns can have either a singular or a plural meaning. When referring to the group as a unit, the noun has a singular meaning and takes a singular verb. When referring to the individual members of the group, the noun has a plural meaning and takes a plural verb.

The **team works** on its defensive plays.
The **team go** to their individual lockers.

▶ **Exercise 1** Underline the verb form in parentheses that best completes each sentence.

The audience (leaves, <u>leave</u>) their seats.

1. The book club (discusses, discuss) their personal opinions of the plot.

2. The class (is, are) going on a bus to the art museum.

3. The choir from East High School (sings, sing) the loudest.

4. The elephant herd (makes, make) a thundering noise during a stampede.

5. The baseball team (boasts, boast) an excellent batting average.

6. The budget committee (reaches, reach) a final decision.

7. The entire class (takes, take) a trip to Washington, D.C.

8. The theater troupe (comes, come) out separately at the end of the play.

9. The bee swarm (buzzes, buzz) around the hive.

10. The jury (argues, argue) among themselves over the verdict.

11. The debating team (wins, win) almost every time.

12. The band (puts, put) their instruments away after practice.

13. The barbershop quartet (knows, know) their individual parts.

Grammar

Grammar

14. The audience (gives, give) the singer a standing ovation.

15. The class (reports, report) on their chosen topics.

16. The math department (decides, decide) which classes they will teach.

17. Boy Scout Troop 10 (raises, raise) money for a camping trip.

18. The Supreme Court (rules, rule) on many of its cases each year.

19. The wolf pack (decreases, decrease) in size after a hard winter.

20. City council (goes, go) to their respective seats before the meeting begins.

21. The flock (flies, fly) in a southerly direction.

22. The restaurant staff (shares, share) their tips with each other.

23. The army platoon (marches, march) on the military base.

24. The U.S. Congress (consists, consist) of members from all fifty states.

25. College athletics (seems, seem) to be a profession in some cases.

26. The crowd (stirs, stir) as the politician takes the platform.

27. The family (sleeps, sleep) soundly in their rooms.

28. The orchestra (draws, draw) a big crowd.

29. The track team (runs, run) well as a whole.

30. The subcommittee (calls, call) for a meeting with the entire committee.

31. The band (appeals, appeal) to people of all ages.

32. The school board (presents, present) its proposal to the superintendent.

33. The volleyball team (practices, practice) their serving techniques.

34. The Music Club (listens, listen) to operas together every Tuesday.

35. The public (supports, support) its mayor.

36. The herd (roams, roam) the countryside aimlessly.

37. The jury (submits, submit) its verdict to the judge.

38. The mob of protestors (is, are) getting out of hand.

39. The Senate (contains, contain) fewer members than the House of Representatives.

40. The choir (knows, know) their individual parts.

Lesson 11
Distinguishing Plurals, Possessives, and Contractions

Grammar

A **contraction** is a word made by combining two words into one and leaving out one or more letters from the two words. An apostrophe shows where the letters have been omitted.

can + not = can't   singer + is = singer's

Most plural and possessive nouns and certain contractions end with the letter -*s*. As a result, they sound alike, but their spellings and meanings are different.

Plural Noun	The **singers** wrote the song.
Plural Possessive Noun	The **singers'** song is enjoyable.
Singular Possessive Noun	We heard the **singer's** song.
Contraction	The **singer's** the songwriter.

▶ **Exercise 1** Write *pl.* above each plural noun (not including plural possessives), *poss.* above each possessive noun, and *con.* above each contraction.

            con.   pl.
Ernest Hemingway's one of the most influential American writers of the twentieth

century.

1. Hemingway's won two prestigious awards—the Nobel Prize and the Pulitzer Prize.

2. Hemingway's birthplace was Oak Park, Illinois.

3. As a boy and youth, Hemingway spent many a summer's day in northern Michigan.

4. Hemingway's family owned a cottage on Waloon Lake.

5. Hemingway made many friends there.

6. Native Americans of the region were among his group of friends.

7. Some of his friends' adventures appeared in his books and short stories.

8. The young Hemingway's writing career began in Kansas City.

9. Hemingway was one of many reporters for the city's newspaper, the *Kansas City Star*.

10. Kansas City's one of many cities Hemingway visited.

11. At age eighteen, the young man's thoughts wandered overseas.

12. Hemingway traveled to Milan, Italy, on the first of his transatlantic flights.

13. World War I's battles were still raging.

14. Hemingway's job was ambulance deputy with an American field service unit.

15. The day that Hemingway arrived, a factory full of munitions blew up.

16. After a few months' time, Hemingway was badly wounded in both legs.

17. These wartime experiences provided many of the details for Hemingway's novel about World War I, called *A Farewell to Arms.*

18. Several of his short stories' details can also be traced back to Hemingway's time spent in Milan.

19. After the war, Hemingway took trips to many different cities and countries.

20. Hemingway's known for discovering places that would later become tourist attractions.

▶ **Exercise 2** **Underline the word in parentheses that best completes the sentence.**

One of (<u>Hemingway's</u>, Hemingways') adventures was an African safari.

1. Hemingway made (preparation's, preparations) for the trip.

2. Some of Hemingway's finest (story's, stories) were written as a result of the safari.

3. The (writers', writer's) imagination was also captured by Spain.

4. (Hemingways, Hemingway's) first exposure to a bullfight overwhelmed the writer.

5. Many of his (stories, stories') themes are about bullfighting.

6. Hemingway also journeyed to (Switzerland's, Switzerlands') cities.

7. The writer made several (trips, trip's) to Switzerland as a reporter for the *Toronto Star.*

8. Hemingway wrote stories about the (countries', country's) winter sports.

9. (Readers', Readers) admiration for Hemingway's writing was strong.

10. Hemingway lived in the (United States', United States) for much of his adult life.

11. Hemingway put his (roots, root's) down in Key West, Florida, in the 1920s and 1930s.

12. Key West was a source for a great deal of Hemingway's (writings, writing's).

13. The themes of these stories are as diverse as the (writers, writer's) life.

14. (Boats', Boats) always appealed to Hemingway.

Lesson 12
Appositives

An **appositive** is a noun that is placed next to, or in apposition to, another noun to identify it or add information to it.

Franklin Delano Roosevelt's wife, **Eleanor,** was a famous humanitarian.

An **appositive phrase** is a group of words that includes an appositive and other words that describe the appositive.

Roosevelt, **our thirty-second president,** was the only U.S. president to be elected to the presidency four times.

An appositive phrase that is not essential to the meaning of the sentence is set off from the rest of the sentence by commas. However, if the appositive is essential to the meaning of the sentence, commas are not used.

▶ **Exercise 1** Underline each appositive or appositive phrase, and circle the noun it identifies.

(George Washington) commander of the Continental Army, led troops during the Revolutionary War.

1. Washington's picture is on a coin, the quarter.

2. John Adams succeeded the president, George Washington, as head of the United States.

3. Adams's wife, Abigail, was well read and outspoken.

4. Thomas Jefferson wrote the first draft of a historic document, the Declaration of Independence.

5. Jefferson designed Monticello, his thirty-two room house.

6. Dolly Madison, wife of James Madison, rescued important government documents from the White House before fire could destroy them.

7. James Monroe was said to have nursed the wounds of the famous French soldier the Marquis de Lafayette.

8. Monroe was president when the United States acquired Florida, a populous territory.

9. John Quincy Adams, the son of the second president, served only one term.

10. A former governor of New York, Martin Van Buren capitalized on the popularity of his predecessor, Andrew Jackson.

11. William Henry Harrison's nickname, "Old Tippecanoe," came from his military victory at the Battle of Tippecanoe in 1811.

12. Harrison's successor, John Tyler, was the first person to become president because of the death of the current president.

13. The "dark horse" candidate, James K. Polk, was backed by the Democratic party.

14. Polk wished to acquire California, a Mexican territory.

15. Zachary Taylor, "Old Rough and Ready," achieved much popularity as a general in the Mexican War.

16. Taylor, the twelfth president, died after only a year in office.

17. Franklin Pierce's good friend Nathaniel Hawthorne helped to promote his presidential candidacy.

18. The Supreme Court case *Dred Scott* v. *Sanford* was decided during James Buchanan's presidency.

19. Buchanan was defeated by the Republican candidate, Abraham Lincoln.

20. Lincoln, one of our greatest presidents, had to lead the country during a bloody civil war.

21. Lincoln earned the nickname the "Great Emancipator."

22. The assassin John Wilkes Booth shot and killed Lincoln one month after he began his second term.

23. The vice president, Andrew Jackson, was sworn in as president after Lincoln's death.

24. The celebrated Civil War general Ulysses S. Grant became the eighteenth president of the United States in 1869.

25. Rutherford B. Hayes's wife, Lucy, was the first wife of a president to hold a college degree.

26. The United States battleship *Maine* blew up in Cuba's harbor during William McKinley's presidency.

☑ Unit 2 **Review**

▶ **Exercise 1** Underline each common noun once and each proper noun twice. Write in the blank *plural, possessive, contraction,* or *appositive* to identify the word in italics.

__contraction__   *Neil Armstrong's* a famous astronaut.

_____ **1.** The Empire State Building used to be *America's* tallest building.

_____ **2.** Jon's an excellent skater, and his *brother's* a great swimmer.

_____ **3.** The *buckeye's* a kind of chestnut.

_____ **4.** Edwin Hubble was the first to show that the universe contains other *galaxies* besides the Milky Way.

_____ **5.** The boy's teacher taught him *volleyball's* finer points.

_____ **6.** The crowd at Cape Kennedy cheered the *rocket's* liftoff.

_____ **7.** Neal was born on his *grandfather's* farm in western Oklahoma.

_____ **8.** The Pointer *Sisters* sing songs with complicated harmonies.

_____ **9.** Isaiah, my best *friend,* is moving to Kansas City, Missouri.

_____ **10.** Governor Stevenson is the best governor our state has had in several *years.*

_____ **11.** The campers took backpacks and *flashlights* when they camped out in the Appalachian Mountains.

_____ **12.** *Hillary's* going to try out for the next musical.

_____ **13.** The musical *Oklahoma!* will be presented to the Parent-Teacher Association.

_____ **14.** The contestants had to memorize one of *Robert Frost's* poems.

_____ **15.** The *tourists* attended the rodeo celebrating Annie Oakley.

_____ **16.** *Maureen's* the most talented flutist in the Johnson Middle School Orchestra.

_____ **17.** Mrs. Phillips, the children's *teacher,* has a keen sense of fashion.

_____ **18.** The *fullback's* helmet fell off when he was tackled.

Cumulative Review: Units 1–2

▶ **Exercise 1** Draw a vertical line between the subject and the predicate. Underline the noun in parentheses that best completes each sentence.

The (<u>bicycle's</u>, bicycles) tire |rolled down the street.

1. My dad's scrambled (eggs, eggs') were too runny to eat.

2. The identical (twins, twins') clothes always matched.

3. Madame Dupont taught her (student's, students) how to make Croque Monsieurs.

4. I love to read the Brontë (sisters, sisters') books.

5. Carlos, Isaac, and Hasan sold popcorn at (Saturdays', Saturday's) soccer match.

6. Edgar Allan (Poe's, Poes') story *The Black Cat* is very scary.

7. Shirley and her (friend's, friends) went to the mall after cheerleading practice.

8. John (Hancocks, Hancock's) signature was the first signature on the Declaration of Independence.

9. Many tourists are attracted to (Hawaiis', Hawaii's) beaches.

10. My parents' favorite singing group was the (Beatle's, Beatles).

11. The collie chewed up the (childrens', children's) toys.

12. My mother's (brother-in-laws, brothers-in-law) from Detroit go to the Pistons' games.

13. The five (maid of honors, maids of honor) at my sister's wedding wore pink.

14. The (newspapers, newspapers') headlines were about the earthquake in Japan.

15. The chicken pox attacked both (preschools', preschools) children.

16. Eugene and Jennifer were (runner-ups, runners-up) in the poetry contest.

17. Paul Cézanne painted many still-life (paintings', paintings).

18. The drama club invited all the (actor's, actors') families to the play's dress rehearsal.

19. My (friends', friends) and I had ice cream after dinner and before the concert.

20. Susie and Maria enjoy trying (Grandmother's, Grandmothers) recipes.

Unit 3: Verbs

Lesson 13
Action Verbs

The main word in a complete predicate of a sentence is the verb. An **action verb** is a word that names an action. Action verbs can express either physical or mental actions.

The white cloud **floated** lazily across the sky. (physical action)
Mary **thought** about the painting. (mental action)

Have, has, and *had* are also action verbs when they name what the subject owns or holds.

Jim **has** an entire set of Mark Twain books. (owns)
Jim **has** experience as a character actor. (holds)

▶ **Exercise 1** Draw two lines under the action verb in each sentence. Write *physical* or *mental* in the blank to indicate if the verb expresses physical action or mental action.

_____physical_____   Horses <u>help</u> humans in many ways.

_____   **1.** Long ago, medieval knights fought battles atop powerful horses.

_____   **2.** Lighter horses carried lords and ladies on fox hunts.

_____   **3.** Travelers sometimes rode horses on long journeys.

_____   **4.** Later, the wealthy traveled in horse-drawn carriages.

_____   **5.** Farmers also relied on horses in the past.

_____   **6.** American farms had more than 20 million horses and mules in 1900.

_____   **7.** Today, many persons keep horses.

_____   **8.** Children especially love shaggy, bright-eyed ponies.

_____   **9.** Gentle Shetland ponies delight young children.

_____   **10.** Shetlands stand only four hands (21 inches) high!

_____   **11.** Sturdy and energetic, ponies perform many tasks.

_____   **12.** The Chincoteague ponies run wild on an island off the Virginia coast.

_____   **13.** According to legend, they swam ashore from a Spanish ship.

Grammar

_____ **14.** The Spanish also brought horses to the Native Americans.

_____ **15.** Some Native Americans became skillful horsemen.

_____ **16.** They used horses in bison hunts.

_____ **17.** The Native Americans preferred the colorful Pinto and Appaloosa breeds.

_____ **18.** Bands of wild horses—Mustangs—roamed wild and free in the

American West.

_____ **19.** Other types of horses never left the city.

_____ **20.** Shire horses pull wagons and carts through the narrow streets of London.

_____ **21.** Circus horses perform before appreciative audiences around the world.

_____ **22.** Police officers ride horses through busy city streets.

_____ **23.** Inside or outside the city, people train horses for many kinds of tasks.

_____ **24.** Horses learn signals through constant repetition.

_____ **25.** Eventually they respond to even the slightest signal from the rider.

_____ **26.** A good rider commands his or her mount effortlessly.

_____ **27.** The horse follows the rider's hand, leg, and body signals.

_____ **28.** Horses appreciate a familiar set of rules.

_____ **29.** For example, the rider always mounts a horse from its left side.

_____ **30.** Unfamiliar situations frighten some horses.

_____ **31.** However, horses have many excellent qualities.

_____ **32.** A horse remembers pleasant and unpleasant events from years before.

_____ **33.** Horses enjoy a thorough grooming each day.

_____ **34.** Horses eat grass, hay, and grain.

_____ **35.** Their stomachs hold eighteen quarts of food.

_____ **36.** A horse requires ten to twelve gallons of fresh water daily.

▶ **Writing Link** **Imagine that you can have any horse you want. Use action verbs to describe the horse you would choose.**

_____

_____

Lesson 14
Verbs: Transitive and Intransitive

Depending on its use in a particular sentence, an action verb can be either transitive or intransitive. A transitive verb is followed by a word or words—called the direct object—that answer the question *what?* or *whom?* An intransitive verb is an action verb that does not have a direct object.

Transitive: The pilot **landed** the antique **airplane.** (*Airplane* is the direct object that answers the question *landed what?* after the verb *landed.*)

Intransitive: The pilot **landed** carefully. (There is no direct object answering the question *landed what?* or *whom?*)

▶ **Exercise 1   Draw two lines under each action verb. Circle each direct object. Write *T* in the blank if the verb is transitive or *I* if the verb is intransitive.**

_____T_____   The pilot started the airplane

_____   1. Wilbur and Orville Wright built the first successful airplane.

_____   2. They built their machine in Ohio.

_____   3. They took it to Kitty Hawk, North Carolina, for its first flight.

_____   4. Orville Wright flew the first airplane on December 17, 1903.

_____   5. The winds at Kitty Hawk blew steadily that day.

_____   6. The twelve-horsepower engine sputtered.

_____   7. Soon it lifted the 750-pound plane into the air for a flight of 120 feet.

_____   8. Orville's brother, Wilbur, ran alongside.

_____   9. This first flight lasted only twelve seconds.

_____   10. The Wright brothers made three more flights that day.

_____   11. The longest one lasted fifty-nine seconds.

_____   12. Few newspapers carried news about the first flight.

_____   13. The brothers made improvements on their airplane and their flight techniques.

_____   14. Other designers worked hard.

_____   15. More successful airplanes appeared.

_____ **16.** Of course, the first pilots had no flight instructors.

_____ **17.** Louis Blériot flew across the English Channel in 1909.

_____ **18.** In 1910, Glenn H. Curtiss piloted his craft from Albany to New York City.

_____ **19.** Airplane technology grew quickly.

_____ **20.** At first, persons used open fields as airports.

_____ **21.** Some airports today retain the word *field* in their names.

_____ **22.** Air fields operated as early as 1909.

_____ **23.** Workers built twenty airports in three years.

_____ **24.** In 1914, the First World War began.

_____ **25.** Both sides in the war found new uses for airplanes.

_____ **26.** The number of air fields expanded because of the new airplane technologies.

_____ **27.** After the war, even the U.S. Postal Service realized its need for airplanes.

_____ **28.** In the 1930s, passengers used planes as an important means of transportation.

_____ **29.** The government counted 1,036 airports in the United States in 1927.

_____ **30.** Today more than eleven thousand airports exist in the United States.

_____ **31.** Fewer than one thousand of them serve large planes.

_____ **32.** Planners established airports close to cities for convenience.

_____ **33.** They chose the sites carefully.

_____ **34.** Nonetheless, airports created problems for some persons.

_____ **35.** Jet engines generate more noise than propeller engines.

_____ **36.** Nearby residents complain sometimes about the noise problem.

▶ **Writing Link Would you like to become a pilot someday? Write a paragraph explaining why or why not. Use transitive and intransitive verbs.**

_____

_____

_____

_____

_____

Lesson 15
Verbs with Indirect Objects

Both a direct object and an indirect object may follow an action verb in a sentence. An **indirect object** tells *to whom* or *for whom* the verb's action is done.

Kara sold **Matt** the bicycle. (*Matt* tells *to whom* Kara sold the bicycle. *Bicycle* is the direct object.)

Indirect objects follow certain rules. First, indirect objects are found only in sentences that have direct objects. Second, an indirect object always comes before a direct object. Finally, the prepositions *to* or *for* can be inserted before the indirect object; its position in the sentence can be changed, and the sentence will still make sense.

Levi threw **Jake** the football. (*Jake* is the indirect object before the direct object, *football*.)

Levi threw the football **to Jake**. (The meaning of the sentence is unchanged. *Jake* was an indirect object in the first example.)

▶ **Exercise 1** Write *DO* above each direct object and *IO* above each indirect object. Not every sentence has an indirect object.

              IO   DO
Wrenn left Josh his video.

1. Yuri threw Karen the ball.

2. The jeweler sold the couple two lovely rings.

3. Roberto refunded Rayna the cost of the unused ticket.

4. Mr. Kenja gave Miki and Vance permission for their project.

5. The student council assigned our class the clean-up project.

6. Pablo paid the clerk two dollars for the birthday card.

7. Ted's mom sent our family the photograph.

8. Jean-Luc speaks French fluently.

9. Sarah guaranteed Ali full payment for his work at her print shop.

10. Alicia lent Steve her history book.

11. Mona showed Emilio her new tennis racket.

12. Mr. Hayes presented the team the first-place trophy.

13. Joanna handed the mail carrier her letter.

14. Boris gave Anita the ruler.

15. Seth taught our class sign language last year.

16. Will made his dog a house.

17. During the game, Salahi passed Harry the ball for three lay-ups.

18. Carl approached the intersection cautiously.

19. Sheila asked her teacher the new student's name.

20. We chose Tammi as our team captain.

21. James offered his classmate a ride to the science fair.

22. They refunded Dad the overcharge.

23. Sally owed Tanya a CD.

24. Akira sold a children's magazine his story.

25. Drew told the children a story at the library last Saturday.

26. Alex bought Jean a ticket to the movie.

27. Isabel lent me her portable radio for the picnic.

28. Debra walked her dog after dinner.

29. The carpenter built the Rileys some beautiful kitchen cabinets.

30. The captain showed his troops the plan.

31. She assigned the class a paper that would be due in one week.

32. Ahmed left the rare bird some food on his way to school.

33. The principal often offers students and teachers his advice.

34. Charlie taught the vocalist the new aria.

35. Terry assured the client of his support in the matter.

36. The deer leapt the creek with ease.

37. Philip conceded Kamil the argument.

38. Mrs. Jones brought Henry his homework.

Lesson 16

Linking Verbs and Predicate Words

A **linking verb** joins the subject of a sentence with a noun or adjective in the predicate that identifies or describes the subject. *Be* in all its forms *(am, is, are, was, were)* is the most common linking verb. Other linking verbs include *appear, become, feel, grow, look, seem, smell, sound, taste,* and *turn.*

Corinne **was** captain. (The linking verb *was* links *captain* to the subject, *Corrine.*)

▶ **Exercise 1** Draw two lines under each verb. Place a check in the blank next to each sentence that contains a linking verb.

___✔___   The bird is red.

_____ 1. The grass became brown and dry during the drought.

_____ 2. The delicious dessert was cherry cobbler.

_____ 3. Karen asked for that book for her birthday.

_____ 4. His answer annoyed me.

_____ 5. The exterior of the new auditorium appears stately.

_____ 6. Cally looks hot and weary after mowing the grass.

_____ 7. The wonderful train ride became an impressive memory.

_____ 8. My younger sister played Tiny Tim in the play.

_____ 9. The auctioneer of the old property was Alice's father.

_____ 10. The annual school choral production was a success.

_____ 11. The smell of burning leaves brought memories of the past.

_____ 12. The country church bells sounded across the meadow.

_____ 13. Our old barn is a warm shelter for the cattle in winter.

_____ 14. Colette ran the marathon in record time.

_____ 15. Jamal's new bicycle seemed too large for him.

_____ 16. The long line of school buses became a caravan for the team.

_____ 17. Today the summer skies seem extremely blue.

_____ **18.** The old candy bar tasted stale.

_____ **19.** The novel soon turned dull.

_____ **20.** The movie ended too quickly.

The words that follow a linking verb and identify or describe the subject are called **subject complements.** The two kinds of subject complements are predicate nouns and predicate adjectives. A **predicate noun** follows a linking verb and renames the subject. A **predicate adjective** follows a linking verb and describes the subject. Predicate nouns and predicate adjectives may be compound.

Corinne was a **team captain** and a **friend.** (compound predicate noun)
She sounded **tired** but **hopeful.** (compound predicate adjective)

▶ **Exercise 2** Write *PN* above each predicate noun and *PA* above each predicate adjective.

                                PA
The Grand Canyon is spectacular at any time of the year.

1. Those mountains become a source of water for our city.

2. The toddler sounded fussy and sleepy.

3. Their opinions on the matter turned sour.

4. Manufacturing was the major industry.

5. The new foreign exchange student seems homesick.

6. The young actor's face appeared old and unhappy with the makeup.

7. Ellie looked joyful over her first-place award.

8. The storm grew intense during the early morning hours.

9. The secretary automatically becomes the president the following year.

10. The old trapper's cabin smelled damp and musty.

11. Jamil felt anxious about his driver's test.

12. The proposed program sounds innovative.

13. Professor Kohler became an authority on the Mesozoic era.

14. The tin soldier looked serious and strong in his place on the shelf.

15. The first buds of spring soon became beautiful flowers.

16. Robyn grew nervous before exams.

17. The green apples tasted bitter to everyone.

18. Sonja became the class expert on astronomy.

19. The weather turned sunny during our camping trip.

20. Every other Saturday Mel was the substitute mail carrier.

21. The handblown glass ornament looked fragile.

22. The twin boys sounded excited about their new baby sister.

23. These frogs were tadpoles not too long ago.

24. The authors felt honored by the recognition.

25. The highway was once an old wagon train route.

▶ **Exercise 3** Draw two lines under each verb. Write *PN* above each predicate noun and *PA* above each predicate adjective. Some sentences do not have a predicate noun or a predicate adjective.

PA
My birthday cake looks beautiful.

1. The car appeared old and rusty.

2. Those tulips look fantastic in the spring sunshine.

3. The old stairway in Kelly's house seems long.

4. Jafar convinced Jennifer of his sincerity.

5. The November weather turned cold and miserable.

6. Steve sickened at the thought of missing his plane.

7. The new team member is Laurie's cousin.

8. Last winter began too soon.

9. The shadows were dark and silent.

10. The roads appeared glassy after the ice storm.

11. My little brother begged for the video.

12. The stately bare tree looked eerie against the sky at twilight.

13. In the middle of the street sat a yellow cat.

14. Mr. Smith grew angry at himself.

15. That farm truck is full of golden corn.

16. Teri became the fastest runner on the track team.

17. Mrs. Vaughn sounded confident about the new computer program.

18. Pecan pie tastes rich and sweet.

19. The snow lies heavily on the rooftops.

20. Marcie's father is a firefighter.

21. Vacation time grew short toward the end of August.

22. Buffalo, New York, was their destination.

23. The salty sea air smelled fresh and welcoming to Kirsten.

24. The dinosaurs in the movie appeared lifelike.

25. The small acorn became a giant oak.

▶ **Writing Link** **Write a paragraph describing what you might see on a winter walk in the woods. Use linking verbs and predicate words.**

_____

_____

_____

_____

_____

_____

_____

Lesson 17
Present and Past Tenses

Tense refers to the form of the verb that shows the time of the action.

The present tense refers to an action that is happening now, to an action that happens regularly, or to a situation that is generally true. The present tense and the base form of a verb are the same when used with all subjects except singular nouns or *he, she,* or *it.* In these cases *-s* or *-es* is added to the verb.

I **smell** the fresh bread. (happening now)
The coach **calls** practice daily. (happens regularly, generally true)

The past tense refers to an action that has already occurred. The past tense of many verbs is formed by adding *-ed* to the base form of the verb.

I **smelled** the bread earlier.
Isabel **called** the coach.

▶ **Exercise 1** **Draw two lines under each verb. Write its tense, *present* or *past,* in the blank.**

___present___   Archaeologists study the past.

_____ **1.** Herodotus lived centuries ago in Asia Minor.

_____ **2.** No one knows the exact dates of his birth and death.

_____ **3.** According to historians, he lived between 484 B.C. and 420 B.C.

_____ **4.** The Roman orator Cicero once called Herodotus "the Father of History."

_____ **5.** Today historians study his books about the Persian Empire.

_____ **6.** Herodotus considered his own work an "inquiry."

_____ **7.** Many individuals enjoy his lively style of writing.

_____ **8.** The historian gained knowledge for his books during his journeys.

_____ **9.** He traveled widely through Greece, the Middle East, and North Africa.

_____ **10.** His books show his gift as a storyteller of history.

_____ **11.** Other historians of this period encountered difficulties with some of

Herodotus's accounts.

Grammar

_____ **12.** Herodotus remains the main source of original information on Greek

history between 550 B.C. and 479 B.C.

_____ **13.** Through his travels he learned about the customs and history of other

peoples.

_____ **14.** His books show his boundless curiosity about peoples and their customs.

_____ **15.** Herodotus described his accounts of their customs.

_____ **16.** His first four books describe the history and divisions of the Persian

empire.

_____ **17.** Ancient rulers accumulated large archives of documents and records

about their achievements.

_____ **18.** Archaeologists study records and remains.

_____ **19.** Even Herodotus showed interest in fossils as a link to the past.

_____ **20.** The works of Herodotus preserve the past for all humankind.

▶ **Exercise 2** **Draw two lines under each verb. Correct each sentence by writing in the
blank the past tense form of the verb.**

conducted Archaeologists conduct that excavation in 1936.

_____ **1.** Two travelers first uncover Native American cities in 1839.

_____ **2.** John Lloyd Stephens and Frederick Catherwood discover the lost city of

Copan.

_____ **3.** Stephens and Catherwood persist in their search.

_____ **4.** They notice great stone stairs in the Honduran jungle.

_____ **5.** They hack the jungle undergrowth.

_____ **6.** Amazement grips them at the top of the stairs.

_____ **7.** The two perceive a vast temple below them.

_____ **8.** Catherwood traces outlines on ruled paper.

_____ **9.** He produces drawings and paintings of Copan's monuments.

_____ **10.** Unfortunately, Catherwood contracts malaria.

_____ **11.** Stephens publishes a book about their discoveries.

_____ **12.** He describes the ancestors of the region's Mayan peoples.

_____ **13.** The Mayan civilization thrives from the fourth to the sixteenth centuries.

_____ **14.** More than 1,000 years ago, 100,000 persons live in the ancient city of

Tikal.

_____ **15.** Classic Mayan civilization lasts until the tenth century.

_____ **16.** City centers possess great numbers of pyramids and palaces.

_____ **17.** Civil war weakens the cities, however.

_____ **18.** Eventually, the common citizens abandon their mighty rulers.

_____ **19.** Their greatest contribution improves the lives of everyone.

_____ **20.** They develop foods different from any other foods in the world.

▶ **Exercise 3** **Draw two lines under each verb. Correct each sentence by writing in the blank the present tense of the verb.**

____wonder____ People constantly <u>wondered</u> about life on Earth many years ago.

_____ **1.** Discoveries about prehistoric times on Earth excited even young

children.

_____ **2.** Archaeologists, geologists, and paleontologists provided us with these

discoveries and their revelations about the past.

_____ **3.** Geologists studied the history of Earth and its life through rocks.

_____ **4.** Scientists who collected fossils are paleontologists.

_____ **5.** Archaeologists examined material remains such as fossils, artifacts, and

relics of past human life and activities.

_____ **6.** Rocks contained such fossils and remains of the past.

_____ **7.** Fossils revealed to us the history of life on Earth.

_____ **8.** They formed over long periods of time.

_____ **9.** Fossils such as pieces of bone, a tooth, or an impression in a rock

showed us examples of past life.

_____ **10.** Geologists calculated the ages of the layers of rock.

_____ **11.** From this, they determined the time of existence of the formerly live

material.

_____ **12.** Geologists located the simplest forms of life in the oldest layers of rock.

_____ **13.** Rocks presented an incomplete history of the earth for various reasons.

_____ **14.** Weather and erosion destroyed rocks and their geological records.

_____ **15.** Also, heat and pressure deep in the earth's crust caused changes in the

rocks.

_____ **16.** The history of Earth consisted of five periods of time called eras.

_____ **17.** These eras included the Archeozoic, the earliest of the five periods.

_____ **18.** A chart, or geological time scale, outlined the history of Earth according

to these five eras.

_____ **19.** On such a chart, Earth's earliest history appeared at the bottom and the

most recent at the top.

_____ **20.** Unfortunately, the complete history of Earth remained a secret.

▶ **Writing Link** **Write a paragraph describing what you might see as a traveler in the
ancient Mayan world. Use the past tense of verbs to describe your journey.**

_____

_____

_____

_____

_____

_____

_____

_____

_____

_____

_____

Lesson 18
Main Verbs and Helping Verbs

All verbs have four principal parts that are used to form the tenses.

PRINCIPAL PARTS OF THE VERB *TALK*

BASE FORM	PRESENT PARTICIPLE	PAST	PAST PARTICIPLE
talk	talking	talked	talked

Other tenses are formed by combining the present participle and the past participle with helping verbs. A **helping verb** helps the **main verb** tell about an action or make a statement. One or more helping verbs followed by a main verb is called a **verb phrase**.

They **are talking** to Sheila about the game. (*Are* is the helping verb, and *talking* is the main verb. Together they form a verb phrase.)

Be, have, and *do* are the most common helping verbs. Forms of the helping verb *be* are *am, is,* and *are* in the present and *was* and *were* in the past. These forms combine with the present participle of the main verb. The helping verb that combines with the past participle of a verb is *have*. Its forms include *have* and *has* in the present and *had* in the past.

▶ **Exercise 1** Draw two lines under the correct helping verb in parentheses and two lines under the participle. Write *pres. part.* or *past part.* in the blank to indicate whether the participle is present or past.

__pres. part__   Alonso (is, has) winning the race.

_____ 1. Ricardo and Craig (are, have) arriving tomorrow.

_____ 2. Our team (was, had) worked hard to win the pennant.

_____ 3. Sally (is, has) joining our debate team.

_____ 4. My dog Rusty (is, has) always barking at something.

_____ 5. The class (is, has) going to the museum.

_____ 6. The buses (were, had) arrived late at the auditorium.

_____ 7. The workers (had, were) painted the bleachers for the first time.

_____ 8. My bike (is, has) working fine since it was in the shop.

_____ 9. Mason's sisters (are, have) played many women's sports.

_____ 10. Dad (was, had) looked everywhere for his keys.

Grammar

_____ **11.** Georgia's friends (have, are) receiving the awards.

_____ **12.** Trent (were, had) printed the poster.

_____ **13.** The new student (is, has) registering at school.

_____ **14.** My friends (have, are) watching the video this afternoon.

_____ **15.** The Sanchez family (is, has) moving in next door.

_____ **16.** Mr. Chen (is, had) reserving the tickets.

_____ **17.** Isabel (are, was) awarded a prize.

_____ **18.** Someone (is, has) marked up my new book.

_____ **19.** The horses (are, have) running across the park.

_____ **20.** The sailboats (were, had) tossed by the storm.

_____ **21.** Anne (is, had) walking to the store.

_____ **22.** Don and Karen (have, are) joining us for the trip.

_____ **23.** Jodi and Hasan (are, have) experimented with a glider.

_____ **24.** The teachers (were, had) evaluating the students.

_____ **25.** The clouds (are, have) gathering to produce a shower.

_____ **26.** The jet planes (is, had) soared over the town.

_____ **27.** The airplane (is, has) replaced the train for rapid travel.

_____ **28.** Our pen pals (are, have) enjoyed the video of our school.

_____ **29.** Artists (have, are) coming to give us a presentation.

_____ **30.** Music (are, has) ranked among my favorite subjects.

_____ **31.** The sleek cat (is, had) crouching as if ready to pounce.

_____ **32.** The birthday gifts (were, had) covered in shiny paper.

_____ **33.** We (were, have) exposed to excellent sound quality at the concert.

_____ **34.** Tina (is, had) succeeded in every sport she tried last year.

_____ **35.** Languages (are, has) fascinating to me.

_____ **36.** I (were, had) suspected that it would rain.

_____ **37.** The garden (is, has) remained my parents' pride and joy.

_____ **38.** The owners (are, have) placed the sheep in their pens.

Lesson 19

Verb Forms: Present Progressive and Past Progressive

The present tense of a verb describes an action that occurs repeatedly. The **present progressive form** of a verb refers to an action that is continuing in the present. The present participle of the main verb and the helping verb *am, are,* or *is* combine to make up the present progressive form.

PRESENT PROGRESSIVE FORM

SINGULAR	PLURAL
I **am painting**.	We **are painting**.
You **are painting**.	You **are painting**.
He, she *or* it **is painting**.	They **are painting**.

The **past progressive form** of a verb refers to an action that was continuing at some point in the past. The present participle of the main verb and the helping verb *was* or *were* combine to make up the past progressive form.

PAST PROGRESSIVE FORM

SINGULAR	PLURAL
I **was painting**.	We **were painting**.
You **were painting**.	You **were painting**.
He, she, *or* it **was painting**.	They **were painting**.

▶ **Exercise 1** If the verb in italics is in the present tense, write its present progressive form in the blank. If it is in the past tense, write its past progressive form.

_____was looking_____ Brett *looked* at the history book.

_____ **1.** The rain *hindered* our plans yesterday.

_____ **2.** I see Carl's father *greets* visitors at the door today.

_____ **3.** Sally *paces* her sports training wisely.

_____ **4.** Ted *placed* first in the finals this year when he won the meet.

_____ **5.** Duwane *missed* the announcement.

_____ **6.** If you *move* tomorrow, let me know.

_____ **7.** Apparently, our grass *survives* the long dry spell.

_____ **8.** Carrie *regulates* her study time.

_____ **9.** The summer sun *heats* up the morning.

Grammar

_____ **10.** The ants in Margo's ant farm *labor* ceaselessly.

_____ **11.** Chet *registers* before the game begins.

_____ **12.** I *recommend* you see that movie before its run is over.

_____ **13.** My parakeet *sings* while I study.

_____ **14.** The play-off game *measures* up with the one last year.

_____ **15.** You *tie* the package securely.

_____ **16.** Harry *touches* on the main point of the idea.

_____ **17.** The birds *scolded* me for disturbing their nest.

_____ **18.** The exchange students *settled* down in their new homes.

_____ **19.** I *treat* my bike better than my brother treats his car.

_____ **20.** Susan *thanked* us before she left.

_____ **21.** Naomi *walks* to school every day this term.

_____ **22.** Ali *washes* his uniform after every competition.

_____ **23.** Linda *wavers* between majoring in chemistry and majoring in

biology.

_____ **24.** The neighbors *wrestle* with the move.

_____ **25.** They *urge* us to see the play.

_____ **26.** I *return* your book to the library.

_____ **27.** Elizabeth *watched* that program after the news.

_____ **28.** When you *utilize* your best speed on the turn, be careful.

_____ **29.** Ophelia *shapes* the clay into the beautiful figurine.

_____ **30.** The sun *smiled* warm and bright on the afternoon.

_____ **31.** The stars *sparkle* on a cloudless night.

_____ **32.** It *occurs* every evening before sunset.

_____ **33.** Our efforts *merited* a break in our work schedule.

_____ **34.** I *oil* the machine more often now.

_____ **35.** She *guessed* about the time.

_____ **36.** Sonia *hummed* that tune during art class.

Grammar

Lesson 20
Perfect Tenses: Present and Past

The **present perfect tense** of a verb names an action that happened at some time in the past. It also names an action that happened in the past and is still occurring. The past participle of the main verb and the helping verb *have* or *has* make up the present perfect tense.

PRESENT PERFECT TENSE

SINGULAR	PLURAL
I **have studied.**	We **have studied.**
You **have studied.**	You **have studied.**
He, she, *or* it **has studied.**	They **have studied.**

The **past perfect tense** of a verb names an action that was completed before another action or event in the past. The past participle of the main verb and the helping verb *had* make up the past perfect tense.

PAST PERFECT TENSE

SINGULAR	PLURAL
I **had studied.**	We **had studied.**
You **had studied.**	You **had studied.**
He, she, *or* it **had studied.**	They **had studied.**

▶ **Exercise 1 Draw two lines under each verb. Write its present perfect tense in the blank.**

__**have offered**__   I offered my services for their anniversary celebration.

_____ **1.** They remember the gifts for the guest speakers.

_____ **2.** Kenji refers to the book on the top shelf.

_____ **3.** Kara performs the dance already.

_____ **4.** The old sailing ship navigates the difficult shallows.

_____ **5.** I follow Marty's suggestions.

_____ **6.** The neighbor's dog growls at me each morning.

_____ **7.** That cat naps every chance he gets!

_____ **8.** That old movie influences many people.

_____ **9.** James loves that book.

_____ **10.** They demolish our team every year!

_____ **11.** We attend Mr. Kumba's class regularly.

_____ **12.** You confine your campfire to this small area.

_____ **13.** Connie's track victories attract press attention.

_____ **14.** At sunset the clouds amaze me with their beautiful colors.

_____ **15.** In the story, Gilgamesh wanders forever.

_____ **16.** The plot of the play unites the friends in the end.

_____ **17.** The tree turns a brilliant red.

_____ **18.** These pictures demonstrate Sunee's artistic style.

_____ **19.** Logic rules our scientific thought.

_____ **20.** Jay and Dave serve the class project well.

▶ **Exercise 2** **Fill in the blank using the verb and tense given in parentheses.** *Past perf.* **indicates past perfect tense, and** *pres. perf.* **indicates present perfect tense.**

Jake and Luis _____*have rafted*_____ down the river in Colorado. (*raft,* pres. perf.)

1. She _____ him before school started. (*telephone,* past perf.)

2. The dog _____ out of its collar. (*slip,* pres. perf.)

3. The waters of the lake _____ in the sunlight. (*sparkle,* pres. perf.)

4. The tulips _____ before the frost. (*sprout,* past perf.)

5. Native Americans _____ a basketball-like game for many years.
   (*play,* pres. perf.)

6. If you _____, you would have had a better view. (*move,* past perf.)

7. If I _____ it before, I wouldn't have to hunt for it now. (*notice,* past perf.)

8. When you _____ the package, will you open it? (*obtain,* pres. perf.)

9. Simon _____ toward running the race. (*lean,* past perf.)

10. The dog _____ the cat once before. (*harm,* pres. perf.)

11. The wind _____ my hat before I could react. (*grab,* past perf.)

12. When you _____ it, did the model shine? (*clean,* past perf.)

Grammar

Lesson 21
Expressing Future Time

The **future tense** of a verb is formed by adding the helping verb *will* before the main verb. When the subject is *I* or *we,* the helping verb *shall* is sometimes used.

Our big tournament **will begin** next week.

Time words such as *tomorrow, next year,* and *later* are used to refer specifically to future time to show that an action has yet to occur. They are used with the present tense of the verb.

Our big tournament **starts next week.**

The present progressive form can also be used with time words to express future actions.

Our big tournament **is starting next week.**

The **future perfect tense** of a verb refers to an action that will be completed before another future action begins. The future perfect tense is formed by inserting *will have* or *shall have* before the past participle of the verb.

By that time, our big tournament **will have started.**

▶ **Exercise 1 Draw two lines under each verb or verb phrase. In the blank write the tense of the verb:** *present, pres. prog.* **(present progressive),** *future,* **or** *fut. perf.* **(future perfect).**

_____fut. perf._____   Trent will have received the award by eight o'clock.

_____ **1.** I will unhook the chain.

_____ **2.** Gina will have walked home by now.

_____ **3.** Ted is advising us about our leaky roof tomorrow.

_____ **4.** They will watch a video on that classic story.

_____ **5.** The school's chess match is beginning tomorrow afternoon.

_____ **6.** By then, I shall have tired of it.

_____ **7.** Camilla will smooth over the problem.

_____ **8.** The dancers are settling on a program next week.

_____ **9.** I will perform up to my instructor's expectations.

Name _____ Class _____ Date _____

_____ **10.** Juan will have persisted until the end of the match.

_____ **11.** Chen practices his violin every day.

_____ **12.** We shall respect his achievements.

_____ **13.** Tomorrow they will mutter about the team's loss.

_____ **14.** Karen will organize the class project.

_____ **15.** They are responding to our suggestion soon.

_____ **16.** Our relatives will stop at our house on their vacation.

_____ **17.** They will have measured the right amount in chemistry class.

_____ **18.** He will have impressed everyone with his vocal talents.

_____ **19.** The store will have inscribed the ring before delivery.

_____ **20.** I shall have earned the coach's respect.

_____ **21.** Kyle distinguishes one of that group's songs from another.

_____ **22.** Jeanne is gathering her books together.

_____ **23.** The station will have fulfilled its promise by Tuesday.

_____ **24.** Next season we debate the other teams in our conference.

_____ **25.** I will describe the plot in my oral book report on Friday.

_____ **26.** Your efforts will have contributed to the environment.

_____ **27.** Sheila advises everyone on financial matters.

_____ **28.** Saturday I will clean my room.

_____ **29.** The marathon runners compete next fall.

_____ **30.** Farm horses will astonish you with their size.

_____ **31.** Before evening, I will have looked everywhere.

_____ **32.** Our team will turn around yet.

_____ **33.** We shall have suggested several options by then.

_____ **34.** Your science project will stimulate great interest.

_____ **35.** Maybe then he will have perceived the solution.

_____ **36.** Darla opposes a picnic in that park every year.

Lesson 22
Active and Passive Voices

A sentence is in the **active voice** when the subject performs the action of the verb.

Neil Armstrong **landed** the *Apollo* lunar module on the moon in 1969.

A sentence is in the **passive voice** when the subject receives the action of the verb. The verb in a passive-voice sentence consists of a form of *be* and the past participle. Often a phrase beginning with *by* follows a verb in a passive-voice sentence.

The *Apollo* lunar module **was landed** on the moon in 1969 **by** Neil Armstrong. (*was* and the past participle of *land* followed by a phrase beginning with *by*)

The active voice is stronger and emphasizes the performer. Use the passive voice when you want to emphasize the receiver of the action or de-emphasize the performer. Also, use the passive voice if you do not know who the performer is.

The moon **was reached** in 1969. (focuses on the event)
The spacecraft **was landed**. (You do not want to state who landed it.)

▶ **Exercise 1** Write in the blank whether the sentence is in the *active* or *passive* voice. Draw a line under the receiver of the action.

_____passive_____ The heavens were studied by ancient astronomers.

_____ **1.** A solar eclipse was predicted by Thales of Miletus in 585 B.C.

_____ **2.** Hipparchus established an observatory in the third century B.C.

_____ **3.** A supernova, or exploding star, was recorded by Chinese astronomers in 1054.

_____ **4.** According to the Greek astronomer Ptolemy, the sun and the planets circled Earth once a day.

_____ **5.** In 1543, a new theory was suggested by a Polish astronomer, Copernicus.

_____ **6.** In this theory, Earth and other planets orbited the sun.

_____ **7.** The use of Copernicus's theory was forbidden by religious leaders until 1757.

Grammar

_____ **8.** However, persons were convinced about Copernicus's theory by the
discoveries of other astronomers.

_____ **9.** The law of universal gravitation was discovered by Sir Isaac Newton.

_____ **10.** The Copernican theory gained support after this discovery.

_____ **11.** Uranus was found by Sir William Herschel in 1781.

_____ **12.** Pluto was discovered by Clyde William Tombaugh in 1930.

_____ **13.** The closest planet to the sun, Mercury, orbits the sun in eighty-eight
Earth days.

_____ **14.** Venus is called "the Morning Star" by many persons.

_____ **15.** An American space probe, *Mariner II,* reached Venus in 1962.

_____ **16.** It sent back data about conditions on and near Venus.

_____ **17.** The surface of Venus has been mapped by succeeding American space
probes.

_____ **18.** We call Mars "the Red Planet."

_____ **19.** This planet was named by ancient Romans after the red god of war in
Roman mythology.

_____ **20.** Limonite, a brick-colored mineral, gives Mars its red color.

_____ **21.** Mars orbits the sun in about 687 Earth days.

_____ **22.** Mars was observed by the U.S. spacecraft *Mariner IV* in 1965.

_____ **23.** In 1976, the United States landed *Viking I* near the planet's equator.

_____ **24.** Photographs of the surface of Mars were sent back to Earth by both
Viking I and *Viking II.*

_____ **25.** They showed the canyons, deep gorges, and "dry river beds" on the
surface of Mars.

_____ **26.** The first space shuttle, *Columbia,* was launched by the United States in
1981.

_____ **27.** Two big booster rockets launch the space shuttle into orbit.

_____ **28.** It uses its wings to land like a glider.

Lesson 23

Irregular Verbs I

These irregular verbs are grouped according to the way they form their past and past participles.

IRREGULAR VERBS

PATTERN	BASE FORM	PAST	PAST PARTICIPLE
One vowel changes to form the past and the past participle.	begin	began	begun
	drink	drank	drunk
	ring	rang	rung
	sing	sang	sung
	spring	sprang *or* sprung	sprung
	swim	swam	swum
The past form and past participle are the same.	bring	brought	brought
	buy	bought	bought
	catch	caught	caught
	creep	crept	crept
	feel	felt	felt
	get	got	got *or* gotten
	keep	kept	kept
	lay	laid	laid
	leave	left	left
	lend	lent	lent
	lose	lost	lost
	make	made	made
	pay	paid	paid
	say	said	said
	seek	sought	sought
	sit	sat	sat
	sleep	slept	slept
	teach	taught	taught
	think	thought	thought
	win	won	won

▶ **Exercise 1 Complete each sentence with the past tense or past participle of the irregular verb in parentheses.**

Wendy had ____sat____ down before the music began. (sit)

1. Ethan had _____ late that morning. (sleep)

2. Ria _____ her new book yesterday. (get)

Grammar

3. Harry _____ me waiting for an hour. (keep)

4. Mai-Lin had _____ about her topic before she wrote the report. (think)

5. My cat just _____ there while the mouse escaped. (sit)

6. I had _____ too much for the CD at the mall. (pay)

7. Akira _____ the art prize last year. (win)

8. Jessica _____ success to our track team last season. (bring)

9. I _____ this cold last week. (catch)

10. Mary had _____ the homework before I arrived. (begin)

11. The horse never _____ a race until yesterday. (lose)

12. Duwana had _____ in the choir before. (sing)

13. We had _____ before the buses arrived. (leave)

14. Mr. Hasan _____ that class last year. (teach)

15. My front tire had _____ a leak. (spring)

16. Cal _____ bad about the test. (feel)

17. Susan's dog _____ a sunny nook in which to sleep. (seek)

18. They have always _____ new books for their birthdays. (get)

19. The cat _____ up on me before he pounced playfully. (creep)

20. They _____ they thought the snow was too good to be true. (say)

21. My little brother had _____ all the orange juice. (drink)

22. The door bell _____ sharply against the quiet. (ring)

23. Sheila _____ across the lake last year. (swim)

24. Shawn had _____ one last week. (buy)

25. I _____ the book down somewhere and lost it completely. (lay)

26. Yesterday Tama _____ her science project. (begin)

27. Two of the art students have _____ the set for this play. (make)

28. He had _____ his jacket to another member of the team. (lend)

Lesson 24
Irregular Verbs II

The following irregular verbs are grouped according to the way their past form and past participle are formed.

IRREGULAR VERBS

PATTERN	BASE FORM	PAST FORM	PAST PARTICIPLE
The base form and the past participle are the same.	become	became	become
	come	came	come
	run	ran	run
The past form ends in *-ew* and the past participle ends in *-wn.*	blow	blew	blown
	draw	drew	drawn
	fly	flew	flown
	grow	grew	grown
	know	knew	known
	throw	threw	thrown
The past participle ends in *-en.*	bite	bit	bitten *or* bit
	break	broke	broken
	choose	chose	chosen
	drive	drove	driven
	eat	ate	eaten
	fall	fell	fallen
	give	gave	given
	ride	rode	ridden
	rise	rose	risen
	see	saw	seen
	speak	spoke	spoken
	steal	stole	stolen
	take	took	taken
	write	wrote	written
The past form and the past participle do not follow any pattern.	am, are, is	was, were	been
	do	did	done
	go	went	gone
	tear	tore	torn
	wear	wore	worn
The base form, past form, and past participle are all the same.	cut	cut	cut
	let	let	let

Grammar

Name _____ Class _____ Date _____

▶ **Exercise 1** Complete each sentence with the past tense or past participle of the irregular verb in parentheses.

I had _____chosen_____ the gift before you called. (choose)

Grammar

1. We _____ names to select a winner. (draw)

2. My friends had _____ all the pizza by the time I arrived. (eat)

3. I _____ the pictures to class yesterday. (take)

4. They had _____ the horses before riding them. (see)

5. Rick _____ to Mr. Tanabe last week. (write)

6. You could have _____ if you had tried. (rise)

7. I had _____ happy to hear from her. (be)

8. Carlos _____ to the grocery store yesterday. (go)

9. Sandra had _____ her finger on the paper. (cut)

10. The wind _____ until the trees looked like green banners. (blow)

11. Davina has _____ her picture many times. (draw)

12. The yard _____ a dreamland of shapes due to the snow drifts. (become)

13. Had you ever _____ a bonsai tree before? (grow)

14. I should never have _____ them use the car. (let)

15. We _____ to Yellowstone Park for our vacation last year. (drive)

16. The temperature had _____ drastically during the night. (fall)

17. The butterfly _____ lazily to another bright flower. (fly)

18. Last summer, I had been _____ all over by mosquitoes. (bite)

19. The old tree _____ bare as winter approached. (grow)

20. Had you _____ at a seminar before? (speak)

21. The moon had _____ before the sky grew black. (rise)

22. Have you ever _____ a roller coaster? (ride)

23. Seth had _____ the answers to all the questions. (know)

24. Judi _____ a huge party for her daughter's sixteenth birthday. (throw)

25. Mom and Dad _____ away for a quiet weekend at the beach. (steal)

26. We _____ the brilliant winter sunrise this morning. (see)

27. Kate _____ the school's free throw shooting record. (break)

28. We had never _____ anything like this safari before. (do)

29. Cheryl had _____ every ounce of energy to the successful performance. (give)

30. The morning has _____ by too quickly for us to enjoy it. (go)

31. My aunt had _____ her new dress to the theater. (wear)

32. Chen _____ upon his memories to write that story. (draw)

33. Jennifer had _____ her best in the hurdles event. (run)

34. Seth _____ the picture out of the magazine. (tear)

35. Have you ever _____ a model airplane like that one before? (fly)

36. We _____ cross-country instead of trying out for baseball. (run)

37. Who _____ the crossword puzzle? (do)

38. Jodi has _____ a famous singer. (become)

39. Unfortunately, I _____ to throw out my old comic book collection years ago. (choose)

40. The snow had _____ in the night, silently, unexpectedly. (come)

▶ **Exercise 2 Underline the word in parentheses that best completes each sentence.**

Ms. Joyce has (wrote, <u>written</u>) several successful novels.

1. If I had (knew, known) you were coming, I would have cleaned my room.

2. Cynthia (gave, given) her sister a fabulous birthday present.

3. George and Mike have often (spoke, spoken) of their trip to Japan.

4. The rainbow (grew, grown) more brilliant as the sky cleared.

5. Unfortunately, Julia (tore, torn) her favorite blouse.

6. The entire family (ate, eaten) some of Aunt Vivian's peach cake.

7. Louis had (became, become) bored with his hobby.

8. Simone had (took, taken) some flowers to her cousin in the hospital.

9. Jeff (ran, run) the last four blocks, but he was still late for school.

10. Marcia (threw, thrown) the football back to Peter.

11. The desk had (was, been) Grandfather's favorite place to write.

12. The bridesmaids (wore, worn) pink organza dresses.

13. Fans had (came, come) from many cities to see the historic concert.

14. The birds (flew, flown) north when the weather turned mild.

15. Everyone watching the parade (rose, risen) when they saw the American flag.

16. Linda had (did, done) all the work for the surprise party herself.

17. The breeze had (blew, blown) rose petals across the sidewalk.

18. Alan (stole, stolen) second base when the pitcher wasn't looking.

19. You have (saw, seen) that movie twice already.

20. Celia (chose, chosen) chicken, and Pam ordered fish.

▶ **Writing Link** **Use the forms of irregular verbs to write a paragraph about your first day in kindergarten or in junior high.**

_____

_____

_____

_____

_____

_____

_____

_____

_____

_____

_____

_____

_____

☑ Unit 3 **Review**

▶ **Exercise 1** Write *T* (transitive), *I* (intransitive), or *LV* (linking verb) above each verb. Write *PN* above each predicate noun and *PA* above each predicate adjective.

          LV   **PA**

The dog becomes nervous during each thunderclap.

1. They brought the presents for the party.

2. Sean became content.

3. Charles rode easily and gracefully.

4. Isabel rang the bell.

5. That old white cat is fat and lazy.

6. Mr. Tanaka assigned our group the project.

7. The softball team leaves a great record.

8. The ladybug seems a gentle, harmless creature.

9. Carol paints beautifully.

10. Crystal saw the dead cactus.

11. The trees shaded the park.

12. Camilla sold her cards to Irene.

13. Sally's track record is impressive.

14. Marie taught me a few Breton words.

15. The archery team won first place.

16. Emily makes expressive, moving portraits.

17. We are ready with these clothes.

18. They guaranteed Sandra a place on the team.

19. The airplane taxied before take-off.

20. That rock is quartz.

Grammar

Cumulative Review: Units 1–3

▶ **Exercise 1** Draw two lines under each verb. Write in the blank the tense of the verb: *present, past, present progressive, past progressive, present perfect, past perfect, future,* or *future perfect.*

_____ past perfect _____ An enthusiastic group <u>had given</u> the performance.

_____ 1. Experts were examining the book.

_____ 2. Lennie will call before Tuesday.

_____ 3. Their team had lost the game during the first quarter.

_____ 4. The sun has hidden behind the clouds all day.

_____ 5. Critics praised that animated movie.

_____ 6. He will have torn some of his clothing on the hike.

_____ 7. Ayita pulls weeds in her garden all summer long.

_____ 8. The crowds are flooding the malls every weekend.

_____ 9. Alice had talked about the shop for some time.

_____ 10. We were leaving on a jet plane.

▶ **Exercise 2** Identify each kind of sentence. Write *dec.* (declarative), *int.* (interrogative), *exc.* (exclamatory), or *imp.* (imperative) in the blank. Then write *com.* above each common noun and *prop.* above each proper noun.

                                 com.   prop.
_ int. _   Where will you go after school, Tina?

_____ 1. Had Dara seen the video before the other students?

_____ 2. Belinda, our new president, will have talked to you about our plan.

_____ 3. Hurry! Our dog is barking wildly!

_____ 4. When will you paint the old barn, Winona?

_____ 5. "You will ride your horse in the parade," Father stated firmly.

_____ 6. That famous piece of art was painted by Picasso, who was born in Spain.

_____ 7. Kurt had received a call from the state of New York on Friday.

_____ 8. Was the museum well attended last year?

Unit 4: Pronouns

Lesson 25
Pronouns: Personal

A **pronoun** is a word that takes the place of one or more nouns and the words that describe those nouns. A **personal pronoun** refers to a specific person or thing. When a personal pronoun is the subject of a sentence, it is a **subject pronoun.** When a personal pronoun is the object of a verb or preposition, it is an **object pronoun**

Tito is a sports fan. **He** especially likes football. (subject)

Tito coaches younger players. Tito coaches **them**. (direct object of a verb)

The head coach gave Tito some responsibility. The coach gave **him** responsibility. (indirect object of a verb)

For Tito, football is enjoyable. For **him,** football is enjoyable. (object of a preposition)

SUBJECT PRONOUNS		OBJECT PRONOUNS	
SINGULAR	PLURAL	SINGULAR	PLURAL
I	we	me	us
you	you	you	you
he, she, it	they	him, her, it	them

▶ **Exercise 1** Write *S* above each subject pronoun and *O* above each object pronoun.

  S   O
He gave her a bouquet.

1. They have a black and white cat named Max.

2. The Rangers beat us four to nothing.

3. You might see David and Jeremy at the carnival.

4. Is he the main character in the book?

5. Did Mr. Rodriguez send you the brochure?

6. Dana stood in line in front of her.

7. We gave the first report.

8. The teacher gave them a *B* plus.

9. Are you going to the volleyball game?

10. When training a dog, always speak gently but firmly to it.

11. She thought the geology museum was fascinating.

12. I can't remember meeting Sarah's aunt.

13. Just give us a chance!

14. Darren saw him at the youth group meeting.

15. Raquel has the flu and is taking medication for it.

16. Does it include batteries or should Mom buy some?

17. We went to Aunt Martha's house for Thanksgiving.

18. Were they interested in buying a magazine subscription?

19. Angela is coming to the dance with me.

20. It slowly stalked the rabbit out in the field.

21. The Lions Club donated it to our school.

22. It became clear that Robby had missed the bus.

23. Jasmine came with me to the park.

24. When Dad and Mom went canoeing, they had a great time.

25. When the mouse ran out of the hole in the stump, the eagle saw it.

26. Did Jan send you the box of chocolates?

27. The police officer said calmly to the man, "Give me the briefcase, please."

28. Could you repeat those instructions, please?

29. Nicole and Sharon were at the party, which is where Paul saw them.

30. Did the counselor ask to have the application mailed to you?

31. I felt as if Caruso were singing the song just for me.

32. The first speaker said, "You will enjoy four years at Franklin Middle School."

33. Walk right up to the woman at the window and hand her the ticket stub.

34. The Tigers are talented; in fact, they won the state tournament two years in a row.

35. The actors presented scenes from *Our Town* for us.

36. If Judy tells Dad about the broken glass, he will understand.

Lesson 26
Pronouns and Antecedents

The noun or group of words that a pronoun refers to is called its antecedent. Be sure every pronoun agrees with its antecedent in number (singular or plural) and gender. The gender of a noun or pronoun may be masculine, feminine, or neuter (referring to things).

Puccini and Verdi wrote many great operas. **They** wrote **them** in Italian. (The plural pronoun *they* refers to *Puccini* and *Verdi*. The plural pronoun *them* refers to *operas.)*

Mary sent a letter to Aunt Fran. Mary sent **it** to **her.** (The singular pronoun *it* refers to *letter*. The singular pronoun *her* refers to *Aunt Fran.)*

▶ **Exercise 1 Draw an arrow from each italicized pronoun in the second sentence to its antecedent in the first sentence.**

Norway has many mountains and fiords. *It* has little farmland.

1. Norway is a small country in northern Europe. *It* hosted the 1994 Winter Olympics.

2. Many people knew little about Norway before the Olympics. *They* learned more about *it*

   by watching the Olympics on television.

3. Much of Norway is covered by mountains. *They* make transportation difficult.

4. The Norwegians invented the sport of skiing. *They* often ski daily during the long winter.

5. Thousands of skiers participate in the annual Birkebeiner ski race. Many people

   consider *it* the world's toughest ski race.

6. Unlike the United States, Norway is a kingdom. *It* also has a prime minister.

7. Queen Sonja and King Haakon reign in Norway. *They* have little power but serve as

   symbols of the country.

8. Sonja Henie is a famous Norwegian figure skater. *She* won three Olympic gold medals.

Grammar

9. Sonja Henie won the world figure skating championship ten years in a row. *She* practically made *it* her private property!

10. Sonja Henie won the title from 1927 to 1936. Many other skaters tried to beat *her* but were unsuccessful.

11. After an Olympic career, Sonja Henie made many movies. *They* were popular around the world.

12. Trygve Lie is another famous Norwegian. *He* was the first secretary general of the United Nations.

13. Trygve Lie was elected to the top post at the UN in 1946. *He* led *it* for seven years.

14. Sigrid Undset, a Norwegian author, wrote many novels. *They* often describe life in the Middle Ages.

15. In 1928 Undset won the Nobel Prize for literature. *It* is one of the world's most prestigious awards.

16. In northern Norway live the people known as Sami, or Lapp. *They* have raised reindeer for hundreds of years.

17. The ancestors of today's Norwegians were called Vikings. *They* lived from about A.D. 700 to A.D. 1200.

18. Vikings sailed the seas in sailboats with dragon heads for decorations. *They* were carved on the prow, or front, of the boats.

19. A famous Viking is Leif Ericsson. Many historians believe *him* to be the first European to land in North America.

20. Vikings left traces in Newfoundland and Canada. *They* called this area Vinland.

Lesson 27
Using Pronouns Correctly

Subject pronouns are used in compound subjects, and object pronouns are used in compound objects.

Deon and Lisa played chess. **He** and **she** played chess. (*He* and *she* form the compound subject.)

The game of chess interests Deon and Lisa. The game interests **him** and **her**. (*Him* and *her* form the compound object.)

Whenever the subject pronoun *I* or the object pronoun *me* is part of the compound subject or object, it should come last.

Deon and **I** went to a chess tournament. (not *I* and *Deon*)

Sometimes a noun and pronoun are used together for emphasis. The form of the pronoun depends on the function of the noun in the sentence.

We chess players study chess intently. (*Players* is the subject, so the subject pronoun *we* is used.)

That book is the most interesting to **us** chess players. (*Chess players* is the object of the preposition *to,* so the object pronoun *us* is used.)

Some sentences make incomplete comparisons. The forms of the pronoun can affect the meaning of such sentences. In any incomplete comparison, use the pronoun that would be correct if the comparison were complete.

Deon was more interested in chess than **she** (was).
Deon was more interested in chess than (he was interested in) **her**.

In formal writing, use a subject pronoun after a linking verb.

Deon's best friend is **he**.

▶ **Exercise 1** Underline the pronoun in parentheses that best completes each sentence.

(<u>We</u>, Us) athletes need our enthusiastic support.

1. Jan and (she, her) are our class representatives.

2. Are you going to come with Rudy and (I, me)?

3. The tallest player on the team is (he, him).

4. My sister always says (we, us) Kozlowskis stick together!

5. What did (they, them) do for their history project?

Grammar

6. The award was given to Dale and (she, her).

7. If you ask (I, me), there's too much emphasis on winning.

8. Please give (she, her) the letter.

9. The president asked (we, us) citizens to make some sacrifices.

10. If you have any questions, talk to Ms. Ramirez or (I, me).

11. Stefan and Neil saw Aubra and (they, them) at the music store.

12. Were you and (she, her) interested in signing up for the Drama Club?

13. Let's divide the assignment between you and (we, us).

14. The winners of the science competition were Dorreen and (she, her).

15. We make a pretty good team, you and (I, me).

▶ **Exercise 2** Complete each sentence by writing in the blank a pronoun of the type indicated. There may be more than one correct answer for each item.

The coach will give the players and ___them___ the details later. (object)

1. Dad bought _____ kids a camera. (object)

2. _____ members of the park committee are very proud of our work. (subject)

3. Did you and _____ see the soccer game? (subject)

4. I don't understand why no one will help you or _____. (object)

5. Why didn't Nicole and _____ try out for the musical? (subject)

6. You are much more patient than _____. (subject)

7. The last ones to finish were _____ and _____ . (subject)

8. _____ is not a really difficult course. (subject)

9. We returned our applications to _____ and _____. (object)

10. Do my parents and _____ need to sign the form in two places? (subject)

11. When I approached the squirrel, _____ scampered away. (subject)

12. The conductor will need an assistant, either _____ or _____. (object)

13. The woman was standing right behind Don and _____ in the line. (object)

14. _____ and _____ are going to meet in the semifinal. (subject)

15. You can sit with _____ freshmen if you want. (object)

Lesson 28
Pronouns: Possessive and Indefinite

Grammar

A **possessive pronoun** shows who or what has something. Possessive pronouns replace possessive nouns. They may come before a noun or they may stand alone.

His bike was stolen. The bike was **his.**

	USED BEFORE NOUNS	USED ALONE
Singular:	my, your, his, her, its	mine, yours, his, hers, its
Plural:	our, your, their	ours, yours, theirs

An **indefinite pronoun** does not refer to a particular person, place, or thing. The indefinite pronouns *all*, *any*, *most*, *none*, and *some* can be singular or plural depending on the phrase that follows. When an indefinite pronoun is used as the subject of a sentence, the verb must agree with it in number.

Everyone attends the weekly assemblies. (singular)
Several look forward to them very much. (plural)
Most of the assembly **is** interesting to the students. (singular)
Most of the assemblies **are** in the afternoon. (plural)

COMMON INDEFINITE PRONOUNS

Singular:	another	anything	everybody	much	no one	somebody
	anybody	each	everyone	neither	nothing	someone
	anyone	either	everything	nobody	one	something
Plural:	both	few	many	others	several	

▶ **Exercise 1 Underline the correct pronoun in parentheses. In the blank identify the pronoun as *poss.* (possessive) or *ind.* (indefinite).**

__ind.__   (Most, <u>One</u>) of the greatest Chinese explorers was Chang Ch'ien.

_____ **1.** Chang Ch'ien lived during the second century B.C. in China and was an officer

in (its, others) army.

_____ **2.** (Yours, His) explorations helped the Han dynasty to flourish.

_____ **3.** (Its, Some) emperor at the time, Wu-Ti, sent him on many missions.

_____ **4.** During (his, my) lifetime, China was invaded by the Huns, a fierce warrior people.

_____ **5.** Finally, the Chinese emperor, Wu-ti, decided that (something, several) had to be

done about the marauding Huns.

_____ **6.** Wu-ti knew that China needed an ally in (its, either) fight against the Huns.

Grammar

_____ 7. (My, His) choice was a people called the Yueh-chih from central Asia.

_____ 8. (Few, Either) knew the exact location of the Yueh-chih.

_____ 9. To find them, (somebody, their) would have to undertake a dangerous search

through unknown country.

_____ 10. China was a large kingdom, but (its, much) western border had not been

completely explored.

_____ 11. To protect (neither, his) kingdom, an earlier emperor, Shih Huang-ti, had built

the Great Wall, four thousand miles long.

_____ 12. Although the Great Wall was able to slow down the invading Hun army,

(nothing, either) could keep them out completely.

_____ 13. Emperor Wu-ti chose Chang Chien, (one, others) of his best and bravest

officers, to lead the dangerous mission.

_____ 14. Along with one hundred soldiers and precious gifts for the Yueh-chih king,

Chang Ch'ien and his party began (her, their) journey.

_____ 15. However, as soon as they passed the Great Wall on their way west, they were

attacked by Huns and almost (everybody, nothing) was killed.

_____ 16. Chang himself spent ten years as a prisoner but learned much about (its, his)

captors while planning his escape.

_____ 17. When Chang finally escaped, he traveled west, where (several, few) had ever

gone before.

_____ 18. He crossed the vast and deadly Gobi, with (its, their) broiling heat and bitter

cold, and traveled almost ten thousand miles!

_____ 19. He explored areas of present-day Afghanistan and Tibet, heard of faraway

civilizations in Persia, India, and even Rome, and learned (everybody, much)

that would prove valuable to Emperor Wu-ti.

_____ 20. At last in 126 B.C., twelve long years after (their, his) departure, Chang

returned to the emperor's court, where he was welcomed as a great hero and

given the title of the Great Traveler.

Lesson 29
Pronouns: Reflexive and Intensive

Grammar

A **reflexive pronoun** refers to a noun or another pronoun and indicates that the same person or thing is involved. Reflexive pronouns are formed by adding *-self* or *-selves* to certain personal and possessive pronouns.

The cat saw **itself** in the mirror.   We helped **ourselves** to apples.

REFLEXIVE PRONOUNS

Singular: myself   yourself   himself, herself, itself
Plural: ourselves   yourselves   themselves

An **intensive pronoun** emphasizes a noun or pronoun already named.

The president **herself** couldn't be prouder.   We **ourselves** have not yet decided.

▶ **Exercise 1** **Place a check (✔) next to the sentence in each pair that correctly uses a reflexive or intensive pronoun.**

_____ Myself made this quilt.

___✔___ I made this quilt myself.

1. _____ They didn't give themselves enough time to do the job.

   _____ They didn't give theirselves enough time to do the job.

2. _____ The fouled-out player pointed to hisself and asked, "Who, me?"

   _____ The fouled-out player pointed to himself and asked, "Who, me?"

3. _____ She found himself in the middle of a dark forest.

   _____ She found herself in the middle of a dark forest.

4. _____ The governor herself presented the citation.

   _____ The governor she presented the citation.

5. _____ Thomas's cat injured itself when it fell off the roof.

   _____ Thomas's cat injured it when it fell off the roof.

6. _____ The hungry soldiers helped theirselves to the farmer's apples.

   _____ The hungry soldiers helped themselves to the farmer's apples.

7. _____ Mr. Banks offered to make the reservations hisself.

_____ Mr. Banks offered to make the reservations himself.

8. _____ Yourselves agree with the decision, don't you?

_____ You yourselves agree with the decision, don't you?

9. _____ The story itself seemed like a fairy tale come true!

_____ The story it seemed like a fairy tale come true!

10. _____ The soccer players improved them through hard work.

_____ The soccer players improved themselves through hard work.

11. _____ The Russians themselves have become our allies.

_____ The Russians and themselves have become allies.

12. _____ Myself was completely confused by the question.

_____ I myself was completely confused by the question.

13. _____ My best friend herselves was accepted in the honors program.

_____ My best friend herself was accepted in the honors program.

14. _____ We ought to be proud of ourselves for doing the right thing.

_____ We ought to be proud of ourself for doing the right thing.

15. _____ My brother is a good tennis player himself.

_____ My brother is a good tennis player herself.

▶ **Exercise 2** **Complete each sentence by filling in a reflexive or intensive pronoun. In the blank write _R_ if the pronoun you wrote is reflexive. Write _I_ if it is intensive.**

___I___ The movie _____itself_____ was unbelievably good!

_____ **1.** We built the whole model _____.

_____ **2.** I knew the dog had fleas because it was always scratching _____.

_____ **3.** She _____ is the owner of the gas station.

_____ **4.** You boys will have to ask _____ that question.

_____ **5.** They _____ gave us the good news.

_____ **6.** We _____ found homes for the abandoned kittens.

_____ **7.** I decided to try to score the winning goal _____.

_____ **8.** Without oxygen, life _____ would not be possible.

Lesson 30

Pronouns: Interrogative and Demonstrative

Grammar

An **interrogative pronoun** is used to introduce an interrogative sentence. The interrogative pronouns are *who, whose, whom, which,* and *what. Who* is used when the interrogative pronoun is the subject of the sentence. *Whom* is used when the interrogative pronoun is the object of a verb or preposition.

Who saw the accident? (subject)   **Whom** did the driver hit? (direct object)
To **whom** did the police officer give a ticket? (object of a preposition)
That's a beautiful dog. **Whose** is it? (shows possession)
What bothers you? **Which** of those cassettes is it?

A **demonstrative pronoun** is one that points out something. The demonstrative pronouns are *this, that, these,* and *those.*

This is a lovely painting. (singular, refers to something nearby)
These are lovely paintings. (plural, nearby)
That is a tall building. (singular, refers to something at a distance)
Those are tall buildings. (plural, at a distance)

▶ **Exercise 1** Underline each interrogative pronoun. Circle each demonstrative pronoun.

<u>Who</u> will volunteer for (this)?

1. Whom did you see behind the curtain?

2. I think this looks best on her.

3. Which is the Grand Champion ewe?

4. Who ate the last piece of cake?

5. That isn't my backpack!

6. What are Jeff and Kevin talking about?

7. Those are really cool shoes.

8. Whose is the yellow house on Vine Street?

9. I think I'll take four of these.

10. Which of you would like to go bowling?

11. This will do nicely, I think.

12. What is your answer for the last question?

13. That is a plan I fear will never work!

14. Whose is this?

15. I'd love to have a pair of those.

16. Who is at the front door?

17. I'm sorry, these are not for sale.

18. Which is the tape you want to buy?

19. From whom did you get that?

20. What is happening here?

▶ **Exercise 2** **Complete each sentence by writing a pronoun of the type indicated.**

_____What_____ is your favorite after-school snack? (interrogative)

1. _____ is the best pizza I've ever eaten! (demonstrative)

2. _____ is the architect of that building? (interrogative)

3. To _____ did you lend your raincoat? (interrogative)

4. _____ is that green mountain bike? (interrogative)

5. I don't think _____ is a good idea! (demonstrative)

6. Whose boots are _____? (demonstrative)

7. _____ was elected club treasurer? (interrogative)

8. Give _____ to David because he was looking for them. (demonstrative)

9. _____ are you going to meet on Saturday? (interrogative)

10. _____ are those computer printouts? (interrogative)

11. _____ of the candidates do you support? (interrogative)

12. _____ will be at the party tonight? (interrogative)

13. _____ does she mean by that? (interrogative)

14. _____ are my parents standing over there. (demonstrative)

15. _____ should I choose? (interrogative)

16. _____ is probably my favorite color. (demonstrative)

17. _____ is that set of tools on the bench? (interrogative)

18. By _____ is that symphony? (interrogative)

☑ Unit 4 **Review**

▶ **Exercise 1** Underline each pronoun. Above each pronoun write *per.* (personal), *poss.* (possessive), *ind.* (indefinite), *ref.* (reflexive), *int.* (intensive), *inter.* (interrogative), or *dem.* (demonstrative).

inter. per.   poss.
<u>What</u> do <u>I</u> smell coming from <u>your</u> kitchen?

1. Dana laughed hysterically when she saw herself in the fun-house mirror.

2. My uncle owns his own engine repair shop.

3. Many of those were stale.

4. Each of the items on the menu sounds delicious.

5. I myself will finish this tomorrow.

6. That will be something to see!

7. They consider themselves better than we are.

8. Who is coming to your graduation party?

9. You yourself won't be able to decide anything.

10. We can't do anything about his refusal to help.

11. I heard several of them scurrying under a rock.

12. That is theirs, so you had better not touch it.

13. Please send these to the McDaniels when you have time.

14. Whose are those?

15. I will tell you this.

16. We ourselves must keep a secret and tell no one about it.

17. If anyone moves, she will be really angry.

18. I am telling you I saw them in Smuggler's Cove around midnight!

Name _____ Class _____ Date _____

▶ **Exercise 1** Write *S* in the blank for each group of words that is a sentence, and write *F* for each fragment. For each sentence, draw one line under the complete subject and two lines under the complete predicate.

_____S_____ <u>My neighbor, Trisha,</u> plays the piano and the flute.

_____ 1. The delivery truck up the street.

_____ 2. The large parking lot across the street was filled.

_____ 3. The Great Wall of China, nearly four thousand miles long, was built entirely

by hand.

_____ 4. One of the visiting students told of his experiences in Thailand.

_____ 5. Hastened quickly up the maple tree in our backyard.

_____ 6. The office building was once a schoolhouse.

_____ 7. My favorite celebrity, Oprah Winfrey, is an inspiration to many.

_____ 8. The rustic lodge at the foot of the scenic mountain.

_____ 9. Designed by several architects.

_____ 10. The first Texas Rangers were hired by settlers to protect them against attacks.

▶ **Exercise 2** Underline each pronoun. Above each pronoun write *per.* (personal), *poss.* (possessive), *ind.* (indefinite), *ref.* (reflexive), *int.* (intensive), *inter.* (interrogative), or *dem.* (demonstrative).

   per.   **poss.**
<u>She</u> opened <u>their</u> gift last night.

1. My aunt knows everyone in her neighborhood.

2. He helped us rehearse our lines for the school play.

3. With whom did you get in touch about that?

4. You yourself should enter the contest.

5. The skunk defends itself by spraying a foul-smelling liquid.

6. This seems riper than the others.

Copyright © by Glencoe/McGraw-Hill

Unit 5: Adjectives and Adverbs

Lesson 31
Adjectives

Grammar

An **adjective** modifies, or describes, a noun or a pronoun. An adjective provides information about the size, shape, color, texture, feeling, sound, smell, number, or condition of a noun or a pronoun.

Brown wrens sometimes build nests above **front** doors.

Most adjectives come before the words they modify. A **predicate adjective** follows a linking verb and modifies the noun or pronoun that is the subject of the sentence.

The clerks in this store are **polite** and **friendly**.

The present participle and past participle forms of verbs may be used as adjectives and predicate adjectives.

A **barking** dog kept me awake all night. (present participle)
The crowd was **excited**. (past participle)

▶ **Exercise 1** Underline each adjective. Draw an arrow to the noun or pronoun it modifies.

Common ants are fascinating insects.

1. Ants are social insects that live in organized colonies.

2. Female ants are either queen ants or worker ants.

3. Male ants mate with young queens and live very short lives.

4. Queens live several years and lay numerous broods of eggs.

5. Ants are also extremely strong and energetic.

6. They are industrious and build structured nests.

7. To do this, they use two sets of powerful jaws that allow them to chew, to dig, and to carry large objects.

8. Ant nests often have several rooms with connecting tunnels.

9. Communication is essential in such complex societies.

10. Ants have interesting ways to share information.

11. Elbowed antennae are extremely active and sensitive; they serve as sense organs for touch and smell.

12. When two ants meet, they rely on antennae to determine if they are nestmates or enemies.

13. If they discover they are true nestmates, they touch mouths and pass on stored chemicals and stored food.

14. Various chemicals give ants full "reports" on colony conditions.

15. Received information then directs behaviors of individual ants.

▶ **Exercise 2** **Complete each sentence by writing an adjective in the blank. You may use a present or past participle form of a verb in some sentences.**

An ____excited____ swarm of bees buzzed around the ____lumbering____ bear.

1. In the spring we see many _____ insects in our yards.

2. The honey bee is a very _____ insect.

3. In springtime honey bees visit the _____ blossoms of plants.

4. They make _____ honey from the flowers' nectar.

5. Butterflies, like honey bees, help pollinate _____ flowers.

6. Some butterflies, such as the monarch, migrate _____ distances from the northern United States or Canada to California, Florida, or Mexico.

7. A butterfly's _____ wings delight people of all ages.

8. Another _____ insect with pretty wings is the ladybug.

9. Ladybugs are _____ because of their bright color and spots.

10. Ladybugs are useful to farmers because they control _____ pests.

Lesson 32
Articles and Proper Adjectives

The words *a, an,* and *the* make up a special group of adjectives called **articles**. *A* and *an* are called **indefinite articles** because they refer to one of a general group of people, places, things, or ideas. Use *a* before words beginning with a consonant sound, and use *an* before words beginning with a vowel sound.

a film **a** bicycle **a** union **an** omelet **an** honor

The is called a **definite article** because it identifies specific people, places, things, or ideas.

The river had flooded **the** nearby fields.

▶ **Exercise 1** Write in the blank the indefinite article that comes before each word or words.

___an___ invigorating hike

_____ 1. arch

_____ 2. scientific experiment

_____ 3. infection

_____ 4. world atlas

_____ 5. art exhibit

_____ 6. underground passage

_____ 7. inside pitch

_____ 8. ball of yarn

_____ 9. avid fan

_____ 10. clever invention

_____ 11. vast empire

_____ 12. honest mistake

_____ 13. emotional response

_____ 14. herd of goats

_____ 15. individual

_____ 16. hour-long film

_____ 17. X ray

_____ 18. application form

_____ 19. egg yolk

_____ 20. university

A **proper adjective** is formed from a proper noun and always begins with a capital letter. In some cases a proper noun keeps the same form when used as a proper adjective.

April is my favorite month.   I enjoy **April** showers.

In other cases, as with names of places, the proper adjective often adds one of the endings listed below. For those not listed, you may need to consult a dictionary.

ENDING	PROPER ADJECTIVE
-an	American, Texan, German, Tibetan, Mexican, Ohioan, Guatemalan, Moroccan, Alaskan, African, Minnesotan
-ese	Chinese, Japanese, Sudanese, Taiwanese, Portuguese, Lebanese
-ian	Canadian, Italian, Brazilian, Californian, Russian, Asian, Australian, Nigerian, Arabian, Egyptian, Austrian, Indian, Bolivian, Floridian
-ish	Spanish, Irish, Turkish, English, Polish

▶ **Exercise 2 Rewrite each group of words by changing the proper noun to a proper adjective. Change the article if necessary.**

a suit from Italy ___an Italian suit_____

1. a skier from Austria _____

2. a heat wave in August _____

3. the flag of Lebanon _____

4. a tour of Alaska _____

5. a river in Asia _____

6. the ambassador from Turkey _____

7. a poem from Japan _____

8. a birthday in November _____

9. a writer from Mexico _____

10. a rug from Egypt _____

11. a painting from China _____

12. the visitor from Morocco _____

13. a meeting on Monday _____

14. a monk from Tibet _____

15. a student from Taiwan _____

Lesson 33
Comparative and Superlative Adjectives

Grammar

The **comparative** form of an adjective compares two things or people. The **superlative** form of an adjective compares more than two things or people. For most adjectives of one syllable and some of two syllables, *-er* and *-est* are added to form the comparative and superlative.

Comparative: Brazil is **bigger** than Venezuela.
Superlative: Brazil is the **biggest** country in South America.

For most adjectives of two or more syllables, the comparative or superlative is formed by adding *more* or *most* before the adjective. Never use *more* or *most* with adjectives that already end with *-er* or *-est.*

Comparative: Marco is **more adventurous** than Kuan.
Superlative: Pete is the **most adventurous** of all.

Some adjectives have irregular comparative forms.

ADJECTIVE	COMPARATIVE	SUPERLATIVE
good, well	better	best
bad	worse	worst
many, much	more	most
little (amount)	less	least
little (size)	littler	littlest

▶ **Exercise 1** Write *C* in the blank if the sentence is correct and *I* if the sentence is incorrect.

___I___ The bestest vacation Sandra ever took was a trip to Wyoming.

_____ **1.** She visited Yellowstone National Park, the most old national park in the world.

_____ **2.** It is also the largest park in the United States.

_____ **3.** Of all the U.S. parks, Yellowstone has the most extensive wildlife preserve.

_____ **4.** The park has much natural wonders that are amazing to behold.

_____ **5.** Among the park's better attractions are huge canyons, cascading waterfalls, and clear blue lakes.

_____ **6.** There are most geysers and hot springs than any other place in the world.

_____ **7.** Geysers are one of nature's most interesting phenomena.

_____ **8.** Geysers make a most spectacular display as they roar high above the ground.

Grammar

_____ 9. While there are over two hundred geysers in Yellowstone, some shoot water more high than others.

_____ 10. Some erupt oftener than others.

_____ 11. Old Faithful is famouser than the other geysers in the park.

_____ 12. It spurts a stream of hot steaming water higher than one hundred feet into the air.

_____ 13. This most splendid geyser erupts from every half hour to every two hours.

_____ 14. For many visitors of Yellowstone, seeing Old Faithful is their funnest memory of the park.

_____ 15. After seeing Old Faithful, Sandra understood more well how the term *geyser* came from the Icelandic word *geysir,* which means "to rush forth."

▶ **Exercise 2** **Complete each sentence by writing in the blank the correct comparative or superlative form of the adjective indicated.**

Yellowstone is the _____ most beautiful _____ park I've ever seen. (beautiful)

1. In 1872 Congress established Yellowstone National Park, the _____ national park in the world. (old)

2. The United States has _____ than fifty national parks. (many)

3. The _____ known include Yellowstone in Wyoming, the Grand Canyon in Arizona, Yosemite in California, and Great Smoky Mountain in Tennessee and North Carolina. (well)

4. The national park system also includes many parks _____ than these four. (famous)

5. The national park system protects some of this country's _____ natural areas. (intriguing)

6. The Everglades in Florida is the _____ subtropical wilderness in the United States. (large)

7. Denali National Park in Alaska is the site of the nation's _____ mountain, Mount McKinley. (high)

8. While a few of the national parks are near cities, _____ parks are far from big towns. (many)

9. Not surprisingly, those parks that are _____ to population centers receive the _____ visitors. (near, many)

10. Among the _____ parks are Great Smoky Mountain and Acadia. (crowded)

Lesson 34
Demonstratives

Demonstrative adjectives point out something and describe nouns by answering the question *which one?* or *which ones?* The words *this, that, these,* and *those* are demonstrative adjectives when they describe nouns. *This* and *that* describe singular nouns. *These* and *those* describe plural nouns.

This, that, these, and *those* can also be used as demonstrative pronouns. They are pronouns when they take the place of nouns.

Grammar

DEMONSTRATIVE ADJECTIVES	DEMONSTRATIVE PRONOUNS
This book is exciting.	**This** is an exciting book.
I enjoy **these** types of stories.	I enjoy **these**.
That plot is convincing.	**That** is a realistic setting.
She writes **those** kinds of books.	Our class liked reading **those**.

▶ **Exercise 1 Underline the word in parentheses that best completes each sentence.**

Did Bella find (that, <u>those</u>) missing shoes?

1. (This, These) window needs to be repaired.

2. (Those, That) man must be over seven feet tall!

3. Did Ashley say she was bringing (this, those) kinds of cookies?

4. I believe (these, this) is what you're looking for.

5. Would you please see that Serafina gets (those, that) reports?

6. I think (these, this) plan of yours is quite practical.

7. (Those, These) animals over there are llamas.

8. Not just anyone can do (this, these) job, you know.

9. Does everyone in the class wear (that, those) kinds of shoes?

10. You often see (this, these) kind of movie during the holiday season.

11. The Computer Club adviser said that (these, this) keyboards were easier to use than the old ones.

12. (That, This) pass was way over his head!

13. How about (them, those) '49ers!

14. The speaker said that (this, these) product is the wave of the future.

15. (These, This) types of illnesses are not common anymore.

16. I didn't really care for (those, them) remarks.

17. (These, This) rose is lighter in color than that one.

18. (Those, Them) rocks contain iron pyrite.

19. (These, This) application form is not complete.

20. (That, Those) hat she's wearing is a little bit unusual.

▶ **Exercise 2** **Underline each demonstrative adjective. Circle each demonstrative pronoun.**

(This) appears to be the lid for that box.

1. Please give them these tickets.

2. Have you been to that new CD and tape store at the mall?

3. The doctor said to take one teaspoon of this twice a day.

4. These are not the right parts.

5. Those new videotapes aren't tracking properly.

6. That speedboat is the fastest on the river.

7. Those are not the runners who finished near the front of the pack.

8. This old clarinet squeaks whenever I try to play it.

9. These cows give more milk than any other type.

10. Without a doubt, this is the best campsite we've had yet.

11. That is a wonderful idea!

12. My mother heard those women speaking Swahili.

13. If you eat any more of those, you'll get a stomachache.

14. These were on the top shelf to the left.

15. That girl by the door has a twin sister.

16. We'll never make it to Denver in this beat-up car.

17. Those boots leak because the rubber has cracked.

18. That was the pony she rode during the fair.

Lesson 35
Adverbs

An **adverb** modifies, or describes, a verb, an adjective, or another adverb. When modifying an adjective or another adverb, an adverb usually comes before the word. When modifying a verb, an adverb can occupy different positions in the sentence.

The woman walked **slowly.** (modifies a verb)
Extremely cold weather can be dangerous. (modifies an adjective)
It snows **very** often in November. (modifies another adverb)

An adverb may tell *when, where,* or *how* about a verb. It may also tell to *what extent* a quality exists. This kind of adverb is called an **intensifier**. *Very, too, rather, quite,* and *almost* are intensifiers.

Many adverbs are formed by adding *-ly* to adjectives. However, not all words that end in *-ly* are adverbs. The words *kindly, friendly, lively,* and *lonely* are usually adjectives. Similarly, not all adverbs end in *-ly*. Some that do not are *afterward, sometimes, later, often, soon, here, there, everywhere, fast, hard, long, slow,* and *straight.*

▶ **Exercise 1 Draw an arrow from each adverb to the word it modifies. In the blank, write *V* if the adverb modifies a verb, *adj.* if it modifies an adjective, or *adv.* if it modifies another adverb. A sentence may have more than one adverb.**

<u>V, adj.</u>   Lena and Trent thoroughly enjoyed the truly vigorous hike.

_____ **1.** When hiking in the American West, you must proceed carefully.

_____ **2.** People walking in rocky areas sometimes come across rattlesnakes.

_____ **3.** Some people are quite afraid of snakes.

_____ **4.** If not provoked, rattlesnakes are not very dangerous.

_____ **5.** All rattlesnakes are poisonous, but they bite people relatively rarely.

_____ **6.** People often find rattlesnakes in dry, rocky areas.

_____ **7.** They are particularly numerous in the Southwest.

_____ **8.** However, they also exist in the eastern part of the country.

Grammar

_____ **9.** Surprisingly, the largest rattler is native to the East.

_____ **10.** The eastern diamondback rattlesnake lives there.

_____ **11.** Practically all eastern diamondbacks live on the southeast coast, from North

Carolina to Florida.

_____ **12.** This largest of rattlers can grow to almost eight feet!

_____ **13.** Rattlesnakes have adapted well to their environment.

_____ **14.** A snake's body temperature depends entirely on the temperature of the air

around it.

_____ **15.** If the temperature drops quickly, a rattlesnake can die.

_____ **16.** Snakes will often lie in the sun to get warm.

▶ **Exercise 2 Complete each sentence by writing an adverb in the blank.**

Emilio and Zina will meet us at the zoo _____ later _____.

1. Rattlers, like all snakes, are _____ misunderstood.

2. Snakes are often killed because _____ many people have a fear of them.

3. Some people _____ assume that snakes are evil.

4. _____, all snakes, including poisonous ones, are frightened of people.

5. When hiking in rattlesnake country, _____ follow a few safety rules.

6. Look _____ before you step into bushes or behind rocks.

7. Before you put your hand on a ledge, look _____ .

8. _____ wear leather boots when you are hiking in rattlesnake country.

9. Rattlers are unable to bite _____ enough to penetrate boot leather.

10. _____ try to chase or pick up a snake.

11. If you see a rattlesnake, walk _____ from it.

12. _____, carry a first-aid kit.

Lesson 36
Comparative and Superlative Adverbs

The **comparative** form of an adverb compares two actions. The **superlative** form of an adverb compares more than two actions. Long adverbs and adverbs ending in *-ly* require the use of *more* or *most*. Shorter adverbs need *-er* or *-est* as an ending.

Comparative: She records the experiment **more accurately** than he does.
Alicia studied **harder** than Rex did.

Superlative: She recorded the experiment **most accurately** of all the students.
Alicia studied **hardest** of all.

Some important adverbs have irregular comparative and superlative forms.

ADVERB	COMPARATIVE	SUPERLATIVE
well	better	best
badly	worse	worst
little (amount)	less	least

The words *less* and *least* are used before both short and long adverbs to form the negative comparative and negative superlative.

Jarrett sings **less well**. Amie sings **least rhythmically** of all.

▶ **Exercise 1** Fill in each blank with the correct form of the adverb.

ADVERB	COMPARATIVE	SUPERLATIVE
swiftly	more swiftly	most swiftly
1. easily	_____	_____
2. _____	more rapidly	_____
3. _____	farther	_____
4. _____	_____	best
5. _____	_____	most dangerously
6. fast	_____	_____
7. neatly	_____	_____
8. _____	_____	most happily

9. badly _____ _____

10. straight _____ _____

11. recklessly _____ _____

12. _____ _____ most truly

13. _____ more incredibly _____

14. often _____ _____

15. _____ _____ least

16. _____ _____ most proudly

17. _____ more closely _____

18. _____ _____ most fully

19. soon _____ _____

20. _____ more quickly _____

▶ **Exercise 2** **Complete each sentence by writing in the blank the correct form, comparative or superlative, of the adverb in parentheses.**

I sat _____closer_____ to the window than Stuart did. (close)

1. That's the _____ I've ever seen our cat run! (fast)

2. Tornadoes occur _____ in the Midwest and Plains states than in other areas of the country. (often)

3. Mandy performed _____ in the gymnastics meet than Robert did. (well)

4. The soprano section sings _____ of all. (strongly)

5. Talk _____ so we can hear you! (loudly)

6. I'm sure she did _____ on the math test than I did. (badly)

7. The DeAngelos had to walk _____ of all to school. (far)

8. Spot approached the food dish _____ than the hungry stray did. (enthusiastically)

9. No one was running around _____ than Lisa! (frantically)

10. My brother plays that blues song _____ of all. (well)

Grammar

Lesson 37
Using Adverbs and Adjectives

Adverbs and adjectives are often confused, especially when they appear after verbs. A predicate adjective follows a linking verb. An adverb follows an action verb.

The teachers in our school are **enthusiastic.** (adjective describing *teachers*)
Teachers in our school must work **hard.** (adverb describing *work*)

The words *bad, badly, good,* and *well* can be confusing. *Bad* and *good* are adjectives. They are used after linking verbs. *Badly* and *well* are adverbs. They describe action verbs. When used after a linking verb to describe a person's health, *well* is an adjective.

ADJECTIVE	ADVERB
This movie is **bad.**	The actors performed **badly.**
The popcorn is **good.**	The seats recline **well.**
I don't feel very **well.**	

People also confuse *real* and *really*, *sure* and *surely*, and *most* and *almost*. *Real, sure,* and *most* are adjectives. *Really, surely,* and *almost* are adverbs.

ADJECTIVE	ADVERB
Skating is a **real** workout.	Skating is **really** fun.
A skater needs **sure** feet.	To go fast is **surely** the most fun.
Most skaters are careful.	I **almost** never fall.

▶ **Exercise 1 Underline the word in parentheses that best completes the sentence.**

Jordan's (<u>sure</u>, surely) delivery guaranteed the success of his speech.

1. Josh had (most, almost) completed the lifesaving class at the YMCA.

2. We didn't do too (bad, badly), all things considered.

3. Learning bird songs and calls is a (good, well) way to identify them.

4. My geometry test is today, and I don't feel very (well, good).

5. Janelle was (real, really) glad to hear from them.

6. Always walk (quiet, quietly) in the woods in case you come upon some deer.

7. (Sure, Surely), he isn't serious about dropping out of the Camera Club!

8. All the staff members felt this issue of the paper turned out fairly (good, well).

Grammar

9. (Most, Almost) guitars have six strings, but some have twelve.

10. Making the yearbook staff is a (real, really) accomplishment.

11. That group of kids is so (loud, loudly) I can barely hear the film.

12. The coach said the team played just (good, well) enough to win.

13. She seemed very (sure, surely) of herself when she walked into the classroom.

14. Kari finished the quiz (most quick, most quickly) of all.

15. The baby ducklings (ready, readily) took to the water.

16. The nurse took her temperature after noticing she didn't look very (good, well).

17. Tina wanted very (bad, badly) to make the softball team.

18. Pete was (most, almost) finished with lunch when I arrived.

19. The plan is (possible, possibly) to carry out, although it will be quite risky.

20. I (sure, surely) will not go there with you!

21. The twelfth of November last year was (real, really) chilly.

22. Luis tried to look at his chances (realistic, realistically).

23. Frankly, this Chinese food doesn't taste (good, well) to me.

24. The judges felt his singing was (more beautiful, more beautifully) than Ellen's.

25. They're not (sure, surely) they'll be able to participate in the math contest.

26. The sound quality at that concert was very (bad, badly).

27. My dad looked (real, really) happy when we gave him his present.

28. Marianne was (extreme, extremely) surprised when she heard who had called her.

▶ **Writing Link** **Write a short paragraph about your favorite extracurricular activity. Include several adjectives and adverbs.**

_____

_____

_____

_____

_____

_____

Lesson 38
Avoiding Double Negatives

The adverb *not* is a negative word. **Negative words** express the idea of "no." *Not* often appears in a shortened form as part of a contraction.

CONTRACTIONS WITH *NOT*

is not=isn't	will not=won't	do not=don't	had not=hadn't
was not=wasn't	cannot=can't	did not=didn't	would not=wouldn't
were not=weren't	could not=couldn't	have not=haven't	should not=shouldn't

Other negative words are listed below. Each negative word has several opposites. These are **affirmative words**, or words that show the idea of "yes."

NEGATIVE	AFFIRMATIVE	NEGATIVE	AFFIRMATIVE
never	ever, always	no one	everyone, someone
nobody	anybody, somebody	nothing	something, anything
none	one, all, some, any	nowhere	somewhere, anywhere

Be careful to avoid using two negative words together in the same sentence. This is called a **double negative**. Correct a double negative by removing one of the negative words or by replacing one with an affirmative word.

Incorrect: That isn't no beautiful sofa.
Correct: That isn't a beautiful sofa.   That is no beautiful sofa.

▶ **Exercise 1 Place a check next to the sentence in each pair that is correct.**

_____   Soto hasn't never saved that amount of money.

___✔___   Soto hasn't ever saved that amount of money.

_____ **1.** I haven't never met my great-grandfather because he lives in Korea.

_____   I haven't ever met my great-grandfather because he lives in Korea.

_____ **2.** You can't go anywhere in New York City without seeing tall buildings.

_____   You can't go nowhere in New York City without seeing tall buildings.

_____ **3.** He didn't do anything about that cut on his arm.

_____   He didn't do nothing about that cut on his arm.

_____ **4.** It wasn't no big deal when we won the game.

_____   It was no big deal when we won the game.

16. The clowns in the parade _____ as they greeted the children. (past progressive form of *smile*)

17. Coach Rodriguez _____ more games than any coach in our school's history by the end of the season. (future perfect tense of *win*)

18. Ms. Kotlinski _____ herself plenty of time to drive to Canada. (past tense of *allow*)

19. Most of the trees in our neighborhood _____ their leaves in October. (present tense of *shed*)

20. This _____ to be the longest winter yet. (present perfect tense of *appear*)

▶ **Exercise 3** **Draw one line under each adjective. (Ignore the articles *a*, *an*, and *the*.) Draw two lines under each adverb. Draw an arrow from each adjective or adverb to the word it modifies.**

A playful squirrel ran quickly to the tree.

1. Julius joyfully delivered presents to eager nieces.

2. Falling snow already has covered the landscape.

3. Church bells rang merrily.

4. The humble director graciously accepted her two awards.

5. To please the young birds, the red cardinal went in search of food.

6. That music store hardly ever has what I am looking for.

7. Purple wildflowers danced in the spring breeze.

8. Light from the sun bathed the sandy beach sooner than we expected.

9. Neighbors often bring me marvelous apples.

10. Grandmother served a delicious meal of wedding soup and manicotti.

11. The soccer team almost won a difficult game.

12. She carefully chose a new piece of jewelry.

Unit 6: Prepositions, Conjunctions, and Interjections

Lesson 39
Prepositions and Prepositional Phrases

A preposition is a word that relates a noun or a pronoun to another word in a sentence. Prepositions of more than one word are compound prepositions

The magazine **on** the table just arrived.
Darlene will perform the solo **instead of** Retta.

COMMONLY USED PREPOSITIONS

about	at	by	like	over	up
above	before	down	near	since	upon
across	behind	during	of	through	with
after	below	for	off	throughout	within
against	beneath	from	on	to	without
along	beside	in	onto	toward	
among	between	inside	out	under	
around	beyond	into	outside	until	

COMPOUND PREPOSITIONS

according to	aside from	in front of	instead of
across from	because of	in place of	on account of
along with	far from	in spite of	on top of

▶ Exercise 1 **Underline each preposition or compound preposition.**

The development <u>of</u> flea markets <u>in</u> the United States is an outgrowth <u>of</u> the bazaar.

1. A bazaar is an Asian marketplace held inside the city.

2. Here, traders in small stalls or shops sell miscellaneous goods.

3. Some bazaars are located along a single, narrow street.

4. Others spread throughout a number of streets.

5. For example, there might be a street of coppersmiths beside two streets of booksellers.

6. One section could house a huge covered bazaar with four hundred shops.

7. The bazaar originated in early times.

8. During that period, it served for gossip and trade.

9. One city known for its colorful bazaars since ancient times is Istanbul, Turkey.

10. It is the only major city located on two continents—Asia and Europe.

11. Istanbul, called Constantinople from A.D. 330 to 1453, is Turkey's leading center of industry, trade, and culture.

12. Tourists visit the city to see its museums and palaces, along with its bazaars.

13. A lucky sightseer might find an antique beneath the many wares or trinkets at one of these unique shops.

14. Some shopkeepers might expect the tourist to bargain over the cost instead of paying a fixed price.

15. Aside from the large crowds, many one-of-a-kind items can be found throughout the bazaar-laden streets.

A **prepositional phrase** is a group of words that begins with a preposition and ends with a noun or pronoun called the **object of the preposition**.

The pitcher **in the rear** is filled **with sweetened tea**.

▶ **Exercise 2** Draw one line under each prepositional phrase. Draw a second line under each object of the preposition.

Sadie Jenkins hired Heloise and me to clean the large shed behind her house.

1. After the discovery of many antiques, we suggested that she sell the items.

2. Three porcelain dolls and a wooden chess set of Renaissance design were among our best finds.

3. Mrs. Jenkins smiled at us and said that along with our pay we could have twenty percent of the money we generated.

4. Diving into our task with new enthusiasm, we searched through every box and container inside the shed.

5. When Dad contacted two antique dealers and told them about the dozens of items, they agreed to come to the house and make an offer.

Lesson 40
Pronouns as Objects of Prepositions

When a pronoun is the object of a preposition, use an object pronoun and not a subject pronoun.

The burly man sang a lullaby to Karen. The burly man sang a lullaby to **her**.

Sometimes a preposition will have a compound object consisting of a noun and a pronoun. Remember to use an object pronoun in a compound object.

I sold tickets to Carrie and Seana. I sold tickets to Carrie and **her**.
Alberto agreed with Willie and **me**.

The subject pronoun *who* is never the object of a preposition; only the object pronoun *whom* can be an object.

The woman to **whom** I spoke is from Colombia.
Of **whom** did you ask directions?

▶ **Exercise 1** Underline the pronoun that best completes each sentence.

For (who, <u>whom</u>) are these party favors intended?

1. Community service is important to Simon and (we, us).

2. Did you give instructions to Waldo and (she, her)?

3. Is this carnation plant intended for (he, him)?

4. For Lee Chan and (he, him), did the lesson present much difficulty?

5. The decision was easy for Michael and (he, him).

6. The stranger to (who, whom) I spoke turned out to be Pietro's brother.

7. I explained the situation to Mickey, Juan, and (her, she).

8. With (who, whom) did you go to the movies?

9. For his brother and (he, him), sleeping late meant rising at eight.

10. The results of the poll were released by Twila, Arthur, and (she, her).

11. They were telling stories about (who, whom)?

12. According to Myron and (she, her), they never watered the lawn during the drought.

13. How many of (they, them) bought tickets for the basketball game?

14. Upon (who, whom) did the blocks collapse?

15. We sat near (they, them) at the band concert.

▶ **Exercise 2** Underline each pronoun that is an object of a preposition. Write *C* in the blank if the pronoun is correct. Write the correct pronoun if necessary.

___me___   John gave a knowing look to Frieda and I̲.

_____ **1.** The party was a surprise to me.

_____ **2.** The newcomers were neighbors of Lisa and she.

_____ **3.** Treg should have called you or I.

_____ **4.** Vacations are boring for whom?

_____ **5.** The waitress spilled juice on I.

_____ **6.** Gently rolling hills are unfamiliar to us in Iowa.

_____ **7.** All of those murals were painted by he.

_____ **8.** Alice introduced her parents to they.

_____ **9.** Shawnda is the person to who we report.

_____ **10.** David raised twenty dollars for us to give to the needy family.

_____ **11.** The map that she drew looked very confusing to Juan and I.

_____ **12.** "To who are you speaking, Richard?" asked the teacher.

_____ **13.** I'll share my lunch with you and they.

_____ **14.** The winner certainly wasn't with me!

_____ **15.** Will you come to the dance with Bill and I?

▶ **Writing Link** Write a paragraph about an interesting place you have visited. Include pronouns as objects of prepositions.

_____

_____

_____

_____

_____

_____

Lesson 41
Prepositional Phrases as Adjectives and Adverbs

A prepositional phrase that modifies or describes a noun or pronoun is an **adjective phrase**. Notice that, unlike most adjectives, an adjective phrase usually comes after the word it modifies.

I noticed a man **with bushy eyebrows.**

A prepositional phrase that modifies a verb, an adjective, or another adverb is an **adverb phrase**. An adverb phrase tells *when, where,* or *how* an action occurs.

The hikers rested **beside a brook.** (describes a verb)
The vista was breathtaking **from this view.** (describes an adjective)
The quartet performed well **for such an early hour.** (describes an adverb)

▶ **Exercise 1** Underline each prepositional phrase. Draw an arrow to the word it modifies.

Movies began in the late 1800s. People experimented with devices to make pictures

move.

1. One of these experimenters was Thomas A. Edison.

2. George Eastman, a pioneer in photographic equipment, helped Edison invent the

kinetoscope.

3. Motion pictures were projected for the first time on December 28, 1895.

4. Early filmmakers photographed almost anything near the camera.

5. Language differences presented no problem because movies, at that time, were silent.

6. Titles, or printed dialogue, were inserted between scenes.

7. Soon audiences became bored, and attendance at the movies declined.

8. One development that saved movies from extinction was that they began to tell stories.

9. One such story, *The Great Train Robbery,* led to the establishment of nickelodeons.

10. A nickelodeon was an early movie theater with a five-cent admission charge.

11. Around 1927, a sound system called Movietone was developed in the studios.

12. These first talkies were awkward and tense compared to the silent films.

13. Many silent film stars had voices unsuited to sound films.

14. New techniques in photography and editing were tried during this time.

15. The most successful movies of the 1930s and 1940s were musicals, gangster films, and horror shows.

▶ **Exercise 2** **Draw one line under each adjective phrase. Draw two lines under each adverb phrase.**

Within the last few years, the quality of home entertainment has changed dramatically.

1. With modern advancements, high-quality sound no longer requires huge speakers.

2. Some of the most advanced systems use only three-inch speakers.

3. "Home theater" sound systems place speakers behind the listeners.

4. With stunning realism, these rear speakers enhance the recordings almost to the level of a live performance.

5. It is difficult to imagine the improvement beyond stereo; you must hear it for yourself.

6. Video images with greater resolution and clarity are also reaching new heights of quality.

7. Until the last two to three years, projection televisions, with their huge screens, were inferior to sets with cathode ray tubes.

8. Manufacturers have responded to consumer demands by building television sets with greater brightness and resolution.

9. As digital recording spreads throughout the industry, one can expect virtually perfect sound reproduction even after years of use; old-style records deteriorate with every play.

10. Superb production within the confines of our homes is a reality within reach of even modest budgets.

Lesson 42
Conjunctions: Coordinating and Correlative

A **coordinating conjunction** is a word that connects parts of a sentence. *And, but, or, for,* and *nor* are coordinating conjunctions.

Allison **and** Rosita have lived in Texas.
Do you remember if Tony plays soccer **or** sings in the choir?
Geraldo chose spaghetti, **but** we ate lasagna.

To strengthen the relationship between words or groups of words, use a correlative conjunction. **Correlative conjunctions** are pairs of words that connect words or phrases in a sentence. Correlative conjunctions include *both ... and, either ... or, neither ... nor,* and *not only ... but also.*

The NFL has franchises in **both** Green Bay **and** San Diego.

When a compound subject is joined by the conjunction *and,* it takes a plural verb.

Wilma **and** Helga **are** class officers.

When a compound subject is joined by *or* or *nor,* the verb agrees with the nearest part of the subject.

Neither the boys **nor** Mr. Ferguson **is** afraid of the rapids.

▶ **Exercise 1** Circle each conjunction. Write in the blank *coord.* if it is a coordinating conjunction and *correl.* if it is a correlative conjunction.

_____coord._____   Rugby (and) cricket are examples of English sports.

_____ **1.** The soil is rich, and the climate is moderate.

_____ **2.** The ceremony was covered by either radio or television.

_____ **3.** Rags and Mittens are litter mates.

_____ **4.** Neither the Johnsons nor the Montoyas are our next-door neighbors.

_____ **5.** Jeremy had English and gym before lunch.

_____ **6.** Neither rain nor snow is in the immediate forecast.

_____ **7.** Erin had a fever, but Maria felt fine.

_____ **8.** Before selecting a computer, Mr. Oleson collected brochures and flyers.

_____ **9.** Hector ate corn and green beans with his steak.

Grammar

_____ **10.** Both her essay and her speech were flawless.

_____ **11.** Molly had an umbrella, but Alfonso was unprepared for the shower.

_____ **12.** Both carnations and chrysanthemums are popular flowers for corsages.

_____ **13.** The whole family not only learned snorkeling but also learned water skiing.

_____ **14.** Herve was an expert in the diagnosis and repair of diesel engines.

_____ **15.** Ford, General Motors, and Chrysler are the three major American auto producers.

▶ **Exercise 2 Draw two lines under the correct form of the verb in parentheses. Circle each coordinating or correlative conjunction.**

(Neither) the volleyball players (nor) their coach (<u><u>likes</u></u>, like) the facility.

1. Red hots and candy corn (is, are) Erika's favorite candy.

2. Neither Ahmed nor the rest of the group (is, are) interested in the side trip.

3. Both Benny and Jerry (dislikes, dislike) winter.

4. Fruits and vegetables (is, are) part of a balanced diet.

5. Neither Fido nor the cats (was, were) to be seen.

6. The band and the soloist (performs, perform) this evening.

7. Either a deer or pheasants (was, were) eating his chicken feed.

8. Chan and her family (drives, drive) Cadillacs.

9. Marcus or one of his sisters (makes, make) these clever posters.

10. (Was, Were) the Jacksons or Kenny involved in the accident?

11. Neither my partner nor I (gives, give) legal advice.

12. To each family reunion, Mom, Uncle Charley, and my aunts (brings, bring) pictures from their childhood.

13. As choices for the banquet entree, steak and chicken (tops, top) the list.

14. Neither the parakeets nor the cockatiel (was, were) trained.

15. Neither Ishmael nor the other scouts (prefers, prefer) hiking to horseback riding.

Lesson 43
Conjunctive Adverbs and Interjections

A **conjunctive adverb** may be used instead of a conjunction in a compound sentence. It is usually preceded by a semicolon and followed by a comma.

Many Asians use chopsticks; **however,** some use forks.

USE CONJUNCTIVE ADVERBS
To replace *and*	also, besides, furthermore, moreover
To replace *but*	however, nevertheless, still
To state a result	consequently, therefore, so, thus
To state equality	equally, likewise, similarly

▶ **Exercise 1** Write in each blank a conjunctive adverb that logically links the two simple sentences.

There is a gazebo in her backyard; _____ also _____, there is a garden.

1. The old museum was drafty and rundown; _____, the exhibits were boring and outdated.

2. The team uniforms faded in the wash; _____, the school colors are now mint green and pale yellow.

3. Our tour bus departed an hour late; _____, we arrived just before the aquarium closed.

4. The Tigers are talented; _____, they have won the state championship three years in a row.

5. Mika doesn't know much about opera; _____, he would like to go.

6. Vern enjoys watching birds; _____, he tries to attract them.

7. Many kinds of dogs are found at the animal shelter; _____, cats are regular inhabitants.

8. Nina was unable to play tennis this season; _____, she attended every match.

9. Margi had her braces removed; _____, she must still wear a retainer.

Grammar

10. All the holiday flights were booked; _____, we drove to Chicago.

11. I enjoy watching old movies; _____, Dan prefers the sports channel.

12. Due to the flu, Kareem had missed several days of history class; _____, he was excused from the test.

13. Janice loves to go shopping; _____, Mai enjoys hunting for a bargain.

14. My brother is very creative with his hands; _____, most of the presents that he gives are homemade.

15. Bird watching is very educational; _____, it is great fun.

An **interjection** is a word or group of words used to express strong feeling or to attract attention. Use interjections sparingly in your writing because overuse spoils their effectiveness.

COMMON INTERJECTIONS

aha	come on	ha	oh	ouch	what	yes
alas	gee	hey	oh, no	phew	whoops	
awesome	good grief	hooray	oops	well	wow	

An interjection that expresses very strong feeling may stand alone. An interjection that expresses milder feeling remains a part of the sentence.

The exams are finally over. **Hooray!**
Oh my, I've lost my key again.

▶ **Exercise 2** Write in the blank an interjection that makes sense.

_____Ha_____, you can't catch me!

1. Cleveland just scored a touchdown. _____!

2. _____, what's going on here?

3. _____! Didn't you understand a word I said?

4. That was a rough test. _____!

5. _____! The door pinched my finger.

6. _____, are you going to play cards or talk?

7. Marsha gasped as Eli limped off the court. "_____, now we'll never win."

8. The shot went in right at the buzzer. _____!

 Unit 6 **Review**

▶ **Exercise 1** Underline each prepositional phrase. Circle each conjunction and conjunctive adverb. Write in the blank *coord.* for coordinating conjunction, *correl.* for correlative conjunction, or *conj.* for conjunctive adverb.

<u>coord.</u>　　　The little girl (and) her dog skipped merrily <u>by the playground</u>.

_____ **1.** Maxwell jumped off the wagon; likewise, Todd followed behind him.

_____ **2.** Neither the Ferrari nor the Porsche is made in America.

_____ **3.** The flag glistened and flapped in the breeze as the national anthem was played.

_____ **4.** The drug store was around the corner from the pet shop and the candy store.

_____ **5.** Alberto not only caught the pass in one hand but also gained four yards before the whistle.

_____ **6.** The store in the mall has higher prices than this one, but I like the clothes here better.

_____ **7.** The music on the radio was making me sleepy; therefore, I did my homework without it.

_____ **8.** Casey wanted a golden retriever; thus, she never stopped hinting for one.

_____ **9.** Either the black car or the car with the blue roof ran the traffic light at the corner.

_____ **10.** After school Raoul went to the dentist and had a cleaning.

_____ **11.** One of the cheerleaders and Myra won the spirit award.

_____ **12.** Underneath the car seat, I found eighty-seven cents and a piece of licorice.

_____ **13.** Computers cannot think; consequently, they will never be a replacement for humans.

_____ **14.** A hawk circled lazily in the evening sky; moreover, the wolves began to howl.

_____ **15.** Not only was the semester finished, but Jeremy also did well on his exams.

_____ **16.** You must choose either the electronic game or a baseball glove made of leather.

Name _____ Class _____ Date _____

Cumulative Review: Units 1–6

▶ **Exercise 1** Write in the blank the past form or past participle of each irregular verb in parentheses. Draw one line under each simple subject.

My <u>brother</u> _____ broke _____ the new vase. (break)

1. The pond has not _____ over. (freeze)

2. Isabel _____ into tears when she heard the news. (burst)

3. Chad had _____ the election by only ten votes. (lose)

4. Dad _____ me how to drive defensively. (teach)

5. Have you _____ all your vegetables? (eat)

6. These shoes _____ twice as much as my old ones. (cost)

7. I have _____ my friend several times. (write)

8. Jane _____ the length of the pool and back. (swim)

9. Hakeem had _____ quite a few inches in the past year. (grow)

10. My grandmother has _____ her quilts to many visitors over the years. (show)

11. A pipe in the basement _____ while we were on vacation. (burst)

12. She grabbed a tissue and _____ her nose. (blow)

13. Someone must have _____ his wallet during gym. (steal)

14. Mr. Tadashi has _____ to Jeff's parents about his behavior in class. (speak)

15. They have finally _____ a name for their new puppy. (choose)

16. The luxury liner _____ during the violent storm. (sink)

17. The bells _____ loudly at the stroke of midnight. (ring)

18. We _____ a quart of water following the race. (drink)

19. Manuel had _____ from the horse and broken his arm. (fall)

20. Unfortunately, Carla _____ the lucky ticket into the trash. (throw)

▶ **Exercise 2** **Draw one line under each adjective (excluding articles) and two lines under each adverb.**

<u>Three</u> <u>old</u> nests fell <u>quickly</u> from the tree.

1. The sharp pencils suddenly broke in the middle of the hard test.

2. Stormy weather severely damaged the playground at the elementary school.

3. The one mother sang awhile as she waited nervously in the lobby.

4. The enormous yacht sailed slowly out to the open sea.

5. I will not receive the best grade in the class today.

6. The lengthy description of the social event made me laugh hysterically.

7. A fragrant bouquet made me sneeze suddenly.

8. The last class listened very silently as the new teacher gave the assignment.

9. Patrick always lived in the same house.

10. The bald assistant carefully cleaned the empty cage.

11. Several friends enjoyed the party yesterday.

12. We work hard for this coach because he is the greatest!

13. We finally found the beautiful new house.

14. The weary professor put the heavy book down.

15. My grades are slowly improving now.

16. The lost dog gradually disappeared over the far horizon.

17. The four musical instruments were badly out of tune.

18. The young baby-sitter reluctantly surrendered to the sorrowful pleas.

19. The wild beasts silently stalk nocturnal prey.

20. A quite strange man drove slowly past the red house.

▶ **Exercise 3 Circle each prepositional phrase and draw an arrow to the word it modifies. For each italicized word, write *correl.* (correlative conjunction), *coord.* (coordinating conjunction), *conj.* (conjunctive adverb), or *int.* (interjection) in the blank provided.**

**coord.**   Do you want the large boxes *or* the small ones that are stacked (in the attic)?

_____ **1.** Please take the picture off the wall *and* hang the new one.

_____ **2.** *Neither* Jake *nor* Paul is participating in the staff meeting.

_____ **3.** I selected ice cream in a cup, *but* Rosa chose ice cream on a cone.

_____ **4.** *Ugh!* I dislike eggs in the morning.

_____ **5.** *Not only* do I disagree with the cost of the antique, *but also* it didn't seem to be

valuable.

_____ **6.** You scored much higher on this test than you did on the last one.

Congratulations!

_____ **7.** Different kinds of birds prefer different kinds of seeds; *therefore,* Juan buys

several mixtures.

_____ **8.** The new exhibit at the art gallery is whimsical, *but* it has a serious side.

_____ **9.** Doctors say that *both* exercise *and* a good diet lead to a healthy life.

_____ **10.** Binoculars allow a closer look at the wild animals; *similarly,* a camcorder

saves their activities for later review.

_____ **11.** A water pipe broke at the high school, *and* classes were cancelled.

_____ **12.** *Ouch!* I slammed my finger in the car door.

_____ **13.** Andy ran up the stairs *and* closed the door to his room.

_____ **14.** Collies are Karen's favorite breed of dog; *however,* she enjoys all of the varieties.

_____ **15.** *Neither* Brett *nor* Samantha got the lead role in the musical.

_____ **16.** *Aha,* look what I found in the drawer.

_____ **17.** You'll find the cows over the hill *and* beside the brook.

_____ **18.** Many flowers and shrubs help attract a large variety of birds; *besides,* they

beautify the yard.

Unit 7: Clauses and Complex Sentences

Lesson 44
Sentences and Main Clauses

A **simple sentence** has one complete subject and one complete predicate. The subject, the predicate, or both may be compound.

SUBJECT   PREDICATE
Lightning   struck our oak.

COMPOUND SUBJECT   PREDICATE
Branches and leaves   fell.

SUBJECT   COMPOUND PREDICATE
The oak   has stood for years and will stand for many more.

A **compound sentence** contains two or more simple sentences. Each simple sentence is called a **main clause**. Main clauses may be joined by a comma followed by a conjunction or by a semicolon. A semicolon is also used before a conjunctive adverb, such as *moreover.*

Lightning struck our oak, **but** it did not fall. (two main clauses joined by a comma and a conjunction)

Lightning struck our oak; it did not fall. (two main clauses joined by a semicolon)

Lightning struck our oak; **moreover,** it fell to the ground. (two main clauses joined by a semicolon and a conjunctive adverb)

▶ **Exercise 1** Write in the blank whether the sentence is *simple* or *compound.*

_____compound_____ Volcanoes can sit idle, or they can erupt frequently.

_____ **1.** Earth's surface seems calm, but its interior seethes with energy.

_____ **2.** Pressure and heat inside the earth melt rock.

_____ **3.** Molten rock is lighter than its surroundings; it rises to the surface.

_____ **4.** Molten rock inside the earth is magma; magma on the earth's surface is lava.

_____ **5.** A volcano is formed from magma.

_____ **6.** Some volcanoes erupt with great power; others are less violent.

_____ **7.** Thick magma is forced from inside the earth by great pressure.

_____ **8.** Thin magma flows more easily; moreover, it contains less explosion-causing gas.

_____ **9.** Kiluaea on Hawaii is an example of a peaceful volcano.

_____ **10.** Scientists from all over the world observe its eruptions.

_____ **11.** Mount Saint Helens is another story; the mountain in the state of Washington literally blew its top in 1980.

_____ **12.** A chain of volcanic mountains lies across the Pacific Northwest.

_____ **13.** It is called the Cascade Range, and it includes Mount Saint Helens.

_____ **14.** Earth is not the only planet with volcanoes.

_____ **15.** Photographs reveal active volcanoes on the moons of Jupiter and Neptune and extinct volcanoes on Venus and Mars.

▶ **Exercise 2 Underline each main clause. Add a comma or a semicolon as needed.**

<u>Peter has a great interest in volcanoes</u>; <u>he hopes to become a volcanologist.</u>

1. Volcanologists study volcanoes.

2. They had always hunted an active eruption and in 1980 they got their chance.

3. Mount Saint Helens is an active volcano in Washington but it had not erupted since 1847.

4. In March of 1980, Mount Saint Helens began shaking moreover, its top began to bulge.

5. Scientists raced to Washington from around the world.

6. They knew the mountain would erupt but they could not tell when or how violently.

7. Officials kept people away from the mountain but some adventurous souls went anyway.

8. Mount Saint Helens erupted early on May 18, 1980 and more than sixty people were killed.

9. The destruction to the earth and wildlife was extreme the blast leveled 150 square miles of forest.

10. The avalanche after the blast killed millions of animals and birds.

Lesson 45
Complex Sentences and Subordinate Clauses

A **complex sentence** contains a main clause and one or more subordinate clauses. A main clause can stand alone as a sentence. A **subordinate clause** has a subject and a predicate, but it is not a complete sentence. It depends on the main clause to complete its meaning.

MAIN CLAUSE	SUBORDINATE CLAUSE
We were sailing on the lake	when the thunderstorm hit.
We didn't know	that the paint was wet.
This is the place	where I dropped my pen.

▶ **Exercise 1** Underline each main clause. Place a check in the blank next to each complex sentence.

✔ _____ <u>The game will be postponed</u> because the rain is falling steadily.

_____ **1.** When it is foggy, driving is very dangerous.

_____ **2.** Before I start my workout, I always do some warmup exercises.

_____ **3.** We were surprised when we learned of the arrest.

_____ **4.** We bought our new sofa during the sale at the local furniture store.

_____ **5.** Although it rained all day, we still enjoyed our trip.

_____ **6.** I will help you with your homework after you watch the baby.

_____ **7.** Jake stared at me as if he had seen a ghost.

_____ **8.** Whenever the wind blows the trees against the windows, the dog howls.

_____ **9.** Our choir went on a field trip to the senior citizens' center.

_____ **10.** Owen felt responsible for the missing book though it was not his fault.

_____ **11.** The new computer and printer really make our work easier.

_____ **12.** You can order whatever you want from the menu.

_____ **13.** We will be on time unless there is a traffic jam.

_____ **14.** If our team wins, everyone will celebrate.

_____ **15.** The police did not arrive until the thieves had left.

_____ **16.** You can leave early tomorrow and go to the game.

_____ **17.** We cannot start the concert until the weather clears.

_____ **18.** Sam can mail these packages if they have enough postage on them.

_____ **19.** Jill had her petition filled out so that she could run for office.

_____ **20.** Our class is making the community more aware of the importance of recycling.

_____ **21.** The road is safe as long as there is no ice.

_____ **22.** The building swayed whenever the wind blew.

_____ **23.** Hasan and Mike clapped their hands to the beat.

_____ **24.** Sandy cried because her beloved dog had run away.

_____ **25.** When the room warms up, we can take off our sweaters.

_____ **26.** The pool will be cleaned when spring comes.

_____ **27.** Because Alison loves jazz, she attends every concert.

_____ **28.** The rain ceased, and the stuffy air cleared.

_____ **29.** Since I first saw you, I have wondered if we ever met before.

_____ **30.** While we waited for the feature, we were annoyed by several ads.

_____ **31.** Because our history class is so large, we meet in the auditorium.

_____ **32.** The mountain climber checked her equipment before she started up the slope.

_____ **33.** Please be quiet when you come in late.

_____ **34.** I will lock the door and turn off the lights before leaving.

_____ **35.** Stu is leaving for vacation when he completes his courses.

_____ **36.** If Stan wants to play hockey, he will need more discipline.

_____ **37.** I'll wear a red hat so that you can recognize me.

_____ **38.** The mice darted underground as the owl dived at them.

▶ **Writing Link** **Write at least three complex sentences about your favorite sport.**

_____

_____

_____

_____

Lesson 46
Adjective Clauses

When a subordinate clause modifies a noun or a pronoun, it is called an **adjective clause**. Often, an adjective clause begins with a relative pronoun. An adjective clause can also begin with *where* or *when*.

Ms. Parker, **who is from Colorado,** is coming for dinner.
She has written a book **that tells the history of the Rocky Mountains.**

RELATIVE PRONOUNS

that	who	whose
which	whom	whomever

▶ **Exercise 1** Draw one line under each adjective clause and two lines under each word that introduces an adjective clause.

The present that Tanya received lifted her spirits.

1. Is this the place where you had the accident?

2. The woman whose briefcase you found is here to pick it up.

3. Is this the toaster that always burns the toast?

4. The phone call that I just answered was for you.

5. The people who own that black dog live around the corner.

6. The cookbooks are in the cupboard where we keep the spices.

7. The doctor who originally saw us was out today.

8. We will leave next Friday, which is my birthday.

9. The band that I like best is The Rovers.

10. Anyone who believes that politician is very gullible.

11. The basement is the last place where I should have stored the film.

12. The excuse that he used to explain his lateness was laughable.

13. The moment when Jason arrives will signal the start of the party.

14. Is this the video that you recommended?

15. Connie, who is the winner, will get the trophy.

16. Lainie, who is the star of the play, is signing autographs.

17. Scientists explore rain forest canopies, where many species live.

18. Is this the location where the battle took place?

19. Harry bought a ten-speed, which is his favorite kind of bike.

20. Is the actor whom you like in the movie?

▶ **Exercise 2 Draw one line under each adjective clause. Draw an arrow to the noun or pronoun that it modifies.**

The student <u>who won the spelling bee</u> donated her prize to the class.

1. The days when thousands of buffalo roamed the plains must have been long ago.

2. Is this the documentary that you wanted?

3. The flood happened at a time when everyone was away from home.

4. King, who smelled the smoke, woke us up by barking.

5. I have seen the movie that you are discussing.

6. My favorite class is the one that Mr. Clark teaches.

7. Simone met our new neighbor who lives down the street.

8. Anyone who disagrees with the proposal should vote no.

9. The crystal vase, which was a present from Aunt Sandra, is filled with roses.

10. Is Ralph the neighbor whom you invited to the party?

11. Boris knows the captain whose team won the tournament.

12. Have you talked to the artist who painted this picture?

13. Uncle Vincent bought the biggest refrigerator that he could find.

14. Bridalveil Falls, which is in Yosemite National Park, is lovely.

15. The person whose place I held wants to get back in line.

Lesson 47
Essential and Nonessential Clauses

Grammar

Adjective clauses may be either essential or nonessential. **Essential clauses** are necessary to make the meaning of a sentence clear. A clause beginning with *that* is essential. **Nonessential clauses** add interesting information but are not necessary for the meaning of a sentence. A clause beginning with *which* is usually nonessential. Use commas to set off nonessential clauses from the rest of the sentence.

The sweater **that you knitted for me** fits perfectly. (essential clause)

Dr. Adams, **whose train arrives today,** is a well-known writer. (nonessential clause)

▶ **Exercise 1** Underline each adjective clause. Write *e* (essential) or *non.* (nonessential) in the blank to identify the type of clause. Add commas as needed.

non.   *Wingless Flight,*<u>which I saw yesterday,</u>depicted space travel.

_____ **1.** The explorers whom I most admire are astronauts.

_____ **2.** One man who made space travel possible was Robert Goddard.

_____ **3.** Goddard who tested many rockets helped develop liquid fuel.

_____ **4.** Space travel which is very dangerous began with uncrewed spacecraft.

_____ **5.** The Soviet Union was the first nation with a space satellite which they called

   Sputnik.

_____ **6.** The United States whose first satellite was called *Explorer I* followed the

   Soviet Union four months later.

_____ **7.** Yuri Gagarin who was the Soviet Union's first astronaut orbited Earth once.

_____ **8.** Alan Shepard became the American astronaut who first traveled into space.

_____ **9.** One event that really captured Americans' attention was the space walk of

   Edward White.

_____ **10.** White who had so much fun on the walk was finally ordered back into the

   spacecraft by Mission Control.

_____ **11.** The Apollo program which we studied this year was the American moon

landing project.

_____ **12.** The astronauts who were selected for this mission had to be in superb physical

condition.

_____ **13.** *Apollo 8* which did not land orbited the moon and sent back pictures of the

surface.

_____ **14.** *Apollo 11* developed as the mission that was to land an American on the moon.

_____ **15.** The astronauts who held Americans' interest in 1969 were Armstrong, Aldrin,

and Collins.

_____ **16.** Neil Armstrong who was the commander of the mission walked on the moon

with Buzz Aldrin.

_____ **17.** People who care about space exploration wonder if we will ever go to the

moon again.

_____ **18.** The argument that we should not continue is partly based on safety.

_____ **19.** The astronauts who died in the *Apollo 1* fire and the *Challenger* tragedy are

reminders of the dangers of space travel.

_____ **20.** Their names which will always be remembered are the names of heroes.

_____ **21.** Other spacecraft which carried no people have also explored the solar system.

_____ **22.** The planet that has long attracted science-fiction writers was not

photographed until the mid-1960s.

_____ **23.** *Viking 1* which photographed Mars in 1976 showed a huge volcano.

_____ **24.** The scientists who analyze photographic data could study Viking photographs

of Mars for years.

_____ **25.** The spacecraft that took the most punishment were the Soviet *Venera* probes.

_____ **26.** The *Venera* probes landed on Venus which has a crushing atmosphere and

took pictures before being destroyed.

Lesson 48
Adverb Clauses

An **adverb clause** is a subordinate clause that gives information about the verb in the main clause of the sentence. It tells *how, when, where, why,* or *under what conditions* the action occurs. An adverb clause can also modify an adjective or another adverb.

Because she was so exhausted, Sheila could not keep her eyes open. (The adverb clause tells *why* Sheila could not keep her eyes open.)

Ed's family lived in Atlanta **after he was born**. (The adverb clause tells *when* Ed's family lived in Atlanta.)

Notice that when an adverb clause begins a sentence, a comma is used. However, a comma is not needed before an adverb clause that completes a sentence. Adverb clauses are introduced by **subordinating conjunctions**. These conjunctions tell you that a clause is subordinate and cannot stand alone as a sentence.

COMMON SUBORDINATING CONJUNCTIONS

after	before	though	whenever
although	if	unless	where
as	since	until	whereas
because	than	when	wherever

▶ **Exercise 1** Underline each adverb clause. Circle the subordinating conjunction.

My little sister rides her bicycle more carefully (since) she fell and scraped her knee.

1. Although Tricia works hard, she always welcomes extra projects.

2. Whenever my aunt is in town, she takes me to lunch.

3. He is thinner than he was the last time.

4. Should we go save seats after you buy some popcorn?

5. Do not make a commitment unless you are sure.

6. If I remember correctly, that street goes only one way.

7. The puppy ran under a chair when it heard the cat hiss.

8. Our spelling team performed well although we did not win.

Grammar

9. Because I had no sleeping bag, I slept in the cabin.

10. I hope we get to the party before they yell "Surprise!"

11. As I told you yesterday, my answer is no.

12. I cannot turn in my paper until I have completed this problem.

13. Mother sat where she could see the stage clearly.

14. Since I broke my leg, I need help getting to school.

15. My favorite team is the Knicks whereas Pablo likes the Suns.

▶ **Exercise 2 Draw one line under the adverb clause and two lines under the verb or verb phrase that the adverb clause modifies.**

Before he ordered his meal, Dad read the menu.

1. When he got off the train, the streets were deserted.

2. I will work all day unless I get a call from Dad.

3. I hope Ken will visit us when he is in town.

4. Plenty of leftovers remain because several people did not come to the party.

5. Do not make any noise unless you want to wake the baby.

6. Since my horse was ill, I stayed all night in her stall.

7. As we approached, the mourning doves fluttered away.

8. The villagers fled the town before the volcano erupted.

9. After the meeting ended, the mayor met with the press.

10. If you cannot stop fighting, study in separate rooms.

11. Because she could not choose, Juliet bought both books.

12. Nell will not skate on the lake until she tests the ice.

13. Move the furniture wherever it looks best.

14. Although the dinner was a success, the cook created a mess!

15. I would like that video when you have finished with it.

Lesson 49
Noun Clauses

Noun clauses are subordinate clauses that act as nouns.

Actors must have good memories. (noun)
Whoever acts on stage must have a good memory. (noun clause)

The clause in the second sentence above replaces the noun in the first sentence. Noun clauses can be used in the same way as nouns—as subject, direct object, object of a preposition, and predicate noun.

Whoever runs for office needs much money. (subject)
Candidates know **that the game of politics is expensive**. (direct object)
This is the candidate about **whom I wrote**. (object of a preposition)
Election day is **when the results are known**. (predicate noun)

WORDS THAT INTRODUCE NOUN CLAUSES

how	what	where	who	whomever
however	whatever	which	whom	whose
that	when	whichever	whoever	why

▶ **Exercise 1 Underline each noun clause.**

<u>Why the posters are not finished</u> is the question Ms. Rivera would like answered.

1. The band will play whatever song we choose.

2. The shopping center is where the old forest stood.

3. Whoever wins the most games wins the trophy.

4. Vicky knows how the VCR is hooked up.

5. Do you know where that new student comes from?

6. Kim wonders when the film opens here.

7. I didn't know where these books belonged.

8. The team didn't realize that their quarterback was ill.

9. The starting point for the hike is where the path follows the cliff.

10. Why you chose to bicycle in the rain is a mystery to me.

11. Pass the refreshments to whomever you want.

12. The reporter will question whatever statement the official makes.

13. Could you tell me how you perform that magic trick?

14. How you survived the snowstorm is beyond me.

15. Ken is wondering what will be served for dinner.

16. What really annoys me is loud rock music.

17. This room is where the band practices its halftime program.

18. I don't know which knob controls the color.

19. Save these papers for whoever is recycling them.

20. The students know that they must study for the test.

▶ **Exercise 2 Underline each noun clause. In the blank, indicate its use in the sentence:** *subj.* **(subject),** *d.o.* **(direct object),** *o.p.* **(object of a preposition), or** *p.n.* **(predicate noun).**

<u>subj.</u>   <u>How Constance could have bought that dog</u> continues to baffle me.

_____ **1.** Do you know who is in charge of counting votes?

_____ **2.** Give your ticket to whoever would enjoy the concert.

_____ **3.** Where we will go on our field trip is the subject of debate.

_____ **4.** This is where the fire broke out.

_____ **5.** Kendra is asking why you are acting that way.

_____ **6.** The best choice for you is whatever you think best.

_____ **7.** How they escaped the flood is something I don't understand.

_____ **8.** Sue believes that her skills in soccer need help.

_____ **9.** We don't understand why the cat likes the rain.

_____ **10.** This mail goes in whichever box is marked "Smith."

_____ **11.** The fish will hide under whatever rock it can find.

_____ **12.** My parents' surprise was what we had hoped for.

_____ **13.** The route for the contest became whichever way they went.

_____ **14.** The boys work long hours for whatever they can earn.

_____ **15.** What the team should do is punt.

_____ **16.** The dogs know where the cat often hides.

✓ Unit 7 **Review**

▶ **Exercise 1** Identify each underlined clause as *main*, *adjective*, *adverb*, or *noun*. If the underlined clause modifies a specific word or words, circle the word or words.

_____adjective_____ (Of Mice and Men,) which is my favorite book, made me cry.

_____ 1. My dog lounges around the house <u>wherever she pleases</u>.

_____ 2. The years <u>when the Great Depression hit</u> were terribly hard for many people.

_____ 3. Did anybody see <u>where that snowball came from</u>?

_____ 4. <u>If the school ever sells its old computers</u>, I will buy one.

_____ 5. <u>I have always liked Eric Clapton's music</u>.

_____ 6. The recreation room in my basement is the place <u>where I relax</u>.

_____ 7. <u>Rance ran to the bus stop</u>, but he missed his ride anyway.

_____ 8. We will go to the new movie <u>unless it is sold out</u>.

_____ 9. <u>Whatever restaurant you choose</u> is okay with me.

_____ 10. Solve the mystery <u>before any other player does</u>.

_____ 11. <u>Whoever sells the most candy</u> receives an award.

_____ 12. Science still cannot explain <u>why some animals behave oddly before earthquakes</u>.

_____ 13. On our way to Texas, <u>our plane flew over the Gulf of Mexico</u>.

_____ 14. My little brother, <u>who still believes in Santa Claus</u>, puts milk and cookies out on Christmas Eve.

_____ 15. Because the movie was sold out, <u>we went home</u>.

_____ 16. Calid is disturbed at <u>how his family reacted to the news</u>.

_____ 17. Please give me the remote control, <u>which is sitting on the television</u>.

_____ 18. <u>I bought the latest newspaper</u>.

_____ 19. Socrates, <u>whose writings are still studied</u>, affected Western philosophy.

_____ 20. I always shower <u>after I exercise heavily</u>.

Cumulative Review: Units 1–7

▶ **Exercise 1** Underline the correct pronoun in parentheses. In the blank, write the tense of the verb that is in italics: *present, past, future, present perfect, past perfect,* or *future perfect.*

___present perfect___ Craig and Julio *have decided* (he, <u>they</u>) will start a recycling campaign.

_____ 1. Wayne *works* for (his, their) father on weekends.

_____ 2. Ms. Rothchild *waited* impatiently for (her, hers) luggage to arrive.

_____ 3. The band *will have begun* playing by the time (they, their) reach the stadium.

_____ 4. Kelly, Steve, and Kwasi *had finished* the entire project by the time Lorna joined (their, them).

_____ 5. Our waiter *forgot* (we, us) wanted some rolls.

_____ 6. Aunt Sophie *will light* the candles on (her, his) own birthday cake and let one of the children blow them out.

_____ 7. *Does*n't (no one, anyone) *know* what time the bus leaves?

_____ 8. (That, Those) *have caught* Marisa's attention.

_____ 9. Mr. Concepción *will demonstrate* how (she, he) performs this dance.

_____ 10. Ms. Stanberg *promised* to help us with (our, her) homework.

_____ 11. The painting is lovely, but (it, they) *seems* a little crooked.

_____ 12. Tessa *will have walked* five miles by the time (she, it) reaches the Chungs' house.

_____ 13. Danny and Pedro *had watched* the game for nearly an hour when (they, them) went to the refreshment stand for a snack.

_____ 14. The audience *had caught* one more glimpse of the beautiful singer before (she, her) left the theater.

_____ 15. Rosalinda (herself, himself) *wrote* that haunting melody.

_____ **16.** Gifts *bring* joy to (those, them) who receive them.

_____ **17.** I *will give* Joe the book that (she, he) left in the car.

_____ **18.** Mr. Kristofic, who *spoke* earlier, is (him, himself) a noted

scientist.

_____ **19.** To (who, whom) *will* Sabrina *take* the broken watch?

_____ **20.** (This, These) *will have been* the longest book I have ever read.

▶ **Exercise 2 Circle each conjunction. In the blank, write whether it is *coordinating* or**
correlative.

___coordinating___   Stephan likes to fish, (but) his brother prefers to hike.

_____ **1.** Uncle Wilhelm and Cousin Janet are planning a surprise party.

_____ **2.** Either ravioli or fettucine is her favorite pasta dish.

_____ **3.** Dr. Ortiz remains kind but firm when dealing with patients.

_____ **4.** Justin will hold the camera, and Tonya will gather everyone

together for the picture.

_____ **5.** Not only did Kristy win the contest, but she also received

some expert advice.

_____ **6.** Ryan is wearing a green shirt, for that is his favorite color.

_____ **7.** The wind began to increase, but the storm veered south.

_____ **8.** Neither roses nor tulips would bloom in that garden.

_____ **9.** The car will have to be covered tonight, or it will be covered

with frost tomorrow.

_____ **10.** The pastry chef will bake and decorate a cake.

▶ **Exercise 3 Underline each subordinate clause. In the blank, identify the clause as**
adjective, adverb,* or *noun.

___adverb___   Although they were tired, the basketball team continued practicing.

_____ **1.** Stacy will meet us at the roller-skating rink unless she has not finished

her homework.

_____ **2.** After she addressed the birthday card, Aunt Rose mailed it.

_____ **3.** Tom's friend, who is a mechanic, showed us how to change a flat tire.

_____ **4.** Greg bought the book that Mr. Harkin recommended.

_____ **5.** That new television program, which aired last night, captured Gabrielle's imagination.

_____ **6.** What Samdi baked was my favorite dish at the potluck.

_____ **7.** Though others performed better, no one worked harder than Colleen.

_____ **8.** Our teacher invited the scientist who made this discovery to speak to our class.

_____ **9.** Sue will check the luggage before Mom gets the boarding passes.

_____ **10.** Nashoba is wondering when this city will develop a professional baseball team.

_____ **11.** Curtis asked how we planned to travel to the festival.

_____ **12.** Dr. Spencer will examine Kendra's eyes before he prescribes glasses for her.

_____ **13.** The play that Rudy and I saw amused both of us.

_____ **14.** Who let the dog out concerns our neighbor, Mr. Martinez.

_____ **15.** Whenever Maria sees a music store, she has to go inside and look around.

_____ **16.** The person who can answer your questions is seated by the window.

_____ **17.** The second floor, which has been vacant for three years, is finally being renovated.

_____ **18.** Give your ticket to the person who is standing at the door.

_____ **19.** James waited as though he had something else to say.

_____ **20.** Since she visited Greece, Wendy cannot stop talking about the customs there.

Unit 8: Verbals

Lesson 50

Participles and Participial Phrases

A **present participle** is formed by adding *-ing* to a verb. A **past participle** is usually formed by adding *-ed* to a verb. Sometimes a participle acts as the main verb in a verb phrase. As a verb, the present participle is used with forms of the helping verb *to be,* and the past participle is used with forms of the helping verb *to have.* A participle can also act as an adjective to describe, or modify, a noun or a pronoun.

The robin was **singing** in the tree. (present participle as a main verb)
Our cat stared at the **singing** robin. (present participle as an adjective)
Tammy has **tossed** the water balloon. (past participle as a main verb)
The **tossed** water balloon hit the sidewalk. (past participle as an adjective)

▶ **Exercise 1** Underline each participle. Write in the blank *pres.* if it is a present participle and *past* if it is a past participle.

_____pres._____ The <u>running</u> guard caught the pass from Troy.

_____ **1.** The nervous bird was pecking at the girl.

_____ **2.** A printout of the results has been taped to the door.

_____ **3.** The freezing lady put on her sweater.

_____ **4.** The spilled oil spread over the floor.

_____ **5.** By evening, they will have finished their assignment.

_____ **6.** Everyone has wondered what the great detective was thinking.

_____ **7.** Carol has rescued the trembling cat.

_____ **8.** The elected chairperson must work hard.

_____ **9.** David is throwing the rings at the milk bottles.

_____ **10.** They found out too late that they had entered by the wrong door.

_____ **11.** I made a running leap to clear the last hurdle.

_____ **12.** The engaging film star has smiled and posed for pictures.

_____ **13.** We were unable to keep warm from the blistering wind.

_____ **14.** Allan should have looked at the price tag first.

_____ **15.** We had recycled our discarded newspapers.

_____ **16.** The new video store had a limited number of foreign films.

_____ **17.** Do you see the antique car that is passing the new car?

_____ **18.** Have you ever watched *Rain Man?*

_____ **19.** I had noticed the necklace on the table.

_____ **20.** The bucket was rapidly filling with water.

▶ **Exercise 2 Write *V* above each participle that is part of a verb phrase. Write *adj.* above each participle that is used as an adjective.**

        adj.   **V**

The forgiving teacher has accepted the boy's apology.

1. I feel as if I've been carrying this backpack for three days!

2. Drew has decided to order a piece of the tempting chocolate cake.

3. The determined police officer chased the thief.

4. The accomplished musician prepared for the approaching concert.

5. We had overlooked the hiding puppy.

6. George had worked a great deal at the amazing water park.

7. Will you be deciding soon about the posted job?

8. The flashing lightning scared the dazed children.

9. The sitting boy believed no one could see him behind the bush.

10. We were thinking about your offer and have decided to accept it.

11. Marcus has uncovered the missing final clue.

12. The rusted door was beginning to break.

13. The startled horse had galloped over the fence.

14. The charging defense team sacked the exhausted quarterback.

15. The following program is my dad's favorite.

16. The winning team waved to the remaining crowd.

17. That dog will be chasing bicyclists for as long as he runs loose.

18. For the organized talent show, Gary will be impersonating Mr. Highfield.

19. I felt sorry for the beached baby whale.

20. What were you thinking when you put the melted caramels in the freezer?

A participial phrase includes a participle and all the other words that complete its meaning. It is used as an adjective and can appear before or after the word it modifies. Place the phrase as close as possible to the modified word to avoid unclear meaning. A participial phrase placed at the beginning of a sentence is set off with a comma. Other participial phrases may or may not need commas, depending on whether or not they are essential to the meaning of the sentence.

The girl **throwing the water balloon** is Tammy DiGiovanni.
Tammy, **throwing the water balloon,** aimed at the target.
Running quickly after Tammy, I threw the balloon back.
Tammy, **scared of getting wet,** hid behind a bush.

▶ **Exercise 3** Underline each participial phrase. Draw an arrow to the word the phrase modifies.

Blackie, catching the stick in mid-air, trotted proudly back to Steve.

1. Surprised by our gift of a new winter coat, Grandmother began to cry for joy.

2. The lot, filled with cars, was enormous.

3. The box of fruit containing pears, apples, and oranges arrived at the door.

4. Homeless families often stayed at a shelter operated by a local church.

5. Carrying plenty of water, we set out for the summit of the mountain.

6. Did they see the train coming around the bend?

7. Urged on by the fans, the basketball team began its comeback.

8. The tall man wearing the gray suit is a judge.

9. That newspaper blowing all over the yard is a real mess.

Grammar

Grammar

10. A banana peel lying on the ground caused the comedian to slip.

11. Giggling like a child, Marie handed the package to her brother.

12. Tapping her way up Pearl Street, Margie was the hit of the parade.

13. The king, unrecognized by all his subjects, walked around his kingdom in disguise.

14. I believe I saw the maid climbing the stairs toward the forbidden room.

15. Confused by the identical twins, Mr. Fatar threw up his hands in wonder.

16. The frog, hopping from one rock to the next, managed to get away from the boy.

17. Beginning with the kitchen, they painted every room in the apartment.

18. My mom told us about the new library planned for this neighborhood.

19. I ordered the special, consisting of a ham sandwich and tomato soup.

20. Alberto, asked by the choir director, agreed to sing in the talent show.

▶ **Writing Link** Write a paragraph about a sport you either like to watch or play. Use both present and past participles.

_____

_____

_____

_____

_____

_____

_____

_____

_____

_____

_____

Lesson 51
Gerunds and Gerund Phrases

In addition to being used as an adjective (as in participles and participial phrases), a verb form ending in *-ing* may also serve as a noun. A gerund is a verb form that ends in *-ing* and is used as a noun. It can be the subject of a sentence, the direct object, or the object of a preposition.

Flying is a skill birds must learn. (subject)
Young birds practice **flying.** (direct object)
They can escape from dangers by **flying.** (object of a preposition)

A gerund phrase is a group of words that includes a gerund and other words that complete its meaning.

Flying in a storm takes practice. (subject)
Birds learn **flying in high winds** at a young age. (direct object)
Many birds owe their survival to **flying away from enemies.** (object of a preposition)

▶ **Exercise 1** Circle each gerund. Underline each gerund phrase.

One way people share good times is by observing holidays together.

1. Some people keep Valentine's Day by sending heart-shaped cards to friends.

2. Sharing valentines with others can brighten a wintry February day.

3. The custom of celebrating Valentine's Day stretches back a long way.

4. Many historians believe the holiday sprang from an ancient Roman custom of honoring two brothers by the name of Valentine.

5. Coloring eggs is an activity that belongs to another holiday.

6. Easter is often associated with the blooming of spring flowers.

7. In Christian traditions, Easter marks the rising of Jesus from the dead.

8. At the same time as Easter, Jews observe Passover by preparing a special meal, a *seder*.

9. By eating the special foods at the seder, Jews remember the flight of their ancestors from slavery in Egypt.

10. Playing jokes on people seems a strange way to celebrate a holiday.

11. However, exchanging gag gifts was a custom in France that grew into our April Fool's Day.

12. A lesser-known spring holiday is dedicated to planting trees—Arbor Day.

13. Various states enjoy observing Arbor Day any time from December to May.

14. Most people would agree that respecting mothers is important every day of the year.

15. In 1914 Congress approved reserving a specific day for mothers.

16. The second Sunday in May is the day set aside for remembering Mom.

17. Remembering our patriotic dead is the purpose of another May holiday, Memorial Day.

18. By decorating the graves of soldiers, we honor their memories.

19. In celebrating Memorial Day at the end of May, we pay tribute to those who died for their country.

20. Honoring all members of the armed services is the purpose of Veterans Day, celebrated in November.

▶ **Exercise 2** **Underline each gerund phrase. Write in the blank how it is used in the sentence: *S* for subject, *DO* for direct object, *OP* for object of a preposition, or *none* if the sentence does not contain a gerund.**

__DO__   Our neighbor, Mr. Montoya, enjoys seeing his sons on Father's Day.

_____ 1. Having a special day for fathers was the idea of a Spokane, Washington, woman.

_____ 2. On the third Sunday in June, Father's Day, children show their fathers how they feel about them by sending cards and giving presents.

_____ 3. A holiday in June features flying the American flag, a tradition that began after the Civil War.

_____ 4. June 14 is Flag Day, a day for remembering the first American flag.

_____ **5.** Just one year earlier, thirteen colonies went to war with England by declaring their independence.

_____ **6.** The colonies knew they were entering a dangerous and fateful time.

_____ **7.** With the signing of the Declaration of Independence, the American Revolution began.

_____ **8.** In winning the War of Independence, the colonies became a new and independent nation.

_____ **9.** Ringing out over the streets of Philadelphia on July 4, 1776, was the historic Liberty Bell.

_____ **10.** Celebrating America's birth is the purpose of our Independence Day.

_____ **11.** In almost every American town, holding parades on the Fourth of July is a tradition.

_____ **12.** Watching fireworks is also a big part of the Fourth.

_____ **13.** However, remembering our country's early days should also be a part of the celebrations.

_____ **14.** Signaling the end of summer, Labor Day comes at the start of September.

_____ **15.** This holiday is also an occasion for honoring the nation's workers.

_____ **16.** Adopting the holiday in 1882, New York City was the first place to celebrate workers.

_____ **17.** For many Americans, having a day off from work is the best way to celebrate Labor Day!

_____ **18.** The keeping of the fast of Ramadan occurs during the ninth month of the Islamic calendar.

_____ **19.** American Muslims celebrate this religious festival by fasting during the day.

_____ **20.** But when the sun sets, Muslims can stop their fasting and celebrate their holy month.

Grammar

▶ **Exercise 3** **Identify the word in italics. Write *V* in the blank if the word is a verb in a verb phrase, *part.* if the word is a participle used as an adjective, or *ger.* if the word is a gerund.**

**ger.**   *Eating* special foods is one way to celebrate special days.

_____ **1.** Americans have many different ways of *celebrating* holidays.

_____ **2.** *Bringing* customs and traditions from their homelands, immigrants add to the rich holiday mix in the United States.

_____ **3.** Holidays *belonging* to three major groups are celebrated.

_____ **4.** *Observing* religious holidays is common throughout the United States.

_____ **5.** *Commemorating* national holidays seems important to most Americans.

_____ **6.** Certain states are *celebrating* regional holidays.

_____ **7.** *Staying* up late the night before makes the first holiday of the year seem like the shortest.

_____ **8.** Many people celebrate New Year's Day by *making* noise.

_____ **9.** *Wearing* funny hats is also a part of New Year's festivities.

_____ **10.** *Singing* songs such as "Auld Lang Syne," people say good-bye to the old year and hello to the new.

_____ **11.** *Making* New Year's resolutions is another tradition.

_____ **12.** By making resolutions, many people are *hoping* to stop old habits or begin new ones.

_____ **13.** Are you *thinking* of making any resolutions this New Year's Day?

_____ **14.** Some of our New Year's traditions come from the ancient Romans, who celebrated the *approaching* year.

_____ **15.** In fact, the first month of the year is named after Janus, the Roman god of *beginnings* and endings.

_____ **16.** *Having* two faces, Janus looked forward and backward.

_____ **17.** January 1—New Year's Day—is a good time for *looking* at both the past and the future.

_____ **18.** The early months of the year are rich in holidays *honoring* important Americans.

Lesson 52
Infinitives and Infinitive Phrases

An **infinitive** is another verb form that may function as a noun. It may also function as an adjective or an adverb. An infinitive is formed from the word *to* followed by the base form of a verb. The word *to* is not a preposition when it is used immediately before a verb.

Jenny is always looking for a chance **to read.** (infinitive)
She goes **to the library** at least once a week. (not an infinitive; the word *to* is used as a preposition)

An infinitive used as a noun can be the subject of a sentence or the direct object of a verb.

To read is enjoyable. (subject) Jenny tries **to read** every day. (direct object)

An **infinitive phrase** is a group of words that includes an infinitive and other words that complete its meaning.

Jenny has decided **to read all of Sue Ellen Bridgers's books this summer.**

▶ **Exercise 1 Circle each infinitive. Underline each infinitive phrase.**

My sister is teaching me (to play) chess.

1. Do you like to eat Chinese food?

2. It's hard to choose a video because the selection here is so large.

3. I'm lucky to go to such a good school.

4. My little brother finds it almost impossible to wait until his birthday.

5. To ignore a sore throat is not a very good idea.

6. We have to leave immediately to go to the meeting at the recreation center.

7. To win the last three games of the season will not be easy.

8. To get a *B* on the next test is her objective.

9. To grow a moustache in time for the play became my dad's plan.

10. Let's get together to watch old Laurel and Hardy movies.

11. I know how to fix the glitch in your computer program.

12. To take a cruise in the Caribbean would be wonderful.

13. We love to wander around the old-fashioned shops at the history museum.

14. I don't want to argue about it now.

15. She said she'd love to hear from us.

16. The hospital chaplain stopped to say hello to Maggie after her operation.

17. Does Jordan like to sing in the Glee Club?

18. Did you ever want to go to a Broadway musical?

19. To wait for dinner doesn't bother me at all.

20. On her family's trip to the ocean, Megan is going to try scuba diving.

21. I'm trying to break my habit of saying *whatever* all the time.

22. I think it would be fun to speak a foreign language.

23. To multiply big numbers in her head is my sister's special talent.

24. The teacher asked William to think about taking algebra.

25. Martin's goal is to play the saxophone as well as Kenny G.

26. Doug went to Florida to see the Everglades.

27. Can you believe we're actually going to make it to the playoffs?

28. I'll bet a young kangaroo—called a *joey*—likes to hang on tightly when its mother jumps around!

▶ **Exercise 2 Place a check (✔) next to the sentence in each pair that contains an infinitive phrase.**

____✔____   Everyone would like to get good grades.

_____   I gave my report card to my mother.

_____ 1. She sent Chanukah cards to many different people.

_____   Christine likes to read historical novels.

_____ 2. I hate to go to bed without brushing my teeth.

_____   Let me say thanks to everyone involved with the project.

_____ 3. To munch on peanuts reminds me of being at the circus!

_____   The raft floated down the Ohio River to the Mississippi River.

_____ **4.** We awarded a prize to the tallest girl in the class.

_____ How are those tiny butterflies able to fly all the way to South America?

_____ **5.** The letter began "To whom it may concern."

_____ It took a lot of courage to speak out about injustice the way she did.

_____ **6.** It's really up to her whether we continue.

_____ It would be safer to put that money in a bank account, don't you think?

_____ **7.** To think that anyone could devote so much time to a painting is beyond my comprehension!

_____ Mr. Barnard was transferred to San Diego.

_____ **8.** It takes a certain kind of person to work in an emergency room.

_____ I gave the leftover tuna to Sandy's cat.

_____ **9.** Please move that chair to the living room.

_____ To sail the skies in a glider would be a fantastic experience.

_____ **10.** I'd like to visit Hawaii someday.

_____ In some countries kids go to school on Saturdays.

_____ **11.** For Thanksgiving my family drove to my grandparents' house.

_____ She ought to pay more attention to the rules.

_____ **12.** One day, I'd enjoy going to the desert.

_____ To pay for anything in cash is rather rare these days.

_____ **13.** He spoke to the manager of the restaurant about a part-time job.

_____ I would like you all to notice the "Wet Paint" sign on the wall.

_____ **14.** Tell Kelly if you're interested in going to Aspen, Colorado, for the ski trip.

_____ She wants to return her new shoes because they feel too big.

▶ **Exercise 3** Underline each infinitive phrase. Write *S* in the blank if it is used as a subject, *DO* if it is used as a direct object, or *none* if the sentence has no infinitive phrase.

__DO__ My uncle Jerry loves to hit golf balls.

_____ **1.** She hadn't even learned to turn on the computer.

_____ **2.** Please don't forget to water the plants while I'm gone.

Grammar

Grammar

_____ 3. We all piled into the car and drove to the garden center.

_____ 4. To say you're not interested seems unfair.

_____ 5. To make a donation to SADD in our names was a nice gesture.

_____ 6. This certainly means a lot to my family and me.

_____ 7. What do you want to do this Saturday?

_____ 8. Going to the moon seemed impossible to our grandparents.

_____ 9. To go swimming in frigid Lake Superior is no picnic!

_____ 10. On the tour, they will travel to Oregon and Washington.

_____ 11. Would you like to lend me a pencil for fifth period?

_____ 12. To be myself is the best advice I have been given.

_____ 13. Have you ever wanted to go on a whale-watching trip?

_____ 14. To eat a crisp apple is one of the joys of autumn.

_____ 15. Lee and I walked to DeShon's dad's house.

_____ 16. When her cousins arrived, Ramona decided to take them on a scavenger hunt.

_____ 17. Colin hopes to be a good friend to everyone.

_____ 18. To us and them, the matter just didn't seem all that important.

_____ 19. Does anyone feel like going to the grocery store?

_____ 20. To build a fire in a strong wind takes skill.

_____ 21. Do you want to go out for a pizza after the concert?

_____ 22. To postpone the wedding will upset everyone's plans.

_____ 23. People sometimes would like to change the weather, but, of course, they can't.

_____ 24. The mayor gave a citation to the members of the rescue squad who saved the

child.

_____ 25. To succeed in gymnastics takes dedication.

_____ 26. To point at people is not polite.

_____ 27. Ethan wanted to go to the theme park with his family.

_____ 28. I wish she could have talked to me about the problem.

✓ Unit 8 **Review**

▶ **Exercise 1** Underline each participial, gerund, or infinitive phrase. Write in the blank what kind of phrase it is: *part.* for participial phrase, *ger.* for gerund phrase, or *inf.* for infinitive phrase. Write *none* if the sentence has none of these phrases.

ger.   Lila greatly enjoys <u>planting rose bushes</u>.

_____ **1.** The news showed pictures of houses destroyed by the hurricane.

_____ **2.** Would you ever want to go on a two-week trip to Colorado?

_____ **3.** Taking it easy is my brother's idea of a good vacation.

_____ **4.** To eat too many desserts is not a very good idea.

_____ **5.** Rod is playing the piano in the school jazz band.

_____ **6.** Hearing my dad's voice on the phone, I answered quickly.

_____ **7.** She doesn't really enjoy working after school.

_____ **8.** Nicole was wondering which class would be better for her major.

_____ **9.** In soccer, players use their feet to do almost everything.

_____ **10.** Thomas prefers swimming in a pool rather than in the ocean.

_____ **11.** We opened the door for the carolers touring the neighborhood.

_____ **12.** We took the subway to Columbia Square.

_____ **13.** I have talked to almost everyone about the talent show.

_____ **14.** I love to watch the fireworks display on the Fourth of July.

_____ **15.** Accepted by every college she applied to, my sister must make a difficult decision.

_____ **16.** Deciding on one will be hard.

_____ **17.** Please take the laundry basket to the bedroom.

_____ **18.** Finishing all my homework by eight o'clock won't be easy.

_____ **19.** Do you want to go to the early movie or the late one?

_____ **20.** The dog lapping up water so fast must have been very thirsty.

Cumulative Review: Units 1–8

▶ **Exercise 1** Underline the correct pronoun in parentheses. Write in the blank whether the sentence is *dec.* (declarative), *int.* (interrogative), *exc.* (exclamatory), or *imp.* (imperative).

__int.__   Where did (<u>he</u>, him) leave the instructions?

_____   **1.** Don't forget to send an invitation to (they, them).

_____   **2.** What an incredible jump shot (she, her) has!

_____   **3.** The bridge begins on the east side of the river, and (it, they) ends on the west side of the river.

_____   **4.** Looking through a telescope, Imena could see that constellation and (its, their) nearest neighbor.

_____   **5.** Why did you give (they, them) directions to the secret cave?

_____   **6.** Reynaldo promised to give (we, us) students a tour of the television station.

_____   **7.** Place Mother's flowers on the table, and take the card to (its, her).

_____   **8.** I can't believe (our, us) school won the contest!

_____   **9.** Wendy and Jasmine are donating (her, their) old clothing to a local charity.

_____ **10.** Either Alan or Jerome will collect signatures for (his, theirs) petition on Tuesday.

_____ **11.** Young deer roam freely through this park, but Susan worries that (it, they) will wander onto the highway.

_____ **12.** Who can deliver Hector's homework to (her, him)?

_____ **13.** Bring me the plant that is drooping and I will water (it, him).

_____ **14.** Please ask the Fuelas to bring pictures of (his, their) trip to Texas.

_____ **15.** Look how high Marta can throw (her, his) baton!

_____ **16.** When can Ron show (we, us) how to use the new computer?

_____ **17.** (Those, Them) were the best doughnuts Irene had ever tasted.

_____ **18.** (We, Us) travelers sometimes forget to pack everything.

Grammar

_____ **19.** Take Ms. Gorman's tools to (her, his) house.

_____ **20.** Wow! Jerry surprised even (herself, himself)!

▶ **Exercise 2 Draw one line under each main clause and two lines under each subordinate clause. Write in the blank whether the sentence is *simple, compound,* or *complex.***

___complex___ Before they began the concert, the orchestra tuned their instruments.

_____ **1.** Laura baked brownies for the party, and Chad made submarine
sandwiches.

_____ **2.** Tulips and daffodils dotted the hillside.

_____ **3.** Ms. Devereaux may teach her class indoors today, or she may take
everyone outside.

_____ **4.** As Shirlene was entering her house, she noticed the puppy had been
playing with her slippers.

_____ **5.** Several colorful boats lined up for the race.

_____ **6.** The cast will pose for pictures after the performance ends.

_____ **7.** Isabel and Mai Lin waited for nearly an hour, but the bus never came.

_____ **8.** The festival preparations were delayed because high winds blew the
tents over.

_____ **9.** When you leave, be sure to tell the leader where you are going.

_____ **10.** Uncle Dominic insisted that we all try the new Italian restaurant.

_____ **11.** After the Thompsons sent us a fruit basket, we made them some
homemade pies.

_____ **12.** Brigitta found her lost button while she was jogging through the
neighborhood.

_____ **13.** The trees swayed in the breeze, and the wheat danced in the sunlight.

_____ **14.** The department store was crowded, but Natasha and her mother were
able to finish their shopping without difficulty.

_____ **15.** Lesharo finished his chores before his brother returned home.

▶ **Exercise 3** Underline each participial, gerund, or infinitive phrase. Write in the blank what kind of phrase it is: *part.* for participial phrase, *ger.* for gerund phrase, or *inf.* for infinitive phrase.

**ger.**   Omar is looking forward to <u>camping with John and Travis.</u>

_____ **1.** Jason, working on a shrimp boat, enjoyed his summer.

_____ **2.** Sandy needs to sleep at least seven hours.

_____ **3.** Tabitha learned sewing from her mother.

_____ **4.** Approaching at a rapid pace, the storm darkened the western sky.

_____ **5.** Closing the window reminded Amos of the alarm system.

_____ **6.** Trapped in the spider's web, the locust awaited its captor.

_____ **7.** Mashing potatoes has never been Helen's favorite task.

_____ **8.** Did the Lone Ranger learn to speak the Apache language?

_____ **9.** Referring to her notes, Dr. Cordero spoke about the medical profession.

_____ **10.** Mrs. Maxwell knew how to avoid an unpleasant confrontation.

_____ **11.** Martin heard loud knocking at the door.

_____ **12.** Jocelyn wanted to hear the famous guitarist.

_____ **13.** The crowing of the rooster awakened everyone on the farm.

_____ **14.** Sinking like a big red ball, the sun disappeared from the western horizon.

_____ **15.** The goalkeeper lunged to block Jeremy's kick.

_____ **16.** Going to school consumes most of Jim's time.

_____ **17.** Stopping for lunch, Ella was late for her appointment.

_____ **18.** Walking to the downtown mall requires about twenty minutes.

_____ **19.** Carmella enjoys talking to Morris.

_____ **20.** Jesse raised his left foot to tie the shoelace on his basketball shoe.

Unit 9: Subject-Verb Agreement

Lesson 53
Making Subjects and Verbs Agree

If the subject of a sentence is singular, then the verb of the sentence must also be singular. If the subject is plural, then the verb must also be plural. When the subject and the verb are both singular or both plural, they are said to **agree in number**.

Mr. Lawrenz teaches art. (singular subject, singular verb)
Wade and Lee teach art. (plural subject, plural verb)
I walk to the store. (singular subject, singular verb)
She walks to the store. (singular subject, singular verb)
They walk to the store. (plural subject, plural verb)

Whether the irregular verbs *be, do,* and *have* are used as main verbs or helping verbs, they must agree with the subject.

The window **is** stuck. (singular subject, singular verb)
These windows **do** stick in humid weather. (plural subject, plural helping verb)
He **has** saved money. (singular subject, singular helping verb)

▶ **Exercise 1 Draw two lines under the correct form of the verb in parentheses.**

Carla (bake, <u>bakes</u>) brownies once a week.

1. Cows (produce, produces) milk at the dairy farm.

2. This airplane (fly, flies) to Milwaukee.

3. A wave (crashes, crash) against the breakwater.

4. These mountains (appear, appears) taller than the clouds.

5. These lights (do, does) not work.

6. The rodeo (start, starts) next week.

7. Fred and Ginger (dance, dances) very well together.

8. These books (seems, seem) heavy.

9. She (sings, sing) in the school choir.

10. He (was, were) not home when Coach Lewis called.

11. Tony (do, does) not go to the movies very often.

Grammar

Name _____ Class _____ Date _____

12. Forecasters (predicts, predict) many bad storms this year.

13. Two hundred people (was, were) in the audience.

14. You and I (trains, train) for the same position on the team.

15. Two airports (serve, serves) the Washington, D.C., area.

16. This container (hold, holds) one gallon of liquid.

17. These crates (weighs, weigh) twenty pounds.

18. President Smith (leaves, leave) at three o'clock.

19. Redwood trees (grow, grows) very tall.

20. May High School and Brush High School (have, has) been sports rivals for many years.

▶ **Exercise 2 Write in the blank the correct present-tense form of the verb in parentheses.**

Richard _____plans_____ to visit London in the spring. (plan)

1. King Alexander III of Macedonia _____ commonly known as Alexander the Great. (be)

2. Mr. Collins _____ impatiently for the mail to arrive. (wait)

3. Saul and Keith _____ checkers after school. (play)

4. The birds _____ for food by the pond. (hunt)

5. These sandwiches _____ very good. (taste)

6. There _____ only one right answer to this question. (be)

7. Kathy _____ this music. (like)

8. Leonard _____ spring practice will begin soon. (hope)

9. The wall _____ two windows. (have)

10. The Mississippi River _____ through Louisiana. (flow)

11. Light _____ through the stained glass windows. (shine)

12. Art classes _____ Donna develop her skills. (help)

13. West Point and the Naval Academy _____ near the East Coast. (be)

14. Electric guitars _____ extremely well in this city. (sell)

15. Dolphins _____ in water. (live)

16. Only two weeks _____ in the semester. (remain)

Lesson 54
Locating the Subject

Making a subject and verb agree is easy when the verb directly follows the subject. However, sometimes a prepositional phrase comes between the subject and its verb.

The **books** on the table **belong** to Edwina. (The plural verb, *belong,* agrees with the plural subject, *books.*)

To help determine subject-verb agreement, say the sentence without the prepositional phrase.

The **books belong** to Edwina.

Inverted sentences are those in which the subject follows the verb. Some of these sentences begin with a prepositional phrase. Other inverted sentences begin with *here* or *there.* Do not mistake the object of a preposition or *here* and *there* for the subject.

In the ocean **live animals** of many species.
There **is** the **road** into town.
Here in the storeroom **are** the **tapes** you ordered.

Some interrogative sentences may have a helping verb before the subject. The subject is found between the helping verb and the main verb.

Does this **store sell** videotapes? (*Store* is the subject, *sell* is the main verb, and *does* is the helping verb.)

▶ **Exercise 1 Draw two lines under the correct form of the verb in parentheses. Write *S* in the blank if the subject and verb are singular. Write *pl.* if the subject and verb are plural.**

__pl.__   The flowers in Marta's garden (<u>appear</u>, appears) each spring.

_____ **1.** The lands near the South Pole (are, is) very cold.

_____ **2.** The football players, except for John, (are, is) warming up on the field.

_____ **3.** On the wall (hangs, hang) a certificate of appreciation.

_____ **4.** From this junior high (comes, come) tomorrow's graduates.

_____ **5.** The classroom near the north stairs (get, gets) very cold in the winter.

_____ **6.** (Do, Does) the freshmen understand French?

_____ 7. Alaska, before becoming part of the United States, (was, were) called

"Seward's Folly" or "Icebergia."

_____ 8. There (lie, lies) the finest watchdog in the county!

_____ 9. Do the ingredients in these cereals (includes, include) sugar?

_____ 10. Pluto, which is the farthest planet from the sun, (orbit, orbits) the sun every

90,000 days.

_____ 11. The streets in this city (contains, contain) little asphalt.

_____ 12. Here (are, is) your instructions.

_____ 13. Amber, which is used in jewelry, (come, comes) from fossilized tree sap.

_____ 14. Americans in each region of the country (speak, speaks) with distinct accents.

_____ 15. In the back of the room (sit, sits) the next speaker.

_____ 16. There across the hall (are, is) the language lab.

_____ 17. The leaves on the tree (turn, turns) color every fall.

_____ 18. The abacus, although centuries old, (are, is) still used in many parts of the world.

_____ 19. Does he (think, thinks) this is going to work?

_____ 20. The pieces of the puzzle (fits, fit) together perfectly.

▶ **Exercise 2 Underline the simple subject of each sentence. Write in the blank the correct present-tense form of the verb in parentheses.**

The <u>players</u> in the game _____ **rest** _____ at halftime. (rest)

1. Here in our city _____ a world-renowned author. (work)

2. Rivers in Ohio, except for the Ohio River, _____ shallow-draft waterways.

(be)

3. Only one bird in our yard _____ its nest in that tree. (build)

4. Do these lockers _____ numbers? (have)

5. The microphones in the auditorium _____ professional quality. (be)

6. In the desert _____ many plants. (live)

Grammar

Lesson 55
Collective Nouns and Other Special Subjects

A **collective noun** names a group. It has a singular meaning when the group acts as a unit. It has a plural meaning when showing that each member of the group acts as an individual. The meaning of the noun in the sentence determines whether the singular or plural form of the verb is needed. You can determine whether a collective noun takes a singular or plural verb by substituting the pronoun *it* or *they*.

The **team wants** to buy the coach a gift. (one group, singular)
The **team agree** to purchase their own jerseys. (individuals, plural)

Certain nouns, such as *mathematics* and *mumps*, end in -*s* but use a singular verb form. Nouns such as *jeans* and *scissors* also end in -*s* and take a plural verb, yet they are single objects.

The **news is** on the radio now. (singular)
These **jeans are** torn. (plural)

When the subject refers to an amount as a single unit, it is considered singular. When it refers to more than one unit, it is plural.

Two weeks seems like a long time to wait. (single unit, singular verb)
Two weeks have passed since you called. (several units, plural verb)

The name of a company, title of a book, movie, play, song, or work of art is a proper noun and should be treated as singular even if the subject within the title is plural.

The Flintstones **is** a television show that was made into a movie. (single title)

▶ Exercise 1 Underline the simple subject of each sentence. In the blank, write *S* if the subject is singular and *pl.* if the subject is plural.

____S____   Broadcast <u>news</u> continues to be a popular field of study.

_____ **1.** Ms. Tanaka's class is interested in journalism.

_____ **2.** Three weeks have been spent studying newscasts.

_____ **3.** Television news excites several of the students.

_____ **4.** Jeremy's family gives tours of the television station where his mother works.

_____ **5.** The class appreciate the time they each received with Mrs. Ramos, who showed

    them how to operate a video camera.

_____ 6. The group hopes to produce its own news show.

_____ 7. Student council suggests ideas for a school newscast.

_____ 8. The school band volunteers to record music for the show.

_____ 9. A target audience is selected.

_____ 10. The softball team grant their interviews to three student reporters.

_____ 11. *Youth News* is the name chosen for the program.

_____ 12. Faculty assist in obtaining permission for students to videotape background

material for their news stories.

_____ 13. The Art Club volunteers to draw weather maps.

_____ 14. The coaching staff offer advice on the sports report.

_____ 15. Current events fills the top slot in the newscast.

_____ 16. Ratings are unimportant according to Ms. Tanaka.

_____ 17. The public need to be informed about events that affect their lives.

_____ 18. Ten days pass before all the arrangements are made.

_____ 19. Finally, the class is ready to produce a newscast.

_____ 20. "Jobs for Teens" is the first story they will run.

▶ **Exercise 2 Draw one line under the simple subject. Draw two lines under the correct form of the verb in parentheses.**

Television <u>news</u> (<u>explains,</u> explain) what is happening in government.

1. Media (reports, report) on the daily activities of each branch of government.

2. A network team (gathers, gather) the news each day.

3. The press corps (records, record) what the politicians have to say to them.

4. A dedicated group (presents, present) the information they have each obtained.

5. The audience (watches, watch) to find out what their elected officials are doing.

6. Politics (becomes, become) confusing without someone to describe what the

politicians are trying to do.

7. However, a citizens' group (has, have) more power than it might think.

8. A voting bloc (determines, determine) who will win an election.

Lesson 56
Indefinite Pronouns as Subjects

An **indefinite pronoun** is a pronoun that does not refer to a specific person, place, or thing. Most indefinite pronouns are singular. Some are plural, and some can be either singular or plural. When an indefinite pronoun is the subject of a sentence, the verb must agree in number with the indefinite pronoun.

COMMON INDEFINITE PRONOUNS
Singular: another, anybody, anyone, anything, each, either, everybody, everyone, everything, much, neither, nobody, no one, nothing, one, somebody, someone, something
Plural: both, few, many, others, several
Either Singular or Plural: all, any, most, none, some

Nobody lives without air. (singular)
Many study the process of photosynthesis. (plural)

A prepositional phrase can follow the indefinite pronouns *all, any, most, none,* or *some.* The object of the preposition will determine whether the pronoun is singular or plural.

Some of the building **is** brick. (singular)
Some of the sunflowers **are** large. (plural)

▶ **Exercise 1** **Draw two lines under the correct form of the verb in parentheses.**

Few (expects, <u>expect</u>) to win a prize in the contest.

1. Another (wants, want) to look at the bike.

2. Anybody (study, studies) French before taking a trip to France.

3. Anyone (understand, understands) the importance of this issue.

4. One (tell, tells) us about his days in baseball.

5. Each of the members (speak, speaks) for three minutes.

6. Either of these books (convey, conveys) the mood of the 1980s.

7. Everybody (want, wants) a copy of that videotape.

8. Both of these schools (is, are) outstanding.

9. Everyone who participates (receives, receive) an award.

10. Everything in this room (appears, appear) to be an antique.

Grammar

11. Much of what is in the book (is, are) on the test.

12. Neither (becomes, become) a first-place contender.

13. Some of the students (visits, visit) their schools after they graduate.

14. Thankfully, many (returns, return) to inspire new students.

15. Nobody (like, likes) to see rain during a picnic.

16. Most of the dancers (perform, performs) the same steps.

17. No one (know, knows) how hard we worked on this project.

18. Nothing (is, are) going to change my mind.

19. One (wonders, wonder) how that computer program works.

20. Somebody (wants, want) to talk to you.

▶ **Exercise 2 Write in the blank the correct present-tense form of the verb in parentheses.**

All _____ride_____ the rollercoaster first. (ride)

1. Someone _____ at the door. (be)

2. Something _____ not look right in this equation. (do)

3. Others _____ this path each morning. (walk)

4. Several _____ the process to us. (describe)

5. Much of this course work _____ outside study. (require)

6. Few _____ the trombone. (play)

7. Many _____ the importance of clean air. (understand)

8. Much _____ during a space shuttle launch. (occur)

9. Another _____ to ride the horse. (wait)

10. Some of the questions _____ reading comprehension. (test)

11. Many _____ several items. (contain)

12. One _____ to understand the reasons for making such a rule. (need)

13. None of the stores _____ that brand. (carry)

14. Neither _____ the play as well as the movie. (like)

15. No one in this class _____ painting. (study)

Lesson 57
Agreement with Compound Subjects

A **compound subject** contains two or more simple subjects that have the same verb. It requires a singular or plural verb, depending on how the parts of the subject are connected. When two or more simple subjects are joined by the coordinating conjunction *and* or by the correlative conjunction *both...and*, the verb is plural. Sometimes *and* is used to join two words that are part of a single unit or refer to a single person or thing. In this case, the subject is considered to be singular. When two or more subjects are joined by the coordinating conjunction *or* or *nor*, or the correlative conjunction *either...or* or *neither...nor*, the verb agrees with the subject that is closest to it.

Lakes, rivers, **and** streams **have** fish. (plural)

Both rivers **and** streams **carry** silt. (plural)

Our chief cook **and** bottle-washer **wants** to see you! (singular)

The printout **or** the disks **contain** the information. (plural; one singular and one plural subject; the verb agrees with the subject closest to it)

Either the disks **or** the printout **contains** the information. (singular; one plural and one singular subject; the verb agrees with the subject closest to it)

▶ **Exercise 1** Draw two lines under the correct form of the verb in parentheses. In the blank, write *S* if the verb form is singular or *pl.* if it is plural.

__pl.__   Both the Atlantic Ocean and the Indian Ocean (meets, meet) the African

continent.

_____ 1. The second-largest continent and the most diverse one (is, are) Africa.

_____ 2. Both the east and west coastlines (is, are) smooth.

_____ 3. Africa's northernmost and southernmost points (extend, extends) almost equal

distances from the equator.

_____ 4. The Northern Plateau, Central/Southern Plateau, and Eastern Highlands (is, are)

the three major continental regions.

_____ 5. Both the Senegal and Niger rivers (empties, empty) into the Sudan drainage

basin.

_____ 6. Africa's most famous mountain and highest peak (is, are) Mt. Kilimanjaro.

_____ 7. Either the desert or the tropical rain forest (has, have) an average temperature of 80°.

_____ 8. Neither the Sahara nor the Kalahari (is, are) a cold desert.

_____ 9. Desert and semidesert conditions (prevail, prevails) in northern Africa.

_____ 10. Tall grasses and low trees (grows, grow) on grasslands called savannas.

_____ 11. Giraffes, elephants, and zebras (lives, live) on these savannas.

_____ 12. Both flooding and drought (plague, plagues) Africa.

_____ 13. The forests and grasslands (serves, serve) as home to several species of antelope.

_____ 14. Either the lion or the elephant (stand, stands) guard over his territory.

_____ 15. Insects and diseases (attack, attacks) plants and animals.

_____ 16. National parks and game reserves (protects, protect) Africa's endangered wildlife.

_____ 17. The baobab, borassus palm, and acacia trees (survives, survive) through underground moisture.

_____ 18. For many years, the only source of either radium or diamonds (were, was) the Congo.

_____ 19. Both the Nile and Congo rivers (is, are) important natural resources.

_____ 20. Either the Nile or the Zaire (begins, begin) at Lake Victoria.

_____ 21. Lake Victoria, Owen Falls, and Kariba Gorge (provide, provides) water for hydroelectric generators.

_____ 22. Irrigation and hydroelectric power (use, uses) water from the Nile.

_____ 23. The treasures and sarcophagus of King Tutankhamen (was, were) discovered in 1922.

_____ 24. South and east Africa (contain, contains) many fossils.

_____ 25. Both the Tibesti and Ahaggar mountains (have, has) prehistoric rock drawings.

_____ 26. Africa's traditional art and stories (tell, tells) about the past.

_____ 27. Either historical realities or mythology (is, are) conveyed through traditional art.

_____ 28. Masks and statues (is, are) the most common forms of African art.

Grammar

Unit 9 **Review**

▶ **Exercise 1** Draw two lines under the correct form of the verb in parentheses.

Neither Tom nor Steve (remember, <u>remembers</u>) leaving his bicycle on the sidewalk.

1. Either a cup or a glass (hold, holds) water.

2. Arizona and New Mexico, particularly in the summer, (is, are) very hot.

3. In the winter (come, comes) frigid air from the north.

4. The budget committee (accept, accepts) your proposal.

5. The pliers (do, does) us no good if we cannot find them.

6. Here on the table (lie, lies) the missing keys.

7. Does this cooler (contain, contains) any ice?

8. Twenty-five cents (was, were) the cost of the phone call.

9. *Duel of Eagles* (give, gives) a good description of the Mexican and American fight for the Alamo.

10. My last and best song (is, are) "Maple Leaf Rag."

11. At the corner of Jefferson Avenue and High Street (occur, occurs) many accidents.

12. Their dedication to their profession (serve, serves) the company well.

13. Bowling, hockey, and basketball (is, are) popular sports.

14. The flock of sheep (graze, grazes) contentedly.

15. Scissors (come, comes) in all sizes.

16. Neither boots nor an umbrella (is, are) necessary in sunny weather.

17. Over the horizon (rise, rises) a beautiful pink sun.

18. Five months (has, have) passed since the last school field trip.

19. Many (think, thinks) this test was easy.

20. Both Joshua and Stacy (dance, dances) in the school ballet.

Name _____ Class _____ Date _____

Cumulative Review: Units 1–9

▶ **Exercise 1** Above each word in italics, label its part of speech: *N* (noun), *V* (verb), *adj.* (adjective), *adv.* (adverb), *pro.* (pronoun), or *prep.* (preposition).

       adj.   V   N   prep.
The *foggy* weather *caused problems with* the traffic.

1. *Clear* and cold Lake Superior *holds* one tenth *of* the world's *unfrozen* fresh water.

2. The *brilliantly* colored butterfly *fluttered lazily* over the bright *flowers.*

3. The late-afternoon sunbeams created *long shadows across* the city park.

4. A chameleon *uses* its *ability* to camouflage *itself* to hide from danger.

5. The tour company *carefully* planned the fabulous *European excursion for* the students.

6. Schools are *rarely* closed in *Thunder Bay* because of the *harsh winter* weather.

7. The little boy *napped peacefully* on a blanket *during* the *long* parade.

8. *Pollution* and over-fishing lead to severe *problems* for the fishing *industry.*

9. The *night-time* temperature *plunged rapidly* to *ten* degrees below zero.

10. The huge airliner *quickly* descended *in preparation* for landing.

11. *Moods* and attitudes *are lifted* by a *bright* and *sunny* day.

12. The *higher* altitude *of* Nairobi quickly *left* us *breathless* during our hikes.

13. The howling of the coyote *echoed early through* the canyon.

14. *She* depended *on* her sophisticated camera for her *scientific research.*

15. The old *Model T's* were equipped *quite differently* from the comfortable cars of *today.*

16. *Our* ancient *past* is *revealed* to *us* through the *efforts* of dedicated archaeologists.

17. The Vietnam *Women's* Memorial *honors* women *who served* during that war.

18. The Statue of Freedom on top of the U.S. Capitol *dome was lowered* and *cleaned* for the *first* time in 130 *years.*

19. People *everywhere* enjoy *performances* of Tchaikovsky's *famous* ballet, *The Nutcracker.*

20. The northern *resort offered* fishing in the *summer* and snowmobiling *in the winter.*

▶ **Exercise 2** Draw a line under each adjective clause, adverb clause, and noun clause.
In the blank, indicate the kind of clause by writing *adj., adv.,* or *noun.*

<u>adv.</u>   <u>Whenever you write your name on these forms</u>, please print it.

_____ 1. Our state parks and reserves, which make excellent natural classrooms, hold
exciting discoveries for students and families.

_____ 2. Fritz saw the same car at a lower price after he had already bought his car.

_____ 3. Mrs. Rovtar explained that she would be taking early retirement.

_____ 4. Whoever joins an environmental club will learn much.

_____ 5. Pearl S. Buck, who wrote *The Wave,* won the 1938 Nobel Prize for literature.

_____ 6. Priorities for your life are whatever you decide.

_____ 7. Scott stopped his exercise routine early since he had another obligation.

_____ 8. Jessica loved to read whenever she had free time.

_____ 9. Wherever they are, animals love to play.

_____ 10. She wanted to go into whichever shop they came to first.

_____ 11. The train that travels at midnight carries coal.

_____ 12. Muffin, who is a finicky eater, turned up her nose at the new cat food.

_____ 13. The costume designer will help us with whatever costume changes are
needed.

_____ 14. Whatever choice you make is fine with me.

_____ 15. Wherever he went, the man's happy whistling could be heard.

_____ 16. The ski runs were closed until the wind diminished.

_____ 17. Troy's German shepherd is one dog that is truly faithful to its master.

_____ 18. I don't know why he stayed home.

_____ 19. Shana cherished the family heirloom that she received from her grandmother.

_____ 20. The fisherman wished to remain by the sea because his entire life had
revolved around the water.

▶ **Exercise 3** Draw two lines under the verb in parentheses that agrees in number with the subject.

Painting houses (<u><u>is</u></u>, are) their family's business.

1. Young chimps and baboons often (become, becomes) playmates in the wild.

2. Vacationing in the mountains (remain, remains) a favorite get-away for many families.

3. Each of his many songs (is, are) a favorite of my dad's.

4. Neither their old gramophone nor their antique chairs (go, goes) to the moving sale.

5. Five dollars (seem, seems) too much to pay for a student admission.

6. The members of the new theater group (perform, performs) tonight.

7. The cowboy and rodeo star (walk, walks) safely out of the arena after being thrown from his horse.

8. The largest piece of luggage (weigh, weighs) eighty pounds.

9. Does this book on foreign cities (appeal, appeals) to you?

10. In the wilderness (lie, lies) undiscovered treasures.

11. Each of the four opportunities (offer, offers) valuable experience.

12. Houston, New Orleans, and Atlanta (is, are) located in the southern part of the United States.

13. The principal or the teachers always (arrive, arrives) at school before the students.

14. Their family (organize, organizes) a reunion every five years.

15. Sometimes four weeks (pass, passes) before I see another movie.

16. In the corner of the flower bed (remain, remains) one lone blossom.

17. There (leave, leaves) the train on its daily journey.

18. In Grandfather's day, trousers (was, were) worn after a boy was too big for knickers.

19. Both old merchant vessels and old warships (interest, interests) our world history teacher.

20. Mathematics, as well as science and reading, (is, are) offered during the summer session.

Unit 10: Diagraming Sentences

Lesson 58
Diagraming Simple Subjects and Predicates

To diagram a sentence, draw a horizontal line with a vertical line going through it. Write the simple subject to the left of the vertical line and the simple predicate to the right of the line.

Diagramed below are only the simple subject and simple predicate of the four basic kinds of sentences. Regardless of the word order in the sentence, the location of the simple subject and simple predicate in a sentence diagram is always the same.

DECLARATIVE

People ride horses.

People	ride

IMPERATIVE

Ride the horse.

(you)	Ride

INTERROGATIVE

Do people ride horses?

people	Do ride

EXCLAMATORY

How those horses run!

horses	run

▶ **Exercise 1** Diagram only the simple subject and simple predicate in each sentence.

1. Cally had spoken.

2. The old barn collapsed.

3. Buy that video.

4. Did you give it to her?

5. The dog damaged the flowers.

6. When did you wake him?

7. I took my team jacket.

8. You are muttering.

9. Hand me the book.

10. Are you motivated?

11. Duwana felt sorry.

12. Our team desires a win.

13. Earn the money for it.

14. Have you examined your notes?

15. How the ice glitters!

16. Enter the contest.

17. I have prepared for the quiz.

18. He wrecked my bike!

19. Where is my CD?

20. Quartz is beautiful.

Lesson 59
Diagraming Direct and Indirect Objects and Predicate Words

Place the direct object to the right of the verb and next to a vertical line that does not extend below the horizontal line. Locate indirect objects on a horizontal line below and to the right of the verb, connected to the verb by a slanted line.

Do take a free sample.

| (you) | Do take | sample |

Shana gave her brother a video.

| Shana | gave | video |
| brother |

Use a slanted line to separate a predicate noun or predicate adjective from the linking verb.

Kyle was sorry.

| Kyle | was \ sorry |

Priscilla does seem very friendly.

| Priscilla | does seem \ friendly |

▶ **Exercise 1** Diagram the subject, predicate, direct object, indirect object, and any predicate words in each sentence.

1. You look hungry.

2. Ruth thanked him.

3. I sent Susan the notes.

4. Henry overtook the other runners.

5. Fred brought Sarah the money.

6. Camilla seemed happy.

Grammar

7. We love that movie.

8. Candrika told us the story.

9. They remained angry.

10. Wrenn did me a favor.

11. Jennifer threw Sam the ball.

12. Mr. Hassan is nice.

13. Aaron grasped the discus.

14. Rebecca was pleasant.

15. Tiffany lent Cal the recorder.

16. Our work advanced the school's reputation.

17. My dog fetched me the stick.

18. When did you drink it?

19. Carol will be ready.

20. Boil the potatoes.

Lesson 60
Diagraming Adjectives and Adverbs

Place adjectives, including articles, and adverbs on slanted lines beneath the words they modify. Predicate adjectives remain on the horizontal line.

Social customs quickly change.

The black cats are very beautiful animals.

Grammar

▶ **Exercise 1 Diagram each sentence.**

1. Cumulus clouds are fluffy.

5. Sunee paints wonderful portraits.

2. The parade featured historical vehicles.

6. Mr. Martinez runs fast.

3. He eagerly ate the green grapes.

7. Our old tree has become rotten.

4. Bret is a fine student.

8. Sailboats always look lovely.

9. The round balloons were absolutely huge.

15. Competitive sports greatly influence our clothes.

10. We will eat pepperoni pizza tomorrow.

16. Adam is our best pitcher.

11. The artisans made beautiful shell necklaces.

17. We happily sang our school song.

18. The maple turned bright red.

12. Tailors designed warm, snug clothing.

19. The spring air smells delightful.

13. The injured boy moved quite gingerly.

20. The squirrel playfully chased a monarch butterfly.

14. The new seeds provided abundant cotton.

Lesson 61
Diagraming Prepositional Phrases

Connect a prepositional phrase to the noun or verb that it modifies. Place the preposition on a slanted line and the object of the preposition on a horizontal line.

Manufacturers make modern automobiles for special needs.

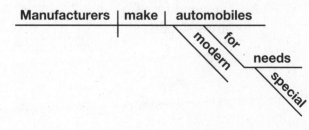

The boat anchored off the beach.

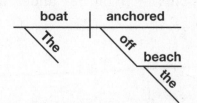

The movie across the street is showing cartoons before noon.

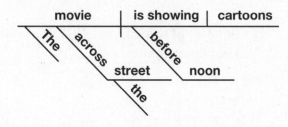

▶ **Exercise 1 Diagram each sentence.**

1. We are waiting for the announcement.

2. She achieved success through hard work.

Grammar

3. The salesclerk offered a refund for the merchandise.

4. Some friends of mine threw me a party for my birthday.

5. Bart reached the store on Shady Lane.

6. Many people opposed the legislation for cultural reasons.

7. The store at the mall is having a sale.

8. The charisma of Hollywood stars also influences modern fashion.

9. The need for affordable childcare grows steadily.

10. His slippers are in the den under the couch.

11. In spite of the bad weather, we will visit Grandma.

12. Power losses occurred after the storm.

Lesson 62
Diagraming Compound Sentence Parts

Coordinating conjunctions such as *and, but,* and *or* are used to join words, phrases, or sentences. Diagram these compound parts of a sentence by placing the second part of the compound below the first. Write the coordinating conjunction on a dotted line connecting the two parts.

Ships and boats carry goods and many passengers.

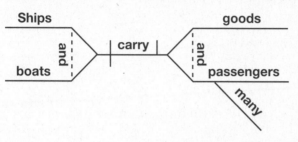

The bus stopped and avoided a collision.   We cut and ate the grapefruit.

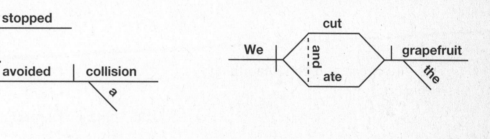

▶ **Exercise 1 Diagram each sentence.**

1. The research team experimented and tested.

2. New designs and models appeared.

3. The soccer team and the baseball team were winners.

4. Pioneers and explorers made canoes and kayaks.

5. Pig skins or cow hides are cured and fashioned.

6. Asian farmers grow rice or bamboo.

7. The editor read and corrected the manuscript.

8. Orville and Wilbur Wright designed and built many airplanes.

9. The train transported grain and coal.

10. I feel very comfortable and quite happy.

11. African explorers made coastal voyages and river trips.

12. Wealth and splendor came to ancient Egypt.

13. The band or orchestra moved the props and scenery.

14. The lumber companies possessed and harvested great forests.

15. He saw a quail and a wild turkey.

Lesson 63
Diagraming Compound Sentences

Diagram each clause of a compound sentence separately. Use a vertical dotted line to connect the verbs of each clause if the main clauses are joined by a semi-colon.

Sparrows flitted among the trees; the cicadas buzzed.

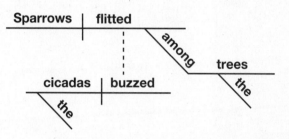

If the main clauses are joined by a conjunction, place the conjunction on a solid horizontal line. Then connect the conjunction to the verb of each clause by vertical dotted lines.

The tractor moved the wagon, and they unloaded the hay.

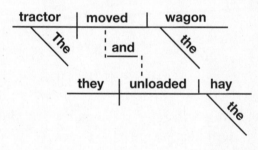

▶ **Exercise 1 Diagram each sentence.**

1. Carla investigated the problem, and she told me the result.

2. Rachel put the canvas on the sled, but she forgot the necessary rope.

Grammar

3. Jane was acquainted with Teri, but she did not know Tiffany.

4. I like the black dress, but it is still too long.

5. Juan obtained the tickets, and he kept them until the game.

6. Jenny will tell the story; Dudley will play the music.

7. The sheep grazed the field, but the grass was very short.

8. The trees give shade on the street, and their leaves renew the air.

9. This frame costs more, but it is the perfect gift.

10. Isabel planned it, but her friends did it.

11. Ann will referee the game, and Barry will keep score.

12. Gum is prohibited here, but it is permitted outside.

Lesson 64

Diagraming Complex Sentences with Adjective or Adverb Clauses

To diagram an adjective clause, draw a dotted line between the relative pronoun that introduces the clause and the noun or pronoun it modifies. Relative pronouns are *who, whom, whose, whoever, whomever, which,* or *that.* Diagram the relative pronoun according to its function in its own clause.

Scientists who study dinosaurs are paleontologists.

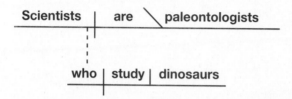

To diagram an adverb clause, draw a dotted line between the verb in the adverb clause and the verb, adjective, or adverb it modifies. Write the subordinating conjunction on the line connecting the verb and the word it modifies.

After he consulted a specialist, he decided against surgery.

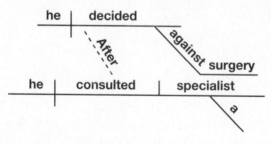

▶ **Exercise 1 Diagram each sentence.**

1. The pen that writes best has blue ink.

2. It was Dr. Robert Koch who first identified the cause of tuberculosis.

Grammar

3. The teacher whom you have for English is excellent.

4. I will wait here until you return from the mall.

5. We ate a delicious dinner before the band played.

6. Amelia Earhart was the first American woman who flew solo across the Atlantic.

7. Willow trees grew where the water was sufficient.

8. Until trees with leaves appeared, giant ferns and conifers were common.

9. While a giraffe eats leaves, hyenas devour a wildebeest.

10. Because the tiger may become extinct, the government enforces strict protection laws.

11. After the cold weather arrived, the tomato plants wilted.

12. It is Chinese food that they prefer for dinner.

Lesson 65
Diagraming Noun Clauses

Noun clauses can be subjects, direct objects, objects of prepositions, or predicate nouns. Diagram a noun clause by placing it on a "stilt" above the main clause.

Diagram the word introducing a noun clause according to its function in the clause. Occasionally the word that introduces the noun clause, such as *that,* is not truly part of either the noun clause or the main clause. Write such a word on its own line above the clause and connect it with a dotted line.

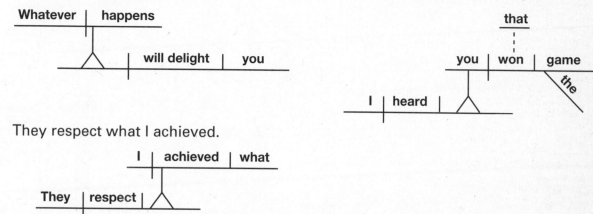

Whatever happens will delight you.

I heard that you won the game.

They respect what I achieved.

▶ **Exercise 1 Diagram each sentence.**

1. Mr. Crosby explained what I am doing wrong.

2. Sheila knows who drew that picture.

3. Whoever takes a boat ride should wear a life jacket.

4. We understand how you lost the book.

5. The apple blossoms show that good weather has finally arrived.

6. I know that Winona is right.

7. The skiers awaited whatever the cold dark clouds brought.

8. Charles thought that he was quite clever.

9. I do not understand whatever it is.

10. Amy wishes that we would stay longer.

11. The travelers patiently observed what the weatherman wrote.

12. Francis feared that I might lose his CD.

13. What we could win seems unbelievable.

14. Her worry is that she will not finish the test.

Lesson 66
Diagraming Verbals

Place a participle or participial phrase beneath the word it modifies. Write the participle on a curve.

The dog, **barking furiously,** woke my family.

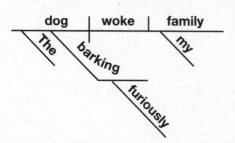

Place a gerund or gerund phrase on a "step" with the gerund written on a curve. Set the step on a "stilt" positioned according to the gerund's role in the sentence. A gerund can be a subject, an object of a verb or preposition, or an appositive.

Cave exploring is an adventure.   Surviving an Alaskan winter takes special precautions.

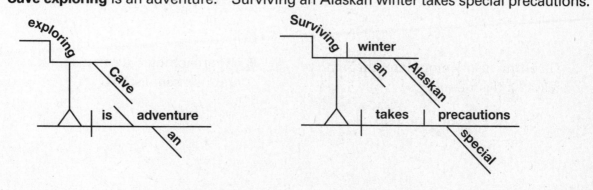

▶ **Exercise 1** **Diagram each sentence.**

1. Hunting can be a means of food production.

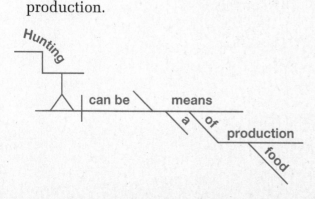

2. Traveling over rugged terrain, many early settlers envisioned a better future.

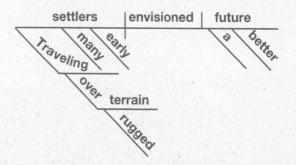

Grammar

3. The growing plant became too large for the pot.

7. Cats enjoy sitting on laps.

4. Fishing provides hours of enjoyment for Frank.

8. The talented potter made a charming jar from clay.

5. Dwelling near a mountain, the family feared a flash flood.

9. Approaching the car, a skunk gave an unmistakable scent.

6. Charles was good at building.

10. Enduring nature's harshness together, the campers felt kinship with the animals.

Lesson 67
Diagraming Infinitives

Place an infinitive or infinitive phrase that is used as a noun on a "stilt" positioned according to its role in the sentence. Then, diagram it as you would a prepositional phrase except that its slanted line should extend below the baseline.

The task of a student is to study hard.

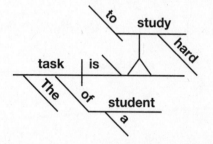

Diagram an infinitive or infinitive phrase that is used as either an adjective or an adverb as you would a prepositional phrase, below the word it modifies, with its slanted line extending below the baseline.

A book **to read** is *The Call of the Wild*.

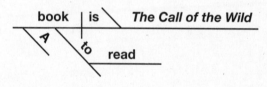

▶ **Exercise 1 Diagram each sentence.**

1. I need to wash my dog.

2. Would you like to include Cal?

3. Henry is ready to launch his project.

4. It is a job to lift those sacks.

5. When do you want to arrive?

6. To fill my class schedule is not easy.

7. Carla and Juan are anxious to leave.

8. Nguyen is happy to hear from us.

9. Camilla failed to receive the package.

10. Do you want to relate to us your version of the story?

11. My parakeets love to scold each other.

12. Look at the tag to find its price.

13. It is your turn to wipe the dishes.

14. I love to feel the spring breezes in the morning.

Unit 10 Review

▶ **Exercise 1 Diagram each sentence.**

1. Teri won the race.

2. Erica told Theresa the story.

3. My dog is an Irish wolfhound.

4. After the embarrassing defeat, Chris ran into the darkened locker room.

5. The horses paced in the paddock, and the mules brayed and stamped.

6. People who are tired cannot study well.

7. I heard the sound of the sea when I walked onto the balcony.

8. Amos remembers how the book ends.

9. Writing is a hobby for Howard.

10. Mario wants to learn about jazz.

Cumulative Review: Units 1–10

▶ **Exercise 1** Write above each pronoun *poss.* (possessive), *ind.* (indefinite), *inter.* (interrogative), or *dem.* (demonstrative).

      dem.   **poss.**
Should this be addressed to her home?

1. What happened to your coat?

2. His brother borrowed her calculator.

3. If anybody knows about this, inform the store manager.

4. Only Gilbert would do something like that.

5. Their efforts to skate on the ice amused everybody.

6. Please take these to her desk.

7. Our plans failed to anticipate everything.

8. To whom will Lloyd go for tutoring?

9. My van had a hole in its muffler, but yours didn't.

10. Melanie's story differs from mine.

11. That can wait until your assignment is finished.

12. Nobody plays soccer like Sarah.

13. What is her last name?

14. Those will have to do until these are ready.

15. Anyone without a ticket will be denied permission to do this.

▶ **Exercise 2** Label each simple subject *SS* and each simple predicate *SP*. Write the type of sentence in the blank: *simple*, *compound*, or *complex*.

              SS SP
___*simple*___ Ira lives in Arizona near the Grand Canyon.

_____ 1. Brad lost the school election to his friend Janet.

_____ 2. Evelyn finished early because Shirley helped her.

_____ 3. Patricia left yesterday, but she plans to return by Friday.

_____ 4. Victor must decide when he will show the film.

_____ **5.** James plans to join Mr. Plant in Kentucky next month.

_____ **6.** If Virginia does not arrive soon, they will leave without her.

_____ **7.** The change in scenery concerned Rosa, but she kept her feelings to

herself.

_____ **8.** Lucius moved toward the microphone as the audience applauded his

accomplishment.

_____ **9.** With the assistance of his math teacher, Terence solved the problem.

_____ **10.** You can cross the Rio Grande at Brownsville, or you can cross it at

Hidalgo.

_____ **11.** Gregory asked us how far we would be going.

_____ **12.** Many French immigrants journeyed to New Orleans; others sailed to

Montreal.

_____ **13.** Early on Tuesday Gordon drove to the airport.

_____ **14.** Sheila believed that our goals were achieved.

_____ **15.** Just before sunset the climbers approached the summit of Mt. Rainier.

▶ **Exercise 3** Underline each participle, gerund, or infinitive phrase. In the blank, identify the kind of phrase: *part.* (participial phrase), *ger.* (gerund phrase), or *inf.* (infinitive phrase).

part. Humming softly, Jody put the baby to sleep.

_____ **1.** Amy hoped to see a well-known actress.

_____ **2.** As he walked through the woods, Dr. Bosch heard chirping overhead.

_____ **3.** Harold asked to receive a receipt for his order.

_____ **4.** Pausing for a few seconds, Yun continued with her recitation.

_____ **5.** Making beds occupies much of a housekeeper's time.

_____ **6.** Pinned helplessly against the ropes, the boxer tried to regain his balance.

_____ **7.** The money deposited in the bank was for Ina's future education.

_____ **8.** Eduardo mastered fencing at school with his coach.

_____ 9. Dawn plans to write her representative about the controversy.

_____ 10. Seth stooped to lift the heavy television.

_____ 11. Jogging to the fairgrounds takes only ten minutes.

_____ 12. Briefly stopping for breakfast, Jerald reviewed his notes for the test.

_____ 13. Practicing basketball dominates Laurie's spare time.

_____ 14. Rachel's father hurried to catch an early bus.

_____ 15. Raymond's nervous whistling made everyone uncomfortable.

Grammar

*U*sage
Glossary

· ·

Unit 11: Usage Glossary

Lesson 68
Usage: *accept* to *a lot*

Words that are similar can easily be misused.

accept, except *Accept* means "to receive" or "to agree to." *Except* means "other than."

I **accept** your help on this project.   Everyone **except** Dena likes to hike.

all ready, already *All ready* means "completely prepared." *Already* means "before" or "by this time."

They are **all ready** for lunch.   The team had **already** warmed up.

all together, altogether *All together* means "in a group." *Altogether* means "completely."

All together we have a total of ten dollars.
We were **altogether** surprised by their actions.

a lot *A lot* is two words meaning "very much." Never write *a lot* as one word. When possible, avoid using this term by replacing it with a specific number.

A lot of cookies were sold at the bake sale.
Fifty dozen cookies were sold at the bake sale. (more specific)

▶ **Exercise 1** Write *C* for correct or *I* for incorrect to indicate whether the word or words in italics are used correctly.

___I___   Our class has *all ready* studied about South America.

_____ **1.** Dana was a member of every club *except* the Chess Club.

_____ **2.** Our teacher was glad to see us *all together* at the pep rally.

_____ **3.** I had *all ready* been there once before.

_____ **4.** Sheila gracefully *accepted* the second-place award.

_____ **5.** We were *altogether* amazed by the news.

_____ **6.** Everyone boarded the bus *accept* David.

_____ **7.** My solo was *already* for the concert.

_____ **8.** The apartment was *altogether* too small for the four of us.

_____ **9.** I like everything on my pizza *except* anchovies.

_____ **10.** *Altogether* the coins totaled one dollar.

_____ **11.** I was allergic to the flowers, so I could not *accept* them.

_____ **12.** Jonah looked happy to *except* the new bike.

_____ **13.** The fire was *already* out by the time the firefighters arrived.

_____ **14.** Our costumes were *all ready* for the play.

_____ **15.** I gathered my friends *all together* to tell them the news.

▶ **Exercise 2** **Underline the word in parentheses that best completes each sentence.**

I really can't eat anything (accept, <u>except</u>) soup.

1. We were (altogether, all together) unprepared for the test.

2. I was (already, all ready) for the dance.

3. Vanessa could not (accept, except) the expensive gift.

4. James bought (a lot, thirty) of the videos.

5. The last time we were (altogether, all together) was two years ago.

6. The baseball card I bought has (already, all ready) increased in value.

7. Everyone (accept, except) Roy went to the soccer game.

8. (A lot, Hundreds) of people watched the parade.

9. Our plans for the trip were (altogether, all together) ruined by the weather.

10. The piano was delivered and is (already, all ready) to be played.

▶ **Writing Link** **Write four sentences about what you do in the morning before school. Include the words *accept, except, all ready, already,* and *altogether.***

_____

_____

_____

_____

_____

_____

Usage

Lesson 69
Usage: *beside* to *less*

---

beside, besides *Beside* means "next to." *Besides* means "in addition to."

The hammer was lying **beside** the toolbox.
Besides carrots, the baby likes peas.

between, among Use *between* for two people or things. Use *among* when talking about groups of three or more.

Echo Avenue is **between** Dancer and Foothill.   It was flying **among** the stars.

bring, take *Bring* means "to carry from a distant place to a closer one." *Take* means "to carry from a nearby place to a distant one."

Bring dessert to the family dinner.   **Take** this letter to the post office.

can, may *Can* indicates ability. *May* expresses permission or possibility.

We **can** finish this Monday.   You **may** work on this inside.   It **may** rain.

choose, chose *Choose* means "to select." *Chose* is the past tense of *choose* and means "selected."

Choose your friends wisely.   Yana **chose** to participate in the debate.

fewer, less Use *fewer* with nouns that can be counted. Use *less* with nouns that cannot be counted.

There were **fewer** hot days this summer.   Traffic is **less** congested tonight.

▶ **Exercise 1** Write *C* for correct or *I* for incorrect to indicate whether the word in italics is used correctly.

___C___   Migration *can* be an interesting topic.

_____ **1.** You probably know that birds are *among* the many animals that migrate.

_____ **2.** Some fish migrate *between* fresh and salt water during their lives.

_____ **3.** Salmon *choose* to live at sea but migrate to fresh water for breeding.

_____ **4.** The European eel lives in fresh water but *brings* to the sea to breed, spawn, and hatch.

_____ **5.** Humpback whales spend summers in polar oceans and in winter *may* move to tropical waters.

_____ **6.** Some land mammals *may* also migrate.

_____ 7. The caribou of Alaska move *among* the tundra and the boreal forest.

_____ 8. Food is available in the tundra during summer, but when the winter *brings* deep snow, the caribou move south.

_____ 9. Some insects also move long distances in search of *less* snow.

_____ 10. In the fall, the North American monarch butterfly *chooses* groves in California, Florida, or Mexico.

_____ 11. A migrating animal *may* expend much energy if the weather is bad.

_____ 12. Migrating birds cannot *bring* their young to the new habitat when they go unless the young birds are strong fliers.

_____ 13. *Among* some species the sun, the moon, and the stars are used for navigation.

_____ 14. Others rely on landscape features, such as rivers or mountain ranges, to *take* them to their distant destinations.

_____ 15. *Beside* these travel aids, some animals are guided by changes in temperature, moisture, and wind direction.

▶ **Exercise 2 Underline the word in parentheses that best completes each sentence.**

There are other interesting behaviors of animals (beside, <u>besides</u>) migration.

1. (Among, Between) these special behaviors is hibernation.

2. You (can, may) study hibernation for your project if you like.

3. Animals do not (choose, chose) to reach this inactive, sleeplike state on their own.

4. (Beside, Besides) the animal's body temperature being lower than normal, its heartbeat and breathing slow down.

5. Because an animal in this state needs (fewer, less) energy to stay alive, it can live off fat stored in its body.

6. A hibernating animal (can, may) more easily survive a harsh winter when food is scarce.

7. (Among, Between) warm-blooded hibernators are such birds as nighthawks and swifts.

8. (Beside, Besides) these birds, we find such mammals as bats, chipmunks, hedgehogs, and marmots (among, between) those creatures that hibernate.

Usage

Lesson 70
Usage: *formally* to *teach*

formally, formerly *Formally* is the adverb form of formal and means "according to certain form." *Formerly* means "in times past."

They **formally** signed a contract.
Formerly, the school had been named after the town.

in, into *In* means "inside." *Into* indicates movement from outside to a point within.

The play will be held **in** the old auditorium.   Pour the milk **into** the bowl.

its, it's *Its* is the possessive form of the personal pronoun *it. It's* is the contraction of *it is.*

Its fur is standing straight up!   **It's** a fantastic place to visit.

lay, lie *Lay* means "to put" or "to place." *Lie* means "to recline" or "to be positioned."

Lay your brush down and come here.   Myra needed to **lie** down.

learn, teach *Learn* means "to receive knowledge." *Teach* means "to give knowledge."

Students **learn** to drive in driver education classes.
Who will **teach** the class?

▶ **Exercise 1 Underline the word in parentheses that best completes each sentence.**

Not everyone wanted to go (in, <u>into</u>) the quilt shop.

1. (It's, Its) not unusual to see zebras at the zoo.

2. I asked the school nurse if I could (lay, lie) down for a few minutes.

3. The clerk put the groceries (in, into) the bag.

4. The puppet shook (it's, its) head as if to say "no."

5. Mrs. Sanders, the teacher of the year, loves to (learn, teach) children.

6. My mother was (formally, formerly) a teacher, but now she works at home.

7. (It's, Its) chocolate candy that I prefer.

8. I poured the solution (in, into) the beaker.

9. Some children (learn, teach) by example.

10. The man argued that the animal should be in (it's, its) natural habitat.

11. (Lay, Lie) the baked goods on the table in the corner.

12. The class is (in, into) room three, across from the biology lab.

13. (It's, Its) unlikely that Peter will decide to go.

14. Barb was happy to (learn, teach) the children to tie their shoes.

15. (In, Into) the living room is a picture of the entire family.

16. The dog's favorite thing to do was to (lay, lie) on the floor and have its stomach scratched.

17. Tomorrow we will (learn, teach) who won the contest.

18. As I walked (in, into) the room, I saw many of my friends.

19. We will wait patiently until (it's, its) time for the dance.

20. My aunt asked me to (lay, lie) white sheets over the furniture in the empty house.

21. The doctor came (in, into) the office.

22. (It's, Its) time for our exercise class.

23. We will (learn, teach) how to jump hurdles in gym class.

24. The room down the hall was (formally, formerly) mine.

25. We were there to (learn, teach) how to use the library.

26. The dog wagged (it's, its) tail when we returned from vacation.

27. Doug tried to (lay, lie) on the hammock, but he fell off.

28. We were (in, into) our places for the choir show.

29. The bird flapped (it's, its) wings and flew away.

30. Joey couldn't wait to (learn, teach) how to drive.

31. The car moved quickly (in, into) the intersection.

32. The path to our camp (lays, lies) ahead of us.

33. Dad told me not to (lay, lie) in the sun without sunscreen.

34. Will Meagan (learn, teach) her sister to swim?

35. My brother and his date were dressed (formally, formerly) for the prom.

Usage

Lesson 71
Usage: *leave* to *sit*

leave, let   *Leave* means "to go away." *Let* means "to allow."

Please don't leave yet.   **Karen lets her brother read her stories.**

loose, lose   *Loose* means "not tightly attached." *Lose* means "to misplace" or "to fail to win."

The bike chain seems loose.   **Did that tire lose air again?**

many, much   Use *many* with nouns that can be counted. Use *much* with nouns that cannot be counted.

Many of the players are ill.   **Much of our time was spent planning.**

precede, proceed   *Precede* means "to go or come before." *Proceed* means "to continue."

Refreshments will precede the recital.   **Please proceed with the agenda.**

quiet, quite   *Quiet* means "calm" or "motionless." *Quite* means "completely" or "entirely."

All was quiet after the storm.   **Alex was not quite finished with his chores.**

raise, rise   *Raise* means "to cause to move upward." *Rise* means "to move upward."

Please raise the window shade.   **The balloons gracefully rise into the air.**

set, sit   *Set* means "to place" or "to put." *Sit* means "to place oneself in a seated position."

We will set out the tulip bulbs.   **We can sit in the front row.**

▶ **Exercise 1   Underline the word in parentheses that best completes each sentence.**

My parents never (<u>let</u>, leave) the dog come into the house.

1. When it was time to (leave, let), we said good-bye.

2. (Many, Much) of Terri's friends visited her in the hospital.

3. If the rope is too (loose, lose), the swing will fall.

4. We were told to (precede, proceed) as if nothing had happened.

5. I (leave, let) my brother borrow my skateboard.

6. The library was very (quiet, quite).

7. Jeff found a place for us to (set, sit) on the grass.

8. Sarah was careful not to (loose, lose) the locket her aunt had given her.

9. (Much, Many) of the human body is made up of water.

10. On Saturday my mother will (leave, let) on a business trip.

11. I (set, sit) the suitcases in the guest room.

12. When I opened the gate, the dog got (loose, lose).

13. The teacher will (leave, let) us use our books during the test.

14. The soldiers will (raise, rise) the flag at noon.

15. Where did you (set, sit) my keys?

16. The flowers were (quiet, quite) beautiful in the spring.

17. My cousin and I (raise, rise) at six o'clock in the morning.

18. The band show will (precede, proceed) the vocal groups.

19. Katrina was (quiet, quite) sure that her answer was correct.

20. Trees that (loose, lose) their leaves in the fall are called deciduous.

21. We had seen that movie (many, much) times before.

22. Be sure to (leave, let) the door unlocked when you go.

23. Uncle Tom always (sets, sits) in the recliner.

24. The choir will (raise, rise) together at the end of the show.

25. Because we lacked some chemicals, we could not (precede, proceed) with the experiment.

26. The old house was (quiet, quite) except for the ticking of a clock.

27. (Much, Many) of Janet's toys were lost during the move.

28. Sheryl will (leave, let) for Europe at the end of the year.

29. There wasn't (many, much) gas left in the car.

30. It was impossible to (let, leave) everyone off work early.

31. Our dance troupe (preceded, proceeded) a float in this year's parade.

32. Isaac was quiet (many, much) of the time.

Usage

Lesson 72
Usage: *than* to *you're*

---

than, then *Than* introduces the second part of a comparison. *Then* means "at that time."

Stew is usually thicker **than** soup.
We skated first and **then** roasted marshmallows.

their, they're *Their* is the possessive form of the personal pronoun *they*. *They're* is the contraction of *they are*.

We attended **their** wedding.   **They're** snorkeling near a coral reef.

theirs, there's *Theirs* means "that or those belonging to them." *There's* is the contraction of *there is*.

Those batons are **theirs**.   **There's** time to play another game.

to, too, two *To* means "in the direction of." *Too* means "also" or "excessively." *Two* is the number after one.

Take Blitz **to** the veterinarian.   That was **too** exciting!   Rafi wants **two** CDs.

where at Do not use *at* after *where*.

Where are my music books? (not *Where* are my music books *at?*)

who's, whose *Who's* is the contraction of *who is*. *Whose* is the possessive form of the pronoun *who*.

Who's going on the class trip?   **Whose** assignments are the longest?

your, you're *Your* is the possessive form of the personal pronoun *you*. *You're* is the contraction of *you are*.

This looks like **your** writing.   **You're** just the person I wanted to see.

▶ **Exercise 1** Write *C* for correct or *I* for incorrect to indicate whether the word in italics is used correctly.

___I___.   Famous composers have enhanced our lives with *they're* music.

_____ **1.** Born in 1756, Wolfgang Amadeus Mozart was a musician *whose* compositions live on today.

_____ **2.** Mozart, *who's* career was filled with ups and downs, began as a child prodigy.

_____ **3.** Mozart was composing minuets by age five and *then* symphonies by age nine.

_____ **4.** *Theirs* was a musical family as Mozart's father was also a composer.

_____ **5.** Maria Anna, Mozart's older sister, was a child prodigy, *two.*

_____ **6.** The Mozarts showed *they're* talents on tours in several countries.

_____ **7.** Wolfgang became accomplished on the piano and the violin, *too.*

_____ **8.** Wolfgang, *whose* friends included Bach, published his first works in 1764.

_____ **9.** *Than,* in 1768, he composed the first of many operas he would write.

_____ **10.** After extensive touring, he returned *too* his native Austria.

_____ **11.** He *then* became a court organist and wrote many religious works.

_____ **12.** *They're* among his most beautiful compositions.

_____ **13.** *Theirs* one great work that is called the "Coronation" mass.

_____ **14.** He *then* wrote music for the Court Opera in Vienna.

_____ **15.** Mozart met Joseph Haydn in 1781 and dedicated some of his works to *they're* friendship.

▶ **Exercise 2 Underline the word in parentheses that best completes each sentence.**

Musicians like Mozart often find (their, <u>they're</u>) gifted in almost every kind of musical composition.

1. Wolfgang Amadeus Mozart is known for writing twenty-two operas, (to, too).

2. If (your, you're) an opera fan, you may already have known this fact.

3. Music can sometimes express emotions better (then, than) the spoken word.

4. Singers, accompanied by an orchestra, use (their, they're) talent to bring a dramatic situation to life.

5. (Theirs, There's) usually an emotional story behind every successful opera.

6. Opera companies attempt to balance (their, they're) season with both comic and tragic operas.

7. (Then, Than), there are musical comedies and operettas that are performed in an opera house.

8. Most musical comedies and operettas have more spoken dialogue (then, than) do operas.

Usage

✓ Unit 11 Review

▶ **Exercise 1** Write in the blank the word or words from the Usage Glossary that are described in parentheses.

_____Between_____ the two houses was a large pear tree. (used for two people or things)

1. We will _____ with the tour when the others arrive. (to continue)

2. I like reading better _____ watching television. (used in comparisons)

3. There are _____ mosquitoes this year than last year. (used with nouns you can count)

4. Please do not _____ your wet jacket on the couch. (to place)

5. We were _____ for the group picture. (in a group)

6. Tony will _____ the responsibility for cleaning up after the party. (to receive)

7. I'm not sure that my parents will _____ me go. (to allow)

8. The hammock hung _____ two trees. (used for two people or things)

9. Is that _____ notebook? (possessive form of *you*)

10. Peter _____ his hand often. (to cause to move upward)

11. After dinner we watched television _____ the family room. (inside)

12. Debra announced that she was able to _____ sign language. (to receive knowledge)

13. My culture is _____ different from yours. (completely)

14. The little girl _____ down her juice and hugged her doll. (to place or to put)

15. _____ something bothering him. (contraction for *there is*)

16. It seems this elevator _____ very, very slowly. (to move upward)

17. Deidre is the girl _____ kitten is missing. (possessive form of *who*)

18. _____ I be excused from the table? (expresses permission)

19. _____ some leftovers home with you. (to carry from nearby to farther away)

20. Derek will _____ the music for his birthday party. (to select)

Unit 12: Capitalization

Lesson 73

Capitalization of Sentences, Quotations, and Salutations

Capitalize the first word of every sentence and the first word of a direct quotation that is a complete sentence.

The poet who won the prize teaches at a nearby college.
Alicia said, "**M**y cat likes to sleep on my desk while I'm studying."

When a quoted sentence is interrupted by explanatory words such as *she said*, do not begin the second part of the quotation with a capital letter.

"I like apples," he said, "**b**ut a good orange can't be beat!"

When the second part of a quotation is a new sentence, put a period after the interrupting expression and begin the second part with a capital letter.

"I think you're right," Warren said. "**T**hat man is a local newscaster."

Do not capitalize an indirect quotation. An **indirect quotation** does not repeat a person's exact words and does not appear in quotations. It is often preceded by the word *that*.

The disc jockey on the radio said **that** this is the number-one song.

Capitalize the first word in the salutation and closing of a letter, the title and name of the person addressed, and a title used in place of a name.

Dear **M**s. **G**arcia: **D**ear **S**ir: **T**o whom it may concern: **S**incerely yours,

 Mechanics

▶ **Exercise 1** Draw three lines under each letter that should be capitalized. Draw a slash (/) through each letter that should be lowercase. Write *C* in the blank if the sentence is correct.

_____   "would you like to go to a presentation about Bats?" my brother asked.

_____ **1.** "the speaker is a famous expert on bats," Jon explained.

_____ **2.** "don't you think bats are a little unpleasant?" I asked Jon.

_____ **3.** "Not at all," Jon replied. "They're one of the most helpful animal species

around."

_____ 4. "They're not too helpful," my friend quipped, "When they swoop down at me."

_____ 5. "Ha-ha-ha," laughed Jon. "You two need a lesson about bats."

_____ 6. He said that If we knew more about bats, we'd understand that they're not
horrible little creatures.

_____ 7. Jon claims They help people in all sorts of ways.

_____ 8. "Let's go," he said smiling. "I'm taking you both to the lecture."

_____ 9. The auditorium was almost full, So we had to sit near the back.

_____ 10. "I prefer to sit here," Jill whispered. "this way we're farther from the bats."

_____ 11. She pointed to a row of small cages on a table on the stage.

_____ 12. "guess what we'd probably find in those!" she said with a smile.

_____ 13. Jon shook his head and told us We were being silly.

_____ 14. "My brother, the bat man!" I whispered to Jill.

_____ 15. "shh," said Jon as a man walked on stage.

_____ 16. "Welcome, bat lovers," said the man, "And all others, too!"

_____ 17. Jon whispered to me, "you and Jill are the others, right?"

_____ 18. "Tonight," he continued, "I hope I can tell you some things that might help
you change your mind about *chiroptera,* the Latin name for the bat."

_____ 19. "Let's ask ourselves," the speaker said, "What we know about bats."

_____ 20. "They're blind," Shouted out one member of the audience. "that's why we say
'blind as a bat.'"

_____ 21. The man on the stage smiled and asked, "how many of you have heard this
saying and thought that bats must be blind?"

_____ 22. almost everyone in the audience raised a hand.

_____ 23. "Well," said the professor, "That's one mistake."

_____ 24. "Bats can't see as well as you or I," he told us, "but they're certainly not blind.
what else do you think you know about bats?"

_____ 25. "Now," he concluded, "If you have time, you may want to see what I have in
these cages."

Mechanics

Lesson 74
Capitalization of Names and Titles of Persons

A **proper noun** names a particular person, place, or thing and is capitalized. Capitalize the names of people and the initials that stand for their names.

Indira **G**andhi   **F. S**cott **F**itzgerald   **B**arbara **W**alters

Capitalize a title or an abbreviation of a title when it comes before a person's name or when it is a substitute for a person's name. Do not capitalize a title in other situations.

I listened to **G**overnor McCormick. "I'm awaiting your orders, **C**aptain." Thomas Worthington was the first **g**overnor of Ohio.

Capitalize the names and abbreviations of academic degrees that follow a person's name. Capitalize *Jr.* and *Sr.*

Elaine Hideyoshi, **Ph.D**.   George Johnson, **M.D.**   Randolph Sears **Jr.**

Capitalize words that show family relationships when used as titles or as substitutes for a person's name. Do not capitalize words that show family relationships when they follow an article or a possessive noun or pronoun.

We sent a letter to **U**ncle Phil.   **G**randma and **G**randpa were married in 1946.
Martha's **a**unt is a dentist.   My **f**ather served in the air force.

Always capitalize the pronoun *I*.

Tricia said, "**I** bought my first home!"

▶ **Exercise 1** Underline the choice in parentheses that best completes each sentence.

We visited my (Grandmother, <u>grandmother</u>) in the hospital.

1. We watched as (General, general) Powell told the nation about the war.

2. The sign on the door read Alvaro de Leon, (M.D., m.d.)

3. Let's ask (Aunt, aunt) Mary to tell us the story again.

4. The woman driving the tank was (Captain, captain) Jenny Monroe.

5. My sister has decided to go to medical school to become a (Doctor, doctor).

6. I'm reading a biography of (Franklin D. Roosevelt, Franklin d. Roosevelt).

7. Please welcome Dr. Leonard Adams, (Ph.D., Ph.d.)

8. He is really no relation, but he seems like an (Uncle, uncle) to us.

9. The man in the video about airplanes is (Professor, professor) Ludwig Hinze, an expert on aviation.

10. I'd like to introduce my (Cousin, cousin), Jason Palmer, from Detroit.

11. I suggest writing to (Senator, senator) O'Leary about this issue.

12. "What do you think, (Grandpa, grandpa), about the 49ers?" asked Rob.

13. The city vehicle had the (Mayor's, mayor's) name on the door.

14. My (Brother, brother) is a guard on the high school basketball team.

15. We visited the home of Dr. Martin Luther King (Jr., jr.)

▶ **Exercise 2** **Draw three lines under each letter that should be capitalized. Draw a slash (/) through each letter that should be lowercase. Write _C_ in the blank if the sentence is correct.**

_____ W.S. donaldson is Mayor of a small town in Illinois.

_____ 1. The candidate from Topeka lost his race for Governor.

_____ 2. The president of the company is Sandra Morris.

_____ 3. Mom said cousin Jane will be staying with us over the holidays.

_____ 4. Sean will have to ask his Mom before he can go to the movie with us.

_____ 5. James k. Polk was president during the Mexican War in the 1840s.

_____ 6. Francie Moyer, M.s.w., is the new school guidance Counselor.

_____ 7. I love this old picture of my great-grandmother standing by her car.

_____ 8. The child cried, "I want to go home, Grandpa, and see uncle Bob."

_____ 9. "Will all students be required to attend the assembly?" Derek asked principal Brower.

_____ 10. The new Minister at our church is Ronald Roberts, D.D.

_____ 11. I could suggest to coach Randolph that i try that play.

_____ 12. David's mother had to go to Austin to talk to one of the Senators.

_____ 13. We have to see dr. Wentworth because my Brother, j.c., is sick.

_____ 14. Emily's Uncle is now known as Matthew Brock, M.D.

_____ 15. James Mueller Jr. is the Captain of our debate team.

Mechanics

Lesson 75
Capitalization of Names of Places

Capitalize the names of cities, counties, states, countries, and continents.

Minneapolis   **M**onroe **C**ounty   **A**labama   **F**rance   **A**frica

Capitalize the names of bodies of water and geographical features.

Lake **H**uron   **B**ay of **B**engal   **S**ierra **M**adre **M**ountains   **E**nglish **C**hannel

Capitalize the names of sections of the country.

the **N**ortheast   the **D**eep **S**outh   the **G**reat **P**lains   **N**ew **E**ngland

Do not capitalize compass points that indicate direction. Do not capitalize adjectives formed from words indicating direction.

east of Toledo   **n**ortherly wind   **s**outhern Illinois   **e**astern Oregon

Capitalize the names of streets and highways, buildings, bridges, and monuments.

Lakeshore **D**rive   **W**ashington **M**onument   **S**ilver **B**ridge   **W**rigley **B**uilding

---

▶ **Exercise 1** Draw three lines under each letter that should be capitalized. Draw a slash (/) through each letter that should be lowercase.

Driving up fifth avenue, we suddenly saw the $ilvery $op of the chrysler building.

1. Two hundred years ago, all of the country's largest cities were located in the northeast and along the Atlantic ocean.

2. These cities, including boston, New york, Philadelphia, and baltimore, are still large and important places.

3. Our nation's Capital is part of this string of Eastern cities.

4. However, as Americans moved West, they built other large cities.

5. Once settlers crossed the appalachian mountains, cities began to grow.

6. Towns such as Buffalo, Pittsburgh, Cincinnati, and cleveland were founded on important Bodies of Water.

7. The Great lakes, the Ohio river, and the Mississippi river were natural places for cities.

Mechanics

8. New states like illinois, missouri, and minnesota had joined the union, and their cities

soon became new Centers of power.

9. For example, St. Louis, near the junction of the missouri river and the mississippi

river, quickly became a vital center of transportation.

10. One of the most important American ports was new orleans.

11. However, even these great cities of the Central United States were surpassed by others

in the 1900s.

12. Large numbers of people moved West and South seeking a good climate and a better life.

13. Because of this explosive growth, the area known as the sun belt is now the fastest-

growing part of the United States.

14. Cities such as los Angeles, San francisco, and Phoenix have grown into important

business and cultural centers.

15. As such cities as Phoenix rise in population, others, such as detroit, fall.

▶ **Exercise 2 Draw three lines under each letter that should be capitalized. Draw a
slash (/) through each letter that should be lowercase. Write *C* in the blank if the
sentence is correct.**

_____ My mother works in the Eastern part of our city near euclid.

_____ **1.** She travels between the Atlantic ocean and the Pacific ocean.

_____ **2.** Her company's main office is in Yonkers, North of New York city.

_____ **3.** She spends much of her time visiting companies in the Midwest.

_____ **4.** That's convenient because we live in Cleveland, ohio, near the Shores of lake

erie.

_____ **5.** Mom can get to the airport by driving west on Lake Shore Drive.

_____ **6.** Once she brought me a model of the Sears tower in Chicago.

_____ **7.** Another time she brought me a pennant from the silverdome in pontiac,

michigan, the home of the detroit Lions.

_____ **8.** She has also been to Pittsburgh, in Western Pennsylvania.

Mechanics

Lesson 76
Capitalization of Other Proper Nouns and Adjectives

Capitalize the names of clubs, organizations, institutions, and political parties.

National Education Association   **Republican party**   **Knox College**

Capitalize brand names but not the nouns following them.

Achilles athletic shoes   **Super cola**   **Beanie jeans**

Capitalize the names of historical events, periods of time, and documents.

World War II   **the Enlightenment**   **the Declaration of Independence**

Capitalize the names of the days of the week, months of the year, and holidays. Do not capitalize the names of the seasons.

Thursday   **August**   **Labor Day**   summer

Capitalize the first word, the last word, and all important words in the title of a book, play, short story, poem, essay, article, film, television series, song, magazine, newspaper, and chapter of a book.

Newsweek   *The Scarlet Letter*   "**Ode to a Nightingale**"   *Schindler's List*

Capitalize the names of ethnic groups, nationalities, and languages.

Thai   **Haitian**   **Welsh**   **Jordanian**   **Pakistani**   **Spanish**

Capitalize proper adjectives that are formed from proper nouns.

Italian restaurant   **Korean flag**   **German shepherd**

▶ **Exercise 1** **Rewrite each phrase using correct capitalization.**

Scottish Folk Music ___Scottish folk music_____

1. japanese restaurant _____

2. *The Turn Of The Screw* _____

3. sunday evening _____

4. Parent-teacher association _____

5. the middle ages _____

6. Flashtron Video Game System _____

7. *Detroit Free press* _____

Mechanics

8. native american groups _____

9. the end of august _____

10. *Popular mechanics* _____

11. jamaican music _____

12. mayflower compact _____

13. french-canadian culture _____

14. *Around The World In 80 Days* _____

15. Independence day _____

16. swifty athletic gear _____

17. *Death Of A Salesman* _____

18. late Spring snowfall _____

19. American medical association _____

20. The American civil war _____

▶ **Exercise 2** **Draw three lines under each letter that should be capitalized. Draw a slash (/) through each letter that should be lowercase.**

The film about The renaissance was held at jefferson college.

1. During the reformation, protestants broke away from the catholic church.

2. T. J. was reading a book called *How to attract bats to your backyard.*

3. We are flying on United airlines flight 289 to los Angeles.

4. In Ohio the Summer Season runs from june through september.

5. At the ethiopian restaurant, we had the most delicious pumpkin dish.

6. Sarah's mom supports the republican Party, but her dad supports the democrats.

7. The exhibit of laotian embroidery was a real eye-opener!

8. Have you ever read the poem "Stopping By Woods On A Snowy Evening"?

9. Our cousins will be staying with us the week before new year's day.

10. The Diplomats were primarily Kenyan and tanzanian.

11. The seminar is sponsored by a united nations organization.

12. Our toughest opponent this season will be hastings middle school.

Mechanics

Copyright © by Glencoe/McGraw-Hill

☑ Unit 12 **Review**

▶ **Exercise 1** Draw three lines under each letter that should be capitalized. Draw a slash (/) through each letter that should be lowercase. Write *C* in the blank if the sentence is correct.

_____ World war I began in the City of sarajevo, bosnia.

_____ 1. Hawaii, with its beaches, rain forests, and beautiful City of Honolulu, is in the Pacific ocean more than 2,000 miles West of Los Angeles.

_____ 2. would any of you like to work on the chess club banquet committee?

_____ 3. Who was president of the United States during the Spanish-American War?

_____ 4. "The detroit lions have neat uniforms," Jason stated. "their colors are silver and blue."

_____ 5. We served mom breakfast in bed on Mothers' Day.

_____ 6. Alaska, our largest state, lies on the Northwest corner of North America.

_____ 7. I asked aunt Maria to show me her new Z-Tron Laptop Computer.

_____ 8. "Don't put your finger into that rabbit's cage," the boy at the fair warned, "unless you want a nasty bite."

_____ 9. The man said, "I am sorry, senator Montgomery, but i think you misunderstood the question."

_____ 10. Our School is presenting *The Man Who Came To Dinner*.

_____ 11. By the time March arrives, I'm more than a little tired of Winter.

_____ 12. Most of alaska's large cities are located along the gulf of alaska.

_____ 13. Begin the letter "Dear Mr. Benson" and end it "Sincerely Yours."

_____ 14. You can see grant's tomb from the Henry Hudson parkway on the West side of Manhattan in New York city.

_____ 15. My aunt said, "Our trip from Juneau to Ketchikan was very exciting."

_____ 16. I'm anxious to eat at the new mexican restaurant at bayshore mall.

Mechanics

Cumulative Review: Units 1–12

▶ **Exercise 1** Underline each adjective, adverb, or noun clause. In the blank, identify the kind of clause by writing *adj.*, *adv.*, or *N*. Circle the word or words that the adjective or adverb clause modifies.

__adj.__   The ⟨package⟩ that Joanne received came by UPS yesterday.

_____ **1.** When the time came, the astronauts climbed into the shuttle.

_____ **2.** The field where they played ball was three miles away.

_____ **3.** Whoever arrives home first will put the soup on to heat.

_____ **4.** Everyone knew why she chose engineering as a career.

_____ **5.** Whenever the bike trail is completed, we will certainly use it.

_____ **6.** The elephants that live in Kenya are protected.

_____ **7.** When the sun rises, beautiful colors appear above the horizon.

_____ **8.** The couple looked at whichever houses were in their price range.

_____ **9.** Where we go on vacation will be determined by a family vote.

_____ **10.** The ballplayers went to the swimming pool after they finished their hot summer practice.

_____ **11.** Though the concert was long, it was enjoyed by all.

_____ **12.** Aimee purchased a type of racquet that is used by the pros.

_____ **13.** How Stonehenge was constructed remains a mystery.

_____ **14.** Vocalists who are serious about their singing careers protect their voices.

_____ **15.** Where the tournament will be held is yet to be determined.

_____ **16.** People who drive a great deal are concerned about rising gasoline prices.

_____ **17.** Sitting around a campfire is what we find very relaxing.

_____ **18.** The gift that Jack bought was a surprise for his dad.

_____ **19.** They slept through the night although there had been a storm.

_____ **20.** The clerk will wait on whoever comes into the store.

▶ **Exercise 2** Identify each word in italics. Above the word write *S* (subject), *V* (verb), *DO* (direct object), *IO* (indirect object), *conj.* (conjunction), or *int.* (interjection).

      conj.   **S**   **V**   **DO**
Although Jacob ate everything on his plate, *he* still *devoured* a big *dessert.*

1. The *president* of the school board *handed* the *graduates* their *diplomas.*

2. *Alas!* The *runner* finally *brought* the *king* the long-awaited *message.*

3. The *menu will include* pie, cake, *or* cookies, *but* not all three.

4. *Neither* the art *teacher nor* the museum *director claimed* to be experts on the Ming dynasty.

5. The *Boston Pops Orchestra gave* the *audience* a delightful *and* entertaining *performance.*

6. I will eat *either spaghetti or meatloaf* for dinner.

7. *Katie gave* the *hospital* all her extra *time.*

8. The *partners were* happy with the deal *after* they discussed it.

9. *Hey, both television and basketball* interfered with his school work.

10. *Janice saved* her *friends* some *tomatoes and peppers* from her garden.

11. *Half* of the class *visited* the *Capitol while* the other half was busy at the White House.

12. *Birds* of prey *include* eagles, falcons, *and* hawks, *whereas* finches, sparrows, *and* pigeons feed mainly on seeds.

13. *Whew! We celebrated* after the game *because* it was our first victory.

14. *Not only* are *they* staying at the beach next summer, *but* they are *also* traveling to Australia in January.

15. The camp *leaders taught* the *campers* many survival *skills, for* these skills were necessary.

16. The *divers refused* to give up the search *because* they knew they would soon find the sunken *treasure.*

Mechanics

▶ **Exercise 3** Draw three lines under each letter that should be capitalized. Make a slash (/) through each letter that should be lowercase. Write *C* in the blank if the sentence is correct.

_____ Our A̸unt and U̸ncle plan to visit southern f̲l̲orida.

_____ **1.** The arctic includes the Northern parts of Europe, Asia, and north America.

_____ **2.** The *Los Angeles Times* was full of reports of earthquake tremors along our country's western coast.

_____ **3.** The world's smallest Continent, Australia, lies between the Indian ocean and the South Pacific ocean.

_____ **4.** We were hungry for both Mexican and Italian Food.

_____ **5.** Jessie's grandma came with aunt Katie on Labor Day Weekend.

_____ **6.** Sign the letter "Sincerely Yours," and mail it to 135 Coconut avenue, Honolulu, Hawaii.

_____ **7.** The Lieutenant spoke to Captain Davis about his wish to visit the U.S. Air Force academy in Colorado springs, Colorado.

_____ **8.** "We can choose our friends," said professor Evans, "But we cannot choose our relatives."

_____ **9.** The newest breakfast treat at the wilsons' house was Pop Crunch Cereal.

_____ **10.** My Uncle enjoys listening to senator Edwards because this Senator is both intelligent and interesting.

_____ **11.** On friday, december 1, we will attend a Winter science fair sponsored by the environmental protection agency.

_____ **12.** "I hope cousin Leroy can come," I said. "he always takes us on a Ferry Boat to Staten island."

Mechanics

Unit 13: Punctuation

Lesson 77
Using the Period and Other End Marks

Different end marks are used with the different types of sentences.

Use a **period** at the end of a declarative sentence. A declarative sentence makes a statement. Also use a period at the end of an imperative sentence. An imperative sentence gives a command or makes a request.

Oak trees can grow very tall. (statement)
Start the motor. (command)   Please identify this tree. (request)

Use a **question mark** at the end of an interrogative sentence. An interrogative sentence asks a question.

Can you show me a black oak?   Is that a chinkapin oak?

Use an **exclamation point** at the end of an exclamatory sentence. An exclamatory sentence expresses strong feeling. Also use an exclamation point at the end of an interjection. An interjection is a word or group of words that expresses strong emotion.

What a tall tree! It would take five people to reach around it!
Wow!   Hey!   Oh, my gosh!   Hooray!   Oops!   Phew!

▶ **Exercise 1 Complete each sentence by adding the correct end mark. In the blank, identify the kind of sentence by writing *dec.* (declarative), *imp.* (imperative), *int.* (interrogative), or *exc.* (exclamatory).**

__int.__   How tall is that oak tree?

_____ **1.** Many people consider oak trees the monarchs of the forest

_____ **2.** Different kinds of oaks are found in most areas of this country

_____ **3.** How many species of oaks can you name

_____ **4.** Make a list of the types you can recognize

_____ **5.** If you live in the eastern United States, you probably see white oaks every day

_____ **6.** They can grow to a height of 100 feet or more

_____ **7.** That's longer than four school buses

Mechanics

_____ 8. Wow What an enormous height that is

_____ 9. Did you know that another name for the white oak is *stave oak*

_____ 10. How this name was given to this tree is an interesting story

_____ 11. Guess how this name came about

_____ 12. *Stave* is the name for a wooden slat in a barrel

_____ 13. In past times, barrels were important for storing liquids

_____ 14. Which tree provided the best wood for making barrel staves

_____ 15. You guessed it—the white, or stave, oak

_____ 16. Today, some liquids are still stored in white oak barrels

_____ 17. Even though we have many high-tech plastics and other materials, some products must still be kept in old-fashioned wooden barrels

_____ 18. That's almost unbelievable

_____ 19. Have you ever seen a model of an 1800s sailing ship

_____ 20. Their sails hung from gigantic masts fifty or sixty feet tall

_____ 21. Where do you think shipbuilders found the wood for these great ships

_____ 22. In the forests of the eastern United States, they found magnificent stands of white oak

_____ 23. In this intriguing way, the monarchs of the forest helped clipper ships become rulers of the high seas; after they were cut down, the mighty oaks reigned over the oceans

_____ 24. It's not difficult to recognize a white oak in a forest or city

_____ 25. Look first for its acorns

_____ 26. Acorns are actually the fruit of an oak tree

_____ 27. Crack one open and find the seeds inside

_____ 28. White oak acorns are egg-shaped and about an inch long

_____ 29. Next, check the leaves

_____ 30. White oak leaves can be as long as nine inches—much bigger than your hand

_____ 31. Don't overlook the easiest way to identify a white oak

_____ 32. Chances are, it's the biggest tree around

Mechanics

Lesson 78
Using Commas to Signal Pause or Separation

Commas signal a pause or separation between parts of a sentence. Use commas to separate three or more items in a series.

The top sellers were Chou, Eve, and Mike.

Use a comma to show a pause after an introductory word, two or more introductory prepositional phrases, or an introductory participle or participial phrase.

Yes, I helped with the class play.
For love of the sport, he sponsored several youth soccer teams.
Crawling through the tunnel, the rescuers reached the trapped men.

Use a comma after conjunctive adverbs such as *however, moreover, furthermore, nevertheless,* and *therefore.*

Our school enrollment has increased; therefore, we need a new building.

Use commas to set off words that interrupt the flow of thought in a sentence and appositives that are not essential to the meaning of the sentence.

My brother, gulping his food, raced through his meal.
The Koreans, comparative newcomers, produce many electronic products.

Use commas to set off names used in direct address.

Marla, you have the highest score on the test.

▶ **Exercise 1** **Complete each sentence by adding commas where necessary. If the sentence is correct as written, write *C* in the blank.**

_____ For thousands of years, people have enjoyed making music.

_____ 1. Modern instruments are made to meet specific standards.

_____ 2. Strings woodwinds brass and percussion are the four families of instruments.

_____ 3. Each family by the way is named for the method it uses to produce sound.

_____ 4. Stringed instruments produce tones when a string is bowed struck or plucked.

_____ 5. Yes the vibrating string makes the sound.

_____ 6. Members of the string family include the violin viola cello and bass.

_____ 7. Pitch is changed by pressing the appropriate spot on the string.

_____ 8. The harp an ancient instrument is often used in an orchestra.

_____ 9. A piano's sound is produced by striking strings with small felt hammers.

_____ 10. Woodwinds the next family produce sound from a vibrating reed.

_____ 11. Clarinets and saxophones are played with a single reed; however oboes and bassoons are played with two reeds fastened together.

_____ 12. Nina why is the flute called a woodwind?

_____ 13. Lacking a reed flutes were originally made of wood.

_____ 14. Of all the instruments in an orchestra the brass ones are the most powerful.

_____ 15. The player produces sound on a brass instrument by vibrating his or her lips in a cup-shaped mouthpiece.

_____ 16. Trumpets and cornets their cousins are the highest pitched brass instruments.

_____ 17. Covering the middle range French horns and trombones add color and depth.

_____ 18. The sousaphone named for the March King is a marching band version of the tuba.

_____ 19. Percussion instruments are struck pounded or beaten; therefore it isn't wrong to think of the piano as a percussion instrument.

_____ 20. Drums an ancient type of music maker come in many shapes and sizes.

_____ 21. Keyboard-style percussion instruments include xylophones vibraphones marimbas and bells.

_____ 22. Symphony orchestras use members from all four families; however marching bands use only woodwinds brass and percussion.

▶ **Writing Link Write a paragraph on a concert you have attended or a recording you enjoy. Be sure to use commas as separators.**

_____

_____

_____

_____

_____

_____

Mechanics

Lesson 79
Using Commas with Clauses

Use a **comma** before *and, or,* or *but* when it joins main clauses.

She is now known as a director, but she also acted on television shows.

Use a comma after an introductory adverb clause. Do not use a comma with an adverb clause that comes at the end of a sentence. Adverb clauses begin with subordinating conjunctions such as *after, although, as, because, before, considering (that), if, in order that, since, so that, though, unless, until, when, whenever, where, wherever, whether,* or *while.*

Unless she gives her approval, we can't proceed. (introductory adverb clause)
She enjoys herself whenever she is dancing. (adverb clause at the end of a sentence)

Use a comma or a pair of commas to set off an adjective clause that is nonessential and merely gives additional information. Do not use commas to set off an essential adjective clause. Essential clauses are those necessary to the meaning of the sentence. Adjective clauses often begin with the relative pronouns *who, whom, whose, which,* and *that.*

The boy over there, whom I think you have met, is fourteen. (nonessential adjective clause)
The sculptor who carved that statue has a delicate touch with a chisel! (essential adjective clause)

▶ **Exercise 1 Complete each sentence by adding commas where necessary. Use the delete symbol (ɣ) to eliminate commas used incorrectly. If the sentence is correct as written, write *C* in the blank.**

_____   While you're visiting San Francisco, be sure to ride on a cable car.

_____ **1.** Make sure you're not late, so that we can get started on time.

_____ **2.** Jeremy enjoys camping and hiking and his best friend does, too.

_____ **3.** Because she wanted to be considered for the job, Ellen filled out an application

form.

_____ **4.** Her older brother whom I've never met goes to Georgetown University.

_____ **5.** Where the snow covers the ground all winter animals have difficulty finding

food.

Mechanics

_____ **6.** People need to help conserve precious natural resources, or we may run short of important materials in the future.

_____ **7.** We went out for pizza, after the volleyball game ended.

_____ **8.** They thought they had arrived too early but I explained that they hadn't.

_____ **9.** Although Iceland is a northerly country, the climate is relatively mild.

_____ **10.** Doris Lessing who is a well-known novelist grew up in South Africa.

_____ **11.** I'll go along, if you want my company.

_____ **12.** The woman, who was wearing the exotic hat, turned out to be the spy.

_____ **13.** Any team, that makes the playoffs, has to be good!

_____ **14.** My brother studies hard but he knows when to take a break.

_____ **15.** Before she started on the test Maya took several deep breaths to relax.

_____ **16.** Jenny, whose mother works part-time, often helps out at home.

_____ **17.** The praying mantis which is an interesting insect can be very helpful to people.

_____ **18.** The man, who will be speaking at the meeting, has lived in Thailand.

_____ **19.** My best friend, whose mother has remarried, was a member of the wedding party.

_____ **20.** Mr. N'Funo called on him, because he raised his hand.

_____ **21.** The woman whom you contacted about the recreation proposal seemed very nice.

_____ **22.** Indonesia which is a large country in Asia includes many islands.

_____ **23.** They can sign up for the audition but they'll have to prepare a short speech from a play.

_____ **24.** When the announcer called my name I was so embarrassed, that my face turned as red as an apple!

_____ **25.** My little sister rides the bus to school, and my older sister rides her bike.

Mechanics

Lesson 80
Using Commas with Titles, Addresses, and Dates

Use **commas** before and after the year when it is used with both the month and the day. Do not use a comma if only the month and year are given.

My great-uncle was born February 3, 1922, in Russia.
Great-Aunt Laura and he were married in June 1946.

Use commas before and after the name of a state or a country when it is used with the name of a city. Do not use a comma after the state if it is used with a ZIP code.

They moved to a farm near Mount Vernon, Ohio, after their marriage.
Their address was 19833 Township Road 44, Howard, OH 43028.

Use a comma or a pair of commas to set off an abbreviated title or degree following a person's name.

Janet Adams, R.N., was a nurse at the local hospital.
Benjamin Paoletti, Ph.D., taught history at a nearby college.

▶ **Exercise 1 Place a check (✔) beside the sentence in each pair that is correct.**

_____ Walt Whitman lived in Brooklyn New York.

__✔__ Walt Whitman lived in Brooklyn, New York.

1. _____ Lateesha's birthday is January 12 1982.

    _____ Lateesha's birthday is January 12, 1982.

2. _____ Samantha Slegeski, D.D.S., is our new family dentist.

    _____ Samantha Slegeski D.D.S. is our new family dentist.

3. _____ Contest entries should be sent to 8340 South Roberts Avenue, Chicago IL, 60617.

    _____ Contest entries should be sent to 8340 South Roberts Avenue, Chicago, IL 60617.

4. _____ When she was in the army, my mother was stationed in Frankfurt, Germany, and Biloxi, Mississippi.

    _____ When she was in the army, my mother was stationed in Frankfurt Germany and Biloxi Mississippi.

5. _____ The first speaker will be Ricardo Flores Ph.D.

    _____ The first speaker will be Ricardo Flores, Ph.D.

Mechanics

6. _____ The first performance of the show was on October 13, 1899.

_____ The first performance of the show was on, October 13 1899.

7. _____ Did you know that Cairo, Illinois is named after the city of Cairo, Egypt?

_____ Did you know that Cairo, Illinois, is named after the city of Cairo, Egypt?

8. _____ The names on the book's title page were Emily Dahlquist Ph.D. and James A. Morris M.A.

_____ The names on the book's title page were Emily Dahlquist, Ph.D., and James A. Morris, M.A.

9. _____ The headquarters of the organization are at 190 20th Avenue, Seattle, WA 98122.

_____ The headquarters of the organization are at 190 20th Avenue, Seattle, WA, 98122.

10. _____ The new model started production in September, 1995.

_____ The new model started production in September 1995.

▶ **Exercise 2 Complete each sentence by adding commas where necessary. If the sentence is correct as written, write *C* in the blank.**

_____ The date on the old letter was June 26, 1902.

_____ **1.** You can get copies of the brochure by writing to 517 S.W. 11th Street Topeka KS 66612.

_____ **2.** The deadline is December 3 1996.

_____ **3.** Robert Nikolai M.S.W. is the director of the regional office.

_____ **4.** Gerald's mom was transferred to Sacramento California in August 1991.

_____ **5.** The university is in Evanston, Illinois, a suburb of Chicago.

_____ **6.** The nurses in charge of the mobile care unit were Shelley Ford R.N. and Allan Cohen L.P.N.

_____ **7.** Who can forget the Bay Area earthquake of October 1990 that interrupted baseball's World Series?

_____ **8.** The sign on the door read Gerald R. Kelly M.D.

_____ **9.** It looks as if the team will move to Baltimore Maryland or St. Louis Missouri.

_____ **10.** The First World War, called the Great War, erupted in Europe in August 1914.

Lesson 81
Using Commas with Direct Quotes, in Letters, and for Clarity

Use a **comma** or commas to set off a direct quotation.

The farmer wiped his forehead and said, "I hope it rains soon."
"I wish," answered the weather forecaster, "I could give you some good news."

Use a comma after the salutation of a friendly letter and after the closing of both a friendly and a business letter.

Dear Dad,   Sincerely,   Your friend,   Cordially,

Use a comma to prevent misreading.

In order to improve the wool, farmers select sheep carefully.

▶ **Exercise 1** Complete each item by adding commas where necessary. If the item is correct as written, write *C* in the blank.

_____   Sincerely, Wendy Peterson

_____ 1. The woman at the window said, "I can help you with that."

_____ 2. Dear Aunt Jenny

_____ 3. "They really ought to do something about their roof" said the inspector.

_____ 4. "Some people prefer cats," stated the woman on the talk show, "while others favor dogs."

_____ 5. "I've never seen anything like it," she cried, "never in my life!"

_____ 6. If they get too large dogs should live outside.

_____ 7. Jillian asked, "Who is going to the carnival with you?"

_____ 8. Yours truly, Denise

_____ 9. "There is little doubt" explained the professor "that we will have to deal with the problem sooner or later."

_____ 10. When damaged trees sometimes have to be taken down.

_____ 11. "I want my daddy," the little girl sobbed with tears in her eyes.

_____ 12. Dear Patrick

Mechanics

_____ 13. The instructor pointed and said, "Don't touch that piece of metal."

_____ 14. Before the movie, stars talked about working with the famous director.

_____ 15. I will need to leave soon" he said "but feel free to stay if you want."

_____ 16. Most cordially, Mr. David Marx

_____ 17. "We shouldn't let a little rain stop us" Ms. Montgomery added.

_____ 18. After Christmas shoppers can often find bargains.

_____ 19. "Step back, please," the major said to the man who got too close to the edge.

_____ 20. Dear Serena

▶ **Exercise 2** **Complete each item by adding commas where necessary. Use the delete symbol (ɣ) to eliminate the commas used incorrectly. If the item is correct as written, write *C* in the blank.**

_____   "Don't forget your keys," said Mom.

_____ 1. In place of her Julia will attend the conference.

_____ 2. "Put the disk, in after you have formatted it" the teacher suggested.

_____ 3. Felipe asked, "What is the population of Puerto Rico?"

_____ 4. Dear Uncle Mark

_____ 5. In case of an emergency, contact the Department of Safety.

_____ 6. "Do you agree with the plan" Corazon asked "or do you think, we should try something else?"

_____ 7. Dad just smiled, and whispered "Let's let Mom find out for herself."

_____ 8. Even though it seems difficult choices must be made.

_____ 9. "I've never worked on a Fourth-of-July parade float," the new girl explained.

_____ 10. Sincerely yours Kevin Conyers

_____ 11. "Raptors—eagles, hawks, falcons, and the like—can be found in every state" the narrator explained.

_____ 12. In place of that one ought to consider this alternative.

_____ 13. "Don't count your chickens" the wise man said "before they're hatched."

_____ 14. When opening, the can be sure not to shake it up.

_____ 15. Nora almost dropped the cake, when she saw the cat on the table.

Lesson 82
Using Semicolons and Colons

Use a semicolon to join the parts of a compound sentence when a coordinating conjunction such as *and, or, nor,* or *but* is not used.

You can use water-based or oil-based paint; both have their advantages.

Use a semicolon to join the parts of a compound sentence when the main clauses are long and subdivided by commas, even if these clauses are already joined by a coordinating conjunction.

Among the most important scientific advances of the twentieth century are telecommunications, computer technology, and space travel; but in no area, including these three, have we achieved all that we might achieve.

Use a semicolon to separate main clauses joined by a conjunctive adverb such as *consequently, furthermore, however, moreover, nevertheless,* or *therefore.*

It was snowing heavily; nevertheless, they left for the holidays.

Use a colon to introduce a list of items that ends a sentence. Use a phrase such as *these, the following,* or *as follows* before the list. Do not use a colon immediately after a verb or a preposition.

These students should report to the office: Christy Schantz, Tony Ramirez, Emily Chou, and Toderick Evans.

Please bring pencils, paper, and an eraser.

▶ **Exercise 1** **Add semicolons or colons where necessary. Use the delete symbol (⅄) to eliminate semicolons and colons used incorrectly. If the sentence is correct as written, write *C* in the blank.**

_____ Glass is a useful material ;it is made from inexpensive raw materials.

_____ **1.** Glass can take these forms fine like a spider web, heavy like a telescope lens, stronger than steel, or more fragile than paper.

_____ **2.** The first human-made glass was used as a glaze on ceramic vessels; but it is not known when, where, or how people first learned the glass-making process.

_____ **3.** Explained very simply, to make glass, use a mixture of sand, soda, and lime cook and cool.

_____ **4.** The result is: a solid with the properties of a liquid that can be blown, molded, spun, or drawn into endless shapes.

Mechanics

_____ **5.** Early glassmaking was slow and costly for these reasons furnaces were small, the heat produced was not enough to melt the materials, and glass blowing and pressing were unknown.

_____ **6.** Merchants soon had a need for glass containers when they discovered that oils, honey, and other liquids could be preserved better in glass.

_____ **7.** There are many kinds of glass each possesses a special quality.

_____ **8.** Flat glass is used when very clear, precise vision is required it comes in the following classifications sheet, plate, and float.

_____ **9.** The strong materials of glass-ceramics can withstand extreme temperatures, strong chemicals, and sudden temperature changes; therefore, this kind of glass is used in cookware, turbine engines, and electronic equipment.

_____ **10.** Flat glass, optical glass, and decorative glass were used prior to this century however, many special types of glass have been invented since 1900.

_____ **11.** The following are some of these types: laminated safety glass, tempered safety glass, colored structural glass, foam glass, and laser glass.

_____ **12.** The properties of ordinary glass that make it useful for electrical purposes are: transparency, heat resistance, resistance to the flow of electricity, and its ability to seal tightly to metal as in light bulbs.

_____ **13.** Fiberglass, which is made of tiny but solid rods of glass, has many uses.

_____ **14.** The fiberglass industry fills the following needs heat insulation, yarn and cloth, electrical insulation, firefighters' suits, and automobile bodies.

_____ **15.** Raw materials used in making optical glass must be pure in order to make flawless lenses for eyeglasses, cameras, and telescopes therefore, the production of optical glass is expensive.

_____ **16.** The shaping of glass can be accomplished by these four methods blowing, pressing, drawing, and casting.

_____ **17.** In glass blowing, a worker uses a hollow iron blowpipe with one end dipped in molten glass she or he blows gently into the pipe until the molten glass bulges out and forms a hollow tube.

_____ **18.** This glass "bubble" can be formed into the desired shape by squeezing, twirling, or stretching it.

_____ **19.** In the pressing method of shaping glass, a hot gob of glass is; dropped in a mold and then pressed with a plunger to fill the mold.

_____ **20.** Both blowing and pressing can be done by hand or by machine moreover, there is a press-and-blow machine, which uses a combination of these methods to form an object.

Mechanics

Lesson 83
Using Quotation Marks and Italics

Use **quotation marks** before and after a direct quotation and with a divided quotation. Use a comma or commas to separate a phrase such as *she said* from the quotation itself. Place a comma or a period *inside* the quotation marks.

"The key," she replied with a laugh, "is having a good instructor."

Place a question mark or exclamation point *inside* the quotation marks when it is part of the quotation. Place a question mark or exclamation point *outside* the quotation marks when it is part of the entire sentence.

Ms. Arnold asked, "Can anyone answer Shawn's question?" (part of the quotation)

Did Shawn say, "The tamarack is a kind of larch"? (part of the entire sentence)

Use quotation marks for the title of a short story, essay, poem, song, magazine or newspaper article, or book chapter.

"To Build a Fire" (short story)   "Directive" (poem)   "Amie" (song)

Use **italics** to identify the title of a book, play, film, television series, magazine, newspaper, or musical work. In handwritten materials, underlining takes the place of italics.

Animal Farm (book)   *Romeo and Juliet* (play)   *Dayton Daily News* (newspaper)

▶ **Exercise 1 Add quotation marks where needed. Draw a line under the items that should be in italics.**

<u>Moby-Dick</u> (book)   "The Road Not Taken" (poem)

1. Model Railroader (magazine)

2. The Wound-Dresser (poem)

3. Twice-Told Tales (book)

4. Incumbents Lose (newspaper article)

5. All's Well That Ends Well (play)

6. The Muppet Movie (film)

7. The Minister's Black Veil (short story)

8. New York Times (newspaper)

9. It Isn't Easy Being Green (song)

10. Dr. Heidegger's Experiment (short story)

11. Home Alone (film)

12. A Winter's Tale (play)

13. Schedules (essay)

14. Leaves of Grass (book)

15. Nantucket (book chapter)

16. Wimoweh (song)

Mechanics

17. Players Vote to Strike (magazine article)   **19.** M☆A☆S☆H☆ (television series)

18. Beat! Beat! Drums! (poem)   **20.** USA Today (newspaper)

▶ **Exercise 2** **Complete each sentence by adding quotation marks and italics (underlining) where necessary.**

"Emily Dickinson is my favorite poet," he told his listeners, "and <u>Moby-Dick</u> is my favorite novel."

1. Did she say, Robert Frost is the greatest poet of our century?

2. Randall had a look of shock on his face as the mayor said, There is a boy here today without whom none of this would have been possible!

3. Do I have to explain again that playing with the deer is not allowed? the park ranger asked.

4. Martin Chuzzlewit, the lecturer explained, is probably Dickens's most underrated novel.

5. The Washington Post featured an article entitled Ways to Increase Your Energy.

6. Where is Apartment B? the woman asked.

7. Go, Panthers! the fans yelled. Beat Tech!

8. Wasn't it David Copperfield who asked for gruel by saying, Please, sir, I want some more?

9. No, Daniel explained, it was Oliver Twist who asked for more at the orphanage.

10. When Mr. Harrison said we didn't need to read those pages, Dawn and Cindy said, Whew!

11. How could she say, No, I don't believe we've met before?

12. I almost fainted when the announcer said, Our winner is Stacy Langham!

13. Felice asked the police officer, Have you seen a little white dog dragging a blue leash?

14. Look out below! Sandy cried as she pushed the hay bale over the edge.

15. What I can't understand, Rudy added, is why no one told us the time of the meeting.

Mechanics

Lesson 84
Using the Apostrophe

Use an **apostrophe** and an *s ('s)* to form the possessive of a singular noun or a plural noun that does not end in s.

box + **'s** = box**'s**   James + **'s** = James**'s**
children + **'s** = children**'s**   men + **'s** = men**'s**

Use an apostrophe alone to form the possessive of a plural noun that ends in *s.*

Holmans + **'** = Holmans**'**   wolves + **'** = wolves**'**   boys + **'** = boys**'**

Use an apostrophe and an *s ('s)* to form the possessive of an indefinite pronoun.

someone + **'s** = someone**'s**   anybody + **'s** = anybody**'s**

Do not use an apostrophe in a possessive pronoun.

The gloves on the floor are his.   Those cookies were ours.

Use an apostrophe and an *s ('s)* to form the plurals of letters, figures, and words when they refer to themselves.

Dot your *i*'s and cross your *t*'s.   No *if*'s, *and*'s, or *but*'s   four *2*'s

Use an apostrophe to replace letters that have been omitted in a contraction. A **contraction** is a word that is made by combining two words into one by leaving out one or more letters.

do + not = don**'t**   it + is = it**'s**   you + are = you**'re**   there + is = there**'s**

Use an apostrophe to show missing numbers in a date.

the class of **'97**   the election of **'92**

▶ **Exercise 1 Write the possessive form of each word. Add a suitable noun.**

jogging shoes <u>jogging shoes' laces</u>

1. fox _____   6. taxes _____

2. women _____   7. vacation _____

3. anyone _____   8. children _____

4. princesses _____   9. members _____

5. Jacksons _____   10. lion _____

Mechanics

11. princess _____   16. bus _____

12. Ms. Davis _____   17. somebody _____

13. nobody _____   18. oxen _____

14. mice _____   19. classes _____

15. player _____   20. computer _____

▶ **Exercise 2** **Add apostrophes where necessary. Use the delete symbol (ꙮ) to eliminate apostrophes used incorrectly.**

Society's needs have led to many inventions throughout its history.

1. Peoples need to eat gave rise to the very first machines.

2. Archaeologists discoveries' of the past include tools that are one million years old.

3. Prehistoric people used crudely chipped stones to form their' axes and spearheads.

4. The inclined planes discovery became the first principle of technology for cutting tools.

5. About 3500 B.C. in the Middle East, the plows invention enabled farmer's to increase crop yields.

6. Its one of humankinds oldest inventions.

7. Theres a device thats found in everyones home that makes use of the principle of the inclined plane.

8. This device is Linus Yales invention in 1848 of the cylinder lock and key.

9. An electronic trimmers blades act as a pair of wedges' to cut hair or stems' like scissors blades.

10. The zippers slide uses wedges' so one can easily open and close this type of fastener.

11. In the 1800s the tin cans invention was useful for preserving and safely transporting canned foods.

12. The consumers problem, however, was how to easily and safely open these' cans.

13. The can opener, with it's sharp-edged cutting blade or wheel, was not invented until the twentieth century.

14. These and other inventions have made peoples lives' easier.

Lesson 85
Using the Hyphen, Dash, and Parentheses

Use a **hyphen** to show the division of a word at the end of a line. Always divide the word between its syllables.

Robert is eagerly looking forward to the day when he can buy a computer.

Use a hyphen in compound numbers and in certain compound nouns.

sixty-four birds   twenty-one points   sister-in-law   great-grandmother

Use a hyphen in a fraction that is used as a modifier. Do not use a hyphen in a fraction used as a noun.

The gymnasium was only **one-half** full for the first game. (modifier)
Almost **one third** of all cars in the parking lot were red. (noun)

Hyphenate a compound modifier only when it precedes the word it modifies.

That's a **well-done** hamburger!   Melanie likes her hamburgers **well done**.

Use a hyphen after the prefixes *all-*, *ex-*, and *self-*. Use a hyphen to separate any prefix from a word that begins with a capital letter.

all-district   ex-governor   self-conscious   mid-Atlantic

Use a **dash** or dashes to show a sudden break or change in thought or speech.

Martin's dog Waldo—he's normally very well behaved—jumped on the table.

Use **parentheses** to set off material that is not part of the main statement but is, nevertheless, important to include.

The container held one liter (1.0567 quarts) of juice.

▶ **Exercise 1** Add hyphens where necessary. If the word or phrase is correct as written, write *C* in the blank.

_____   great-grandfather

_____ **1.** eighty eight

_____ **2.** three fifths majority

_____ **3.** noncritical issue

_____ **4.** self cleaning oven

_____ **5.** dog is poorly behaved

_____ **6.** exteacher

_____ **7.** one half of the students

_____ **8.** fifty four

_____ **9.** all American city

_____ **10.** a well-played game

_____ **11.** preDepression cabin

_____ **12.** postwar

_____ **13.** all wood construction

_____ **14.** seventeen

_____ **15.** selfconfidence

_____ **16.** paper is well written

_____ **17.** two thirds empty

_____ **18.** postRenaissance period

_____ **19.** ex-astronaut

_____ **20.** midPacific island

▶ **Exercise 2 Complete each sentence by adding hyphens, dashes, or parentheses where necessary. Use the delete symbol (⅄) to eliminate those used incorrectly. If the sentence is correct as written, write *C* in the blank.**

_____ Since preColonial times, the black walnut tree has been prized.

_____ **1.** Many people have tasted the delicious nut actually a seed that comes from this important forest tree.

_____ **2.** The husk's peppery aroma caused by oils in the husk is quite strong.

_____ **3.** The husk is, of course, removed—who would want to eat such an odd-tasting thing?—before the nut is shelled and eaten.

_____ **4.** You have to be quick if you want to gather walnuts to eat; many animals squirrels, chipmunks, and other wildlife love walnuts!

_____ **5.** It is work to gather, husk, and shell walnuts that's why most people buy them already shelled or at least husked at the grocery store.

_____ **6.** Some other plants (tomato plants and apple trees, for example) will not grow near a black walnut.

_____ **7.** The tree gives off a poison not harmful to people that kills the roots of certain plants.

_____ **8.** In preRevolutionary days, Americans had many different uses for the black walnut.

_____ **9.** They made a blackish green dye from the husks.

_____ **10.** A pioneer's most important possession may very well have been his musket, and the most prized wood for the gun stock was black walnut.

Mechanics

Lesson 86
Using Abbreviations

Abbreviate a person's title and a professional or academic degree that follows a name.

Dr. Francisco Montoya   Ellen Chang, **D.D.S.**   George Rubashov, **Ph.D.**

Use all capital letters and no periods for abbreviations that are pronounced letter by letter or as words. Exceptions are U.S. and Washington, D.C., which do use periods.

NFL (National Football League)   FBI (Federal Bureau of Investigation)
NASA (National Aeronautics and Space Administration)

Use the abbreviations A.M. (*ante meridiem*, "before noon") and P.M. (*post meridiem*, "after noon") for exact times. For dates use B.C. (before Christ) and, sometimes, A.D. (*anno Domini*, "in the year of the Lord," after Christ).

6:30 A.M.   9:15 P.M.   415 B.C.   A.D. 119

Abbreviate calendar items only in charts and lists.

Oct.   **Jan.**   **Dec.**   **Sat.**   **Wed.**   **Fri.**

Abbreviate units of measure only in scientific writing.

feet **ft.**   inch(es) **in.**   pound(s) **lb.**   kilometer(s) **km**

On envelopes only, abbreviate street names and use the two-letter Postal Service abbreviations for the names of states.

Road **Rd.**   Street **St.**   Avenue **Ave.**   Pennsylvania **PA**   Utah **UT**

▶ **Exercise 1 Underline the word or abbreviation in parentheses that best completes each sentence.**

The man in the *dashiki* works for (U.N.I.C.E.F., <u>UNICEF</u>).

1. The bonsai tree grew to be only eight (in., inches) tall.

2. The (N.A.A.C.P., NAACP) is one of the oldest civil rights organizations.

3. Elaine Howard, (M.D., MD), is the new director of the medical center.

4. Pottery chips from around 2000 (B.C., BC) have been discovered.

5. Suzanne said that Beaumont was about two hundred (km, kilometers) from here.

Mechanics

6. The office building located at 2208 Riverside (Dr., Drive) houses three companies.

7. I'm taking a gymnastics class at the (Y.W.C.A., YWCA) next summer.

8. Rhoda Silber, (Ph.D., PHD), is my mother.

9. A birthday party that began at 6:00 (a.m., A.M.) would be unusual.

10. His ideal weight was between 142 and 158 (lb., pounds) according to the doctor.

11. In (1066 A.D., A.D. 1066) the course of history was changed.

12. Our trip to Houston included a tour of the (N.A.S.A., NASA) headquarters.

13. Joe's family will move into a new apartment on Kingston (Ave., Avenue) tomorrow.

14. The area to be enclosed for the garden was four hundred square (ft., feet).

15. The (IRS, I.R.S.) just sent my mom's company some good news.

16. If you ask me, 10:00 (P.M., PM) is a little late to start your homework.

17. Most of Tim's favorite television shows are on (N.B.C., NBC) this season.

18. The building at 1090 Maryland (Street, St.) is being torn down.

19. The piece of material he bought was only two (yards, yd.) long.

20. Dan and he would love to see an (NFL, N.F.L) game in person.

▶ **Exercise 2** **Rewrite each phrase using the appropriate abbreviation.**

Salt Lake City, Utah <u>Salt Lake City, UT</u> _____

1. 2100 Michigan Avenue _____

2. Mister Alexander Adams _____

3. 7 feet, 2 inches _____

4. 5:15 *ante meridiem* _____

5. Doctor Elizabeth Santos _____

6. 147 pounds _____

7. Hazelton, Pennsylvania _____

8. Arthur Beecham, Doctor of Dental Science _____

9. Wednesday, December 7 _____

10. Frederick La Fontaine Junior _____

Lesson 87
Writing Numbers

Use numerals in charts and tables. In sentences, spell numbers that can be written in one or two words, and use numerals for those requiring more than two words.

The man appeared to be at least seventy-five years old.
More than 650 people attended the education meeting.

Spell out any number that begins a sentence, or reword the sentence so that it does not begin with a number.

Sixty-five thousand four hundred people were at the last game.

Write very large numbers as a numeral followed by the word *million* or *billion.*

The U.S. population is approximately 250 million.

In a sentence, if one number is in numerals, related numbers must be in numerals.

Of the 125 tickets sold, 45 were sold to sophomores.

Spell out ordinal numbers (*first, second,* and so forth).

This is the eighth time I've seen that movie.

Use words for decades, for amounts of money that can be written in one or two words, and for the approximate time of day or when A.M. or P.M. is not used.

| the **seventies** | **fifty** cents | half past **five** | **six** o'clock |

Use numerals for dates; for decimals; for house, apartment, and room numbers; for street or avenue numbers; for telephone numbers; for page numbers; for percentages; for sums of money involving both dollars and cents; and to emphasize the exact time of day or when A.M. or P.M. is used.

| April **1, 1996** | **16** percent | **$207.89** | **2:51** P.M. |

▶ **Exercise 1 Place a check (✔) in the blank next to each sentence that uses numbers or numerals correctly.**

___✔___ LaToya is the third alternate on the drill team.

_____ **1.** The U.S. Senate has 100 members, thirty-four of whom will be elected this year.

_____ **2.** My mom attended her fifteenth high school reunion.

_____ **3.** I read that India's population may soon be as high as 1,000,000,000!

_____ **4.** Six people were waiting in line when I arrived.

Name _____ Class _____ Date _____

_____ **5.** I thought the movie began shortly after 8 o'clock.

_____ **6.** The mayor stated that she believed 75 percent of the voters supported her position.

_____ **7.** You can find the regional director in room forty-two.

_____ **8.** Of the 320 people who work for the company, only twelve have been there more than ten years.

_____ **9.** For information, call four-eight-two-nine-nine-five-zero.

_____ **10.** 19 girls were asked back for the second round of tryouts.

_____ **11.** I think the answer you are looking for is on page 324.

_____ **12.** The airplane was due to arrive from Phoenix at 6:27 P.M.

_____ **13.** She's not the 1st nor will she be the last to fall for that joke.

_____ **14.** The new library has 7 rooms.

_____ **15.** In the late 1980s, the U.S. national debt passed $1,000,000,000,000!

_____ **16.** Carmen's house is at 1345 Wexford Road.

_____ **17.** Less than two percent of the parts were faulty.

_____ **18.** Taking care of twelve hamsters is a lot easier than taking care of twelve cats!

_____ **19.** Sixty-five years had passed since they had met.

_____ **20.** The zoo has eleven baboons, three orangutans, and twenty-one chimpanzees.

_____ **21.** My brother was born on November third, 1979.

_____ **22.** They asked us to be there around seven o'clock.

_____ **23.** Ricky was very pleased with his 2nd-place finish in the backstroke.

_____ **24.** Please take this form to room 68-A.

_____ **25.** Rex's new in-line skates cost seventy dollars.

_____ **26.** The new research facility was built at a cost of $65 million.

_____ **27.** It takes at least 50% of the votes to pass the motion, doesn't it?

_____ **28.** "11 warriors, brave and bold," goes the verse of the famous football fight song.

_____ **29.** The office is located at seven Columbus Avenue.

_____ **30.** Janine has to be home around four o'clock.

✓ Unit 13 **Review**

▶ **Exercise 1 Place a check (✔) next to each sentence that is punctuated correctly.**

_____✔_____   No, I haven't had a chance to see that movie yet.

_____   **1.** "That's the strangest looking dog I've ever seen!" Amanda shrieked.

_____   **2.** At the end of last month, I thought we would be able to succeed; however now I have begun to doubt whether we can.

_____   **3.** Angela, did you remember to feed the gerbils.

_____   **4.** Sweep out the cabin, unplug the refrigerator, and be sure to lock the doors and windows.

_____   **5.** Paul moved here from Portland, Oregon, and Steven moved here from Portland, Maine, they've become best friends over this year.

_____   **6.** The CDs on the shelf are their's, and the CD player is her's.

_____   **7.** The land of Oz would, I suppose, be a good theme for the dance; after all, its such a great movie.

_____   **8.** The positions on a basketball team are: center, forward, and guard.

_____   **9.** The deadline for applying has been extended to Thursday, May 25, 1996.

_____   **10.** Yes, I understand that babysitter's have a lot of responsibility, but we shouldn't have to take children to their doctors appointments, should we?

_____   **11.** The luscious fruit salad contained bananas, strawberries, oranges, peaches, and I don't know what else.

_____   **12.** In some parts of the prairie dogs run wild.

_____   **13.** Was it Romeo who said, "To be or not to be?"

_____   **14.** The skateboard leaning against the wall is either the girls' or James'.

_____   **15.** I'm afraid its going to rain this afternoon before 3 o'clock.

_____   **16.** Unless you want to end up in the water, you shouldn't play on the diving board.

_____   **17.** Send your comments to 345 American Avenue, Room 421, Albuquerque, NM, 87105, or call (505) 555-9872.

_____   **18.** Ms. Ameche said she had received twenty-seven well-written essays and a few that were not so carefully prepared.

Mechanics

Cumulative Review: Units 1–13

▶ **Exercise 1** Write in the blank the correct form (comparative or superlative) of the adjective or adverb in parentheses.

Georgia is considered the ___most (*or* least) thoughtful___ person in our class. (thoughtful)

1. Craig is a _____ runner than Joe. (fast)

2. Florence seemed to be the _____ city we visited during our tour of Italy. (beautiful)

3. Pamela and Christine paddled their canoe _____ than Jim and Ryan paddled theirs. (quickly)

4. Of all the maintenance people, Sylvia worked _____. (feverishly)

5. This is the _____ pasta I have ever tasted. (good)

6. That plant is the _____ to survive a cold night. (likely)

7. The second television program appeared _____ than the first. (bad)

8. Katie's choir rehearsed the _____ song last. (easy)

9. The _____ Miki's family plans to drive is Albuquerque. (far)

10. Sue's essay _____ resembled the example than Will's essay did. (closely)

▶ **Exercise 2** Underline the word in parentheses that best completes each sentence.

Cameron is (<u>altogether</u>, all together) certain the plane will arrive on time.

1. Marta wants to (learn, teach) how her grandmother bakes bread.

2. Give (you're, your) schedule to Ms. Maroukis.

3. The orchestra will now (precede, proceed) to play a new composition.

4. Everyone (accept, except) Joshua volunteered to stay late.

5. Dr. Sorenson found it difficult to choose (between, among) so many worthy applicants for the scholarship.

6. The company checked (it's, its) advertising budget before buying more newspaper ads.

7. (Leave, Let) the lavender material on the counter.

Mechanics

8. Does the committee (choose, chose) the winner of the essay contest?

9. Ms. Cochran (formally, formerly) played professional tennis; now she is our tennis coach.

10. (Set, Sit) the vase of roses in the center of the table.

11. Dennis knows when (theirs, there's) going to be a sale at the electronics store.

12. An-Li says the movie has (all ready, already) begun.

13. The book Janice is looking for is (beside, besides) the encyclopedia.

14. My dog likes to (lay, lie) in front of the television.

15. (Many, Much) of the tickets were sold before Caitlin arrived.

16. Does anyone know (who's, whose) bringing the pizza?

17. Doreen used (fewer, less) ingredients in her sweet and sour chicken than Sid used in his.

18. The skating competition will be held (in, into) Parker Arena.

19. The shopping mall was (quiet, quite) crowded Friday night.

20. Dr. Wyatt explained the procedure and (than, then) began the examination.

▶ **Exercise 3 Add correct end marks. Delete (ϔ) each unnecessary comma, semicolon, or colon.**

Kylee, have you seen ϔ my purple sweater?

1. Anita enjoys writing poetry, but Jean prefers writing stories

2. Carlo's orchard contains orange trees, lemon trees, and cherry trees

3. Take the film to the camera shop, before you stop at the grocery store

4. Have you seen Meg this afternoon

5. Some of the guests were drinking tea on the veranda; others were practicing archery on the lawn

6. Wow Look at all those colorful balloons coming down

7. Can you see snow, on top of that mountain

8. What an extraordinary coincidence that was

9. In the room above the garage, you will find a secret compartment

10. The gentleman with the black umbrella, who is an ambassador to the United Nations, said hello to us as we were entering the hotel

11. Fling the boomerang as far as you can, and see where it lands

12. Though she is proud of all her paintings, Valeria considers this one her masterpiece

13. The directions to the restaurant are as follows: drive north on Lake Shore Drive, turn left at Huron Street, and turn right at Michigan Avenue

14. Did Mr. Hamilton buy a mahogany desk, or an oak table at the antique store

15. That is: an enormous bouquet of flowers

16. The debate team from Garfield Middle School is arguing that the law should be changed; however, the Brookside team believes the law should remain as it is

17. I am taking ceramics, and Judi is studying Japanese

18. Watch out for that snowball, Kelly

19. Where, would the instruction manual be

20. Did Susan, or Roberto, bring the CDs

▶ **Exercise 4** **Write the part of speech above each word in italics:** *N* **(noun),** *V* **(verb),** *pro.*
(pronoun), *adj.* **(adjective),** *adv.* **(adverb),** *prep.* **(preposition), or** *conj.* **(conjunction).**

       N   V   prep.
  Sally waited for Claire *by* the swimming pool.

1. Dexter *and* Nina attended the elegant dance, *but* Alex and Nora *stayed* home.

2. *They* hid their *ambition* until the *proper* moment arrived.

3. Cedric *paced impatiently* while his sister stabled her *horse*.

4. *That* completes our tour *of* the *furniture* factory.

5. *Place* the *silver* tray next to the fine *china*.

6. *She* was introduced to many interesting *people at* the park.

7. Celeste *wants* to plan the party *herself or* at least plan the menu.

8. *Brandon* believes his *sister-in-law* has left *town*.

9. Gina *and* Todd will be attending the *special* gathering *at* Aunt Edna's house.

10. The person *who* sent the flowers *wishes* to speak to you *soon*.

Mechanics

Vocabulary and Spelling

Unit 14: Vocabulary and Spelling

Lesson 88

Building Vocabulary: Learning from Context

Clues to the meaning of a new word can be found in the context, the words and sentences surrounding it.

TYPE OF CONTEXT CLUE	CLUE WORDS	EXAMPLE
Comparison The thing or idea named by the unfamiliar word is compared with something more familiar.	also same likewise similar, similarly identical, identically	His writing is barely *legible.* It is **similar** to chicken scratchings in a barnyard.
Contrast The thing or idea named by the unfamiliar word is contrasted with something more familiar.	but on the other hand on the contrary unlike however	What I'm saying is no *conjecture.* **On the contrary,** I happen to know that it is absolutely true.
Cause and effect The unfamiliar word is explained as a part of a cause-and-effect relationship.	because since therefore as a result consequently	The judge seems *partial* to the debate team from Smathers Middle School **because** she always nods when they give their speeches.

▶ **Exercise 1** Use context clues to determine the meaning of the word in italics. Choose the correct meaning from the list and write its letter in the appropriate blank.

A. a sudden, unexpected desire

B. unimportant

C. untidy

D. avoid doing

E. unconcerned

F. out of style

G. tall and slender

H. bill

I. special vocabulary of a particular group

J. a job that requires little work

K. having to do with veins

L. prove wrong

M. motivation for doing something

N. talk about past experiences

O. gradual increase

P. unsuspicious

__P__ Steven is very *credulous;* he'll believe almost anything.

Name _____ Class _____ Date _____

_____ 1. After we received the shipment of computer paper, the company sent us an *invoice* asking us to pay the amount within thirty days.

_____ 2. That *trifling* problem is just not worth worrying about for one second.

_____ 3. It was fun to listen to the two brothers *reminisce* about their childhood on the farm.

_____ 4. I couldn't understand a word of those computer scientists' technical *jargon*.

_____ 5. Being treasurer of the Spanish Club is definitely not a *sinecure;* on the contrary, it requires a lot of time and effort.

_____ 6. Most of the players on the basketball team are *rangy,* while the members of the football team tend to be husky.

_____ 7. Because they had left a few holes in their argument, we were able to *refute* it.

_____ 8. Tell the captain he can be confident that I will never *shirk* my duty.

_____ 9. A chance to play in the city-wide championship game should be plenty of *incentive* for the volleyball team to work hard.

_____ 10. In response to the *crescendo* of applause, the candidate returned to the stage and waved to her supporters.

_____ 11. Eating too much fatty food can harm the *vascular* system and restrict the flow of blood throughout the body.

_____ 12. When the team went ahead by eighteen points, they grew *complacent* and stopped scoring.

_____ 13. You can tell by looking at his messy room that he is a *slovenly* person.

_____ 14. Don't bring your tapes of that band to the party; their music is so *outmoded* it sounds as if it's from the 1970s.

_____ 15. We hadn't planned to go; we went to the movie purely on a *whim*.

▶ Writing Link **Choose three vocabulary words from the lesson and use them in your own sentences.**

_____

_____

_____

_____

_____

Lesson 89
Building Vocabulary: Word Roots

The **root** of a word is the part that carries the main meaning. Some roots can stand alone. Others make little or no sense without other word parts added to them. Knowing the meanings of roots can help you figure out the meanings of unfamiliar words.

ROOT	WORD	MEANING
audi means "hear"	audible	able to be heard
	audition	tryout where a person's talents are displayed
bio means "life"	biology	study of living things
	biography	story of a person's life
ben means "good"	beneficial	good or positive
	benefit	do something good
meter means "measure"	speedometer	instrument for measuring speed
	chronometer	instrument for measuring time
port means "carry"	portable	able to be carried
	export	goods sold, or carried, outside the country

▶ **Exercise 1** In the blank, write a short definition of the italicized root. Use a dictionary if necessary.

*bio*sphere <u>life</u>

1. *video* _____

2. at*tract* _____

3. *phono*graph _____

4. in*cred*ible _____

5. geo*logy* _____

6. *milli*pede _____

7. *dent*ist _____

8. *son*ic _____

9. tele*vision* _____

10. *photo*graph _____

11. *flex*ible _____

12. im*mortal* _____

13. *astro*nomy _____

14. *cent*ury _____

15. con*vention* _____

16. *lect*ure _____

17. *deca*de _____

18. *chron*icle _____

19. *man*ual _____

20. *tele*phone _____

Vocabulary and Spelling

▶ **Exercise 2** **Complete each sentence by filling in a word that uses the root in parentheses.**

The farmer used his _____tractor_____ to pull our car out of the ditch. (tract)

1. Because Brian is a good _____, he was asked to take pictures for the school newspaper. (photo)

2. The members of the political party came together at their _____ in Houston to nominate their candidates. (ven)

3. If you want to know what the temperature is outside, just look at the _____. (meter)

4. When we watch _____, we see pictures from far away in our own homes. (tele)

5. I'm reading a book about the life of Mother Teresa; it's called _____ *of a Saint.* (bio)

6. Take another look at your essay and _____ it if you think it's necessary. (vis)

7. Our town is holding a _____ to celebrate its founding one hundred years ago. (cent)

8. When the jet plane flew over our neighborhood, it created an unbelievably loud _____ boom. (son)

9. For Spanish class we had to write a _____ between two people; they could talk about anything we wanted. (log)

10. Since the automatic starter on Mom's lawn mower doesn't work, she has to pull the rope to start it _____. (man)

11. Even though we could see the movie, we couldn't hear it because the _____ track was faulty. (audi)

12. I have mostly cassette tapes, but I also like to listen to old records on my dad's _____. (phon)

13. The box says the pet carrier is _____, but when our cat, who weighs 22 pounds, is inside it, I can barely lift it! (port)

14. The _____ table of American presidents lists them in the order they served. (chron)

15. The store tried to _____ more customers by offering a special two-for-one sale. (tract)

Lesson 90
Building Vocabulary: Prefixes and Suffixes

Prefixes and suffixes are word parts that can be added to roots. A **prefix** is added to the beginning of the root. A **suffix** is added at the end.

un (prefix) + kind (root) = unkind ("not kind")
kind (root) + ness (suffix) = kindness (noun form of the adjective *kind*)

Prefixes and suffixes can change, even reverse, the meanings of roots. Suffixes, unlike prefixes, can also change the part of speech of the root word. For example, adding *-ness* to *kind* (an adjective) makes it into *kindness* (a noun). Adding *-ly* makes it into *kindly* (an adverb).

Learning prefixes and suffixes can help you figure out the meaning of unfamiliar words.

PREFIXES	MEANING
co-	with
il-, im-, in-, ir-, dis-, non-, and *un-*	not, the opposite of
post-	after
pre-	before
sub-	below or beneath

SUFFIXES	MEANING
-al, -ly, and *-y*	in the manner of, having to do with
-ee, -eer, -er, -ian, -ist, -or	one who does (something)
-ful, -ous	full of

▶ **Exercise 1** Add a prefix or suffix to each italicized root word. Write the new word in the blank and underline the suffix or prefix.

__logically__ in the manner of being *logical*

_____ **1.** one who *protests*

_____ **2.** not *regular*

_____ **3.** having to do with *grime*

_____ **4.** in the manner of being *angry*

_____ **5.** the opposite of *adequate*

_____ **6.** one who *drives* a car

_____ **7.** to *sign* together

Vocabulary and Spelling

_____ **8.** full of *tact*

_____ **9.** in the manner of being *contented*

_____ **10.** the opposite of *attractive*

_____ **11.** having to do with *sun*

_____ **12.** one who *invests* money

_____ **13.** full of *spite*

_____ **14.** after the *election*

_____ **15.** below *freezing*

_____ **16.** in the manner of being *excited*

_____ **17.** the opposite of *polite*

_____ **18.** one who *plays*

_____ **19.** having to do with the action of *reversing* something

_____ **20.** *arranged* ahead of time

_____ **21.** full of *courage*

_____ **22.** having to do with *music*

_____ **23.** the opposite of *literate*

_____ **24.** in the manner of being *sloppy*

▶ **Exercise 2** **Underline the prefix or suffix in each word. Write the meaning of the word. Use a dictionary if necessary.**

immobile ___not capable of being moved_____

1. unpopular _____

2. postpone _____

3. bravely _____

4. coauthor _____

5. comical _____

6. harpist _____

7. painter _____

Vocabulary and Spelling

Lesson 91
Building Vocabulary: Synonyms and Antonyms

Synonyms are words that have the same, or nearly the same, meaning. For example, *end* and *finish* are synonyms, as are *big* and *large*. When searching for just the right word to use, the best place to find synonyms is in a thesaurus. A dictionary also has information on synonyms and their usage.

Antonyms are words that have the opposite, or nearly opposite, meaning. *Begin* and *finish* are antonyms, as are *big* and *small*. The easiest way to form antonyms is by adding a prefix meaning *not. Un-, il-, dis-, in-, im-, ir-,* and *non-* are all prefixes that reverse the meaning of a root. They form antonyms such as **un**fair, **il**legal, **dis**interested, **in**efficient, **im**perfect, **ir**regular, and **non**fat. Sometimes an antonym can be made by changing the suffix. *Joyful* and *joyless* are antonyms.

▶ **Exercise 1** **Write a synonym in the blank to replace the word or words in italics. Use your dictionary or thesaurus as needed.**

___difficult___   Solving this week's crossword puzzle was *hard*.

_____ **1.** Mei's *enthusiasm* for competition was second to none.

_____ **2.** Eating healthy foods is definitely *good* for the body.

_____ **3.** This beautiful lake is so *calm* at sunrise.

_____ **4.** Their response to the question was one of total *confusion.*

_____ **5.** My throat is so *dry* I could drink a gallon of water.

_____ **6.** The hotel where Christine stayed in New Mexico had a lovely little *patio.*

_____ **7.** My grandfather always talks about how *long-lasting* his first lawn mower was.

_____ **8.** The scorpion *moved* under a rock when we approached it.

_____ **9.** Ray has a *very bad* cold; he ought to be in bed instead of at school.

_____ **10.** Diplodocus, one of the largest dinosaurs, was a *plant-eater.*

_____ **11.** The freeway heading into Los Angeles was absolutely choked with *cars.*

_____ **12.** Martin *thought* about why the character in the novel would have behaved the way she did.

Vocabulary and Spelling

_____ **13.** I knew we had a problem when I noticed that the wall behind the refrigerator was *wet.*

_____ **14.** When Roger first moved to his new school, Jose was the *nicest* person he met.

_____ **15.** Serafina sang her solo last night *very well.*

_____ **16.** Will you *start* dancing when everyone else does?

_____ **17.** The *acute* pain in my stomach didn't go away, so my mom called the doctor.

_____ **18.** I hope you won't *desert* me when I need you.

▶ **Exercise 2** **Write an antonym in the blank to replace the word in italics. Use your dictionary or thesaurus as needed.**

____happy____ Mr. Nakajima seemed *glum* when I visited him in the hospital.

_____ **1.** Rachel's flight was scheduled to *depart* at 4:45 A.M.

_____ **2.** The candidate will be *available* for questions this afternoon.

_____ **3.** The movie was actually *lengthier* than it seemed.

_____ **4.** The *closing* time of the shop was posted in the window.

_____ **5.** What you are suggesting seems *possible.*

_____ **6.** Philip's mood seemed *buoyant* after what he had been through.

_____ **7.** They *believe* the political candidate's remarks.

_____ **8.** Lisa is one of the most *sensitive* people I know.

_____ **9.** Gina told me that Jim's apology was *heartfelt.*

_____ **10.** I couldn't think of going outside on such a *frigid* day!

_____ **11.** Many of the company's activities were *advisable.*

_____ **12.** I was surprised by how *polite* the visitor was.

_____ **13.** The bracelet he gave her for her birthday was very *costly.*

_____ **14.** The goalie on our soccer team moved to a *nearby* town.

_____ **15.** We all felt that Herb expressed his ideas *clearly.*

Lesson 92
Building Vocabulary: Homographs and Homophones

Homographs are words that are spelled alike but have different meanings and sometimes different pronunciations. The root *homo* means "same," and *graph* means "write." *Beat* and *beat* are homographs. You can **beat** an opponent in a game, and you can appreciate a song's **beat**.

Homophones are words that sound alike but are spelled differently and have different meanings. *Male* and *mail* are homophones.

▶ **Exercise 1** Write the italicized homograph's part of speech. Write *N* for noun, *V* for verb, or *adj.* for adjective.

___N___   Sarah carefully opened the fragile *box.*

___V___   I will *box* in the tournament.

_____   **1.** Her dress for the dance was a *pale* shade of purple.

_____   The farmer had to repair a *pale* in the wooden fence.

_____   **2.** Many postal workers sorted the *mail* over the holidays.

_____   Will you please *mail* this letter for me?

_____   **3.** My brother could *yak* on the phone all night.

_____   The *yak* is a large, shaggy-haired wild ox of Tibet.

_____   **4.** A large *bull* charged the toreador as the crowd shouted, "Olé."

_____   The Pope sent out an official *bull* to all his priests.

_____   **5.** Will that sweater *fray* at the seams?

_____   A *fray* started after the football game between the cross-town rivals.

_____   **6.** Walking on the *piled* carpeting was like walking on cushions.

_____   Our neighbor *piled* the firewood along the chain-link fence.

_____   **7.** All passengers will *abandon* the sinking ship.

_____   Following final exams, the students left the school with reckless *abandon.*

_____   **8.** The *slug* slowly crept across the pavement.

_____   Sometimes the boxers *slug* each other during a match.

Vocabulary and Spelling

_____ **9.** The little girl refused to sit on Santa's *lap.*

_____ The waves *lap* quietly against the sides of the boat.

_____ **10.** My best friend, Julie, *won* the writing contest at school.

_____ While sightseeing in South Korea, we had to exchange dollars for *won.*

▶ **Exercise 2 The words in parentheses are homophones. Underline the word that best completes each sentence.**

The harder the wind (<u>blew</u>, blue), the colder it felt on the mountain.

1. The explorers finally discovered the (sight, site) of the ancient temple.

2. Chickens, ducks, and turkeys are all types of (foul, fowl).

3. By the time our friends arrived, they were several (hours, ours) late.

4. Phil was taking his favorite (you, ewe) to the state fair sheep contest.

5. If you don't (need, knead) bread long enough, it won't bake properly.

6. If you can, (would, wood) you please come a few minutes early to help me set up the chairs?

7. I'll never forget my first glimpse of the (sea, see) as we drove over the hill.

8. Finishing a marathon race is a (reel, real) accomplishment, no matter what your time.

9. Don't stand out there freezing—come on (in, inn).

10. Brittany likes to (reed, read) mysteries.

11. Helen should have received that package by now, since we (scent, sent) it last week.

12. Have you ever wanted to (sore, soar) in the sky like an eagle?

13. Sailing around the world alone in a tiny sailboat is an incredible (feet, feat).

14. We watched as the robin hopped down the sidewalk and ate a (whole, hole) fat worm.

15. Jordi is allergic to (bee, be) stings, so she always has to carry a special sting kit.

16. My sister gets up at half past (fore, four) in the morning to deliver newspapers.

17. I'm glad that people can now be (find, fined) for littering the beach.

18. This juice is (made, maid) from Florida oranges, isn't it?

Lesson 93
Basic Spelling Rules I

SPELLING *IE* AND *EI*

The *i* comes before the *e*, except when both letters follow *c* or when both letters are pronounced together as an *ā* sound. However, many exceptions to this rule exist.

bel**ie**ve (*i* before *e*)   rec**ei**ve (*ei* after *c*)   **ei**ght (*ā* sound)   h**ei**ght (exception)

SPELLING UNSTRESSED VOWELS

An unstressed vowel is a vowel sound that is not emphasized when the word is pronounced. For example, in *com-bi-na-tion* the second syllable, *bi,* is unstressed. To determine how an unstressed vowel is spelled, think of a related word in which that syllable is stressed. To determine the spelling of the second syllable in *combination,* think of the word *combine.*

▶ **Exercise 1 Write each word adding the missing vowel or vowels.**

ach—ve _achieve_

1. retr—ve _____

2. v—l _____

3. penc-l _____

4. fant-sy _____

5. attend-nt _____

6. w—rd _____

7. c—ling _____

8. perc—ve _____

9. rel—ve _____

10. influ-nce _____

11. neg-tive _____

12. dram-tist _____

13. mel-dy _____

14. conc—ve _____

15. n—ghbor _____

16. gr—ve _____

ADDING PREFIXES

When adding a prefix to a word, simply keep the spelling of the word and attach the prefix. If the prefix ends in the same letter as the first letter of the word, keep both letters.

un + happy = **un**happy   co + operate = **co**operate

Vocabulary and Spelling

SUFFIXES AND FINAL Y

When a word ends in a consonant + *y*, change the *y* to *i* before adding a suffix. When the word ends in a vowel + *y*, keep the *y*. If the suffix begins with an *i*, keep the *y*.

fly + es = fl**ies**   key + s = ke**ys**   fly + ing = fl**ying**   play + ing = play**ing**

SUFFIXES AND SILENT E

When adding a suffix that begins with a consonant to a word that ends in silent *e*, keep the *e*.

achieve + ment = achie**vement**

When adding a suffix that begins with a vowel or *y* to a word that ends in a silent *e*, drop the *e*.

give + ing = gi**ving**

When adding -*ly* to a word that ends in *l* plus silent *e*, drop the *le*.

possible + ly = possib**ly**

When adding a suffix that begins with *a* or *o* to a word that ends in *ce* or *ge*, keep the *e*.

change + able = chang**eable**

When adding a suffix that begins with a vowel to a word that ends in *ee* or *oe*, keep the *e*.

canoe + ing = cano**eing**

▶ **Exercise 2** **Use the spelling rules in this lesson to spell the words indicated.**

state + -*ment* __statement__

1. *pre-* + wash _____
2. like + -*able* _____
3. reply + -*es* _____
4. hoe + -*ing* _____
5. *co-* + write _____
6. compete + -*ing* _____
7. live + -*ly* _____
8. manage + -*able* _____
9. debate + -*able* _____

10. *post-* + election _____
11. amaze + -*ment* _____
12. try + -*ing* _____
13. *semi-* + formal _____
14. noise + -*y* _____
15. *dis-* + service _____
16. agree + -*able* _____
17. possible + -*ly* _____
18. quote + -*ing* _____

Vocabulary and Spelling

Lesson 94
Basic Spelling Rules II

DOUBLING THE FINAL CONSONANT

Double the final consonant when a word ends in a single consonant following one vowel if the word is one syllable. The same rule applies if the word has an accent on the last syllable and the accent remains there after the suffix is added.

mop + -*ing* = mo**pping**   mad + -*er* = ma**dder**
compel + -*ing* = compe**lling**   admit + -*ed* = admi**tted**

Do not double the final consonant when the suffix begins with a consonant.

color + -*ful* = colo**rful**   kind + -*ness* = kind**ness**   bad + -*ly* = bad**ly**

Special case: When a word ends in *ll* and the suffix -*ly* is added, drop one *l*.

full + -*ly* = fu**lly**   dull + -*ly* = du**lly**

FORMING COMPOUND WORDS

When forming compound words, the spelling rule is very simple. Just put the two words together, even if it means having two consonants together.

book + keeper = boo**kk**eeper   back + pack = bac**kp**ack

▶ **Exercise 1** Write in the blank the new word formed by combining the two words or word and suffix indicated.

jog + -*ing* <u>jogging</u>

1. retreat + -*ing* _____
2. count + -*ed* _____
3. jack + *knife* _____
4. unforget + -*able* _____
5. ship + -*ed* _____
6. war + -*ed* _____
7. shrill + -*ly* _____
8. regret + -*able* _____
9. bold + -*ness* _____

10. win + -*er* _____
11. occur + -*ence* _____
12. light + *house* _____
13. leader + -*ship* _____
14. zoo + *keeper* _____
15. remember + -*ing* _____
16. wrap + -*er* _____
17. busy + *body* _____
18. refer + -*ence* _____

Vocabulary and Spelling

GENERAL RULES FOR FORMING PLURALS

Most nouns form their plurals by adding -s. However, nouns that end in *ch, s, sh, x,* or *z* form their plurals by adding -es. If the noun ends in a consonant + *y,* change *y* to *i* and add -es. If the noun ends in *lf,* change the *f* to a *v* and add -es. If the noun ends in *fe,* change the *f* to a *v* and add -s.

desk**s**   fox**es**   histor**ies**   sel**ves**   kni**ves**

SPECIAL RULES FOR FORMING PLURALS

To form the plural of proper names and one-word compound nouns, follow the general rules for plurals. To form the plural of hyphenated compound nouns or compound nouns of more than one word, make the most important word plural.

Anderson**s**   Montez**es**   doormat**s**   blueberr**ies**
sister**s**-in-law   secretar**ies** of defense

Some nouns have irregular plural forms.

geese   mice   teeth   children   oxen

Some nouns have the same singular and plural forms.

deer   sheep   fish   antelope

▶ **Exercise 2   Write in the blank the plural form of each word.**

brother-in-law   <u>brothers-in-law</u>

1. notch _____

2. buzz _____

3. box _____

4. baby _____

5. studio _____

6. shelf _____

7. giraffe _____

8. belief _____

9. video _____

10. life _____

11. self _____

12. Morris _____

13. passer-by _____

14. goose _____

15. antelope _____

16. head of state _____

17. sheep _____

18. strawberry _____

Vocabulary and Spelling

Name _____ Class _____ Date _____

Unit 14 Review: Building Vocabulary

▶ **Exercise 1** Underline the word or words in parentheses that correctly complete the sentence. Use a dictionary if necessary.

Cara's favorite class is (<u>biology</u>, biography).

1. (*Post, pre*) *meridiem* means "after noon."

2. The United States (exports, imports) grain to Russia.

3. A metronome, ticking rhythmically, helped the piano student keep the music's (beat, beet) consistent.

4. Lynn, a law student, carries class notes in a leather (scolex, portfolio).

5. The postal worker delivers our (male, mail) in the afternoons.

6. Dixie's shovel and (pail, pale) lay abandoned in the hot sand.

7. Did you test the car's (breaks, brakes)?

8. Because they cosigned the bank papers for a loan, (one, both) of them will have to pay it back.

▶ **Exercise 2** Write a synonym and an antonym for each word. Use your dictionary or thesaurus as needed.

WORD	SYNONYM	ANTONYM
remember	recall	forget
1. few	_____	_____
2. choose	_____	_____
3. delight	_____	_____
4. dirty	_____	_____
5. disorder	_____	_____
6. labor	_____	_____
7. assist	_____	_____
8. foolish	_____	_____

Vocabulary and Spelling

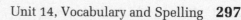

9. true   _____   _____

10. common   _____   _____

11. boring   _____   _____

12. useless   _____   _____

13. merry   _____   _____

14. inspire   _____   _____

15. avoid   _____   _____

16. courage   _____   _____

17. steady   _____   _____

18. bold   _____   _____

19. joy   _____   _____

20. clumsy   _____   _____

21. morning   _____   _____

22. stand   _____   _____

23. last   _____   _____

24. float   _____   _____

▶ **Exercise 3** **Add a prefix or suffix to the root of each italicized word. Write the new word in the blank.**

____unmoved____   not *moved*

_____   **1.** one who *dances*

_____   **2.** in the manner of *meekness*

_____   **3.** the opposite of *matter*

_____   **4.** full of *beauty*

_____   **5.** below the *soil*

_____   **6.** one who makes *music*

_____   **7.** full of *joy*

_____   **8.** in the manner of *boldness*

Vocabulary and Spelling

✓ Unit 14 Review: Basic Spelling Rules

▶ **Exercise 1** Underline the word or phrase that is spelled correctly.

Our school (principle, <u>principal</u>) has many progressive ideas.

1. We will meet our (freinds, friends) at the movie tomorrow night.

2. Owning a dog is a large (responsability, responsibility).

3. The blizzard (delayed, delaid) my dad's flight.

4. Tamara and Vivian are going (shoping, shopping) for bathing suits.

5. The (chiefs of staff, chieves of staff) gathered in the conference room.

6. Pedro's (sister-in-laws, sisters-in-law) organized a surprise party for him.

7. We laughed when Grandpa's (fishook, fishhook) got caught on his pants.

8. Julius was (totally, totaly) stunned to see his cat run up the oak tree.

9. The song says that Wyatt Earp was (couragous, courageous) and bold.

10. Visiting the Grand Canyon was an (unforgettable, unforgetable) experience.

11. I am sure Gracie will (recieve, receive) many compliments on her new purple sweater.

12. The twins plan to attend (seperate, separate) summer camps.

13. Carbohydrates, proteins, minerals, and vitamins are important (nutriants, nutrients) for the body.

14. Is your little brother as (nosei, nosy) as mine is?

15. The (monkies, monkeys) at the zoo entertained our class all afternoon.

16. Fireflies are (becomming, becoming) very active in the evenings now.

17. Please cut the pizza into two (halves, halfs).

18. Juanita (led, lead) our field hockey team to victory.

19. My parents took many (photoes, photos) when we vacationed at Gettysburg.

20. Look at all the (deer, deers) scrambling out of the wood.

21. The weather has been extremely (changable, changeable) lately.

22. Dr. Berkowitz gave Amad (medecine, medicine) to help reduce the swelling of his sprained ankle.

Vocabulary and Spelling

► **Exercise 2** Write in the blank the word formed by combining two words or by combining the word with the prefix or suffix indicated.

skate + -ing __skating_____

1. remarkable + -ly _____
2. incredible + -ly _____
3. broken + -ness _____
4. mis- + spelling _____
5. peace + -able _____
6. benefit + -ed _____
7. back + pack _____
8. use + -able _____
9. fancy + -ful _____
10. employ + -ment _____

11. refer + -ed _____
12. co- + operate _____
13. dis- + service _____
14. imply + -ed _____
15. fly + -ing _____
16. occur + -ence _____
17. grand + child _____
18. busy + -est _____
19. un- + necessary _____
20. sad + -er _____

► **Exercise 3** Write in the blank the plural form of each word.

music box __music boxes_____

1. atlas _____
2. key _____
3. echo _____
4. wife _____
5. fox _____
6. branch _____
7. audience _____
8. blueberry _____

9. sheep _____
10. Jones _____
11. foot _____
12. piano _____
13. Monday _____
14. son-in-law _____
15. roomful _____
16. giraffe _____

Composition

Unit 15: Composition

Lesson 95

The Writing Process: Prewriting

The prewriting stage of the writing process is an idea stage. Before you write, gather ideas and make choices about three things: your topic, your purpose, and your audience. Together, these three things make up the prewriting stage.

There are several ways that you can find a **topic**, or subject to write about. *Freewriting*, writing whatever comes to mind, can lead you to a general topic. You might also *make lists* that relate to one key word or idea or *ask general questions* about a subject that interests you.

Along with choosing a topic, you need to determine the **purpose**, or reason, for writing. Your purpose might be to describe, to amuse, to inform, to narrate, or to persuade.

Finally, you need to choose an **audience**, or who will read your written piece. Ask yourself "Whom am I trying to persuade?" or "Whom am I trying to inform?" The style, the words, and the information you include will depend on who your readers will be.

▶ **Exercise 1 Spend ten minutes freewriting about a recent event that happened in your school.**

Answers will vary.

_____

_____

_____

_____

_____

_____

_____

_____

_____

_____

Composition

▶ **Exercise 2** From your freewriting in Exercise 1, choose a specific topic that you could write about.

Answers will vary but should be related to the writing from Exercise 1.

_____

_____

▶ **Exercise 3** Choose at least two purposes for the topic you chose in Exercise 2. Determine an audience for each purpose.

Answers will vary; check that the chosen purpose and audience are appropriate for the topic.

_____

_____

_____

▶ **Exercise 4** Write one or two questions that you might research before writing about each topic below.

Topic: Your community's activities for teen-agers

What kind of activities do teenagers in our community enjoy?

Does the community provide those activities?

1. **Topic:** Your school's music programs

_____

_____

_____

2. **Topic:** Air pollution

_____

_____

_____

3. **Topic:** Organizations in your community that need young volunteer workers

_____

_____

Composition

4. Topic: Popular hairstyles

_____

_____

_____

5. Topic: Preparing healthful meals

_____

_____

_____

▶ **Exercise 5 Identify two possible purposes for each topic below.**

Topic: How an eighth-grader can earn money during the summer

Purpose 1: to inform an eighth-grade reader of ways to earn money

Purpose 2: to persuade eighth-graders to earn their own money

1. Topic: An abandoned house in your neighborhood

Purpose 1: _____

Purpose 2: _____

2. Topic: Your school's student council elections

Purpose 1: _____

Purpose 2: _____

3. Topic: Resolving fights with friends

Purpose 1: _____

Purpose 2: _____

4. Topic: Your household chores

Purpose 1: _____

Purpose 2: _____

5. Topic: Fixing something that is broken

Purpose 1: _____

Purpose 2: _____

Composition

▶ **Exercise 6 Identify one audience and one purpose for each topic.**

Topic: An increase in allowance

Purpose: To persuade your parents to raise your allowance _____

Audience: Your parents _____

1. **Topic:** A movie you saw last weekend

Purpose: _____

Audience: _____

2. **Topic:** Your commitment to physical fitness

Purpose: _____

Audience: _____

3. **Topic:** An embarrassing moment from elementary school

Purpose: _____

Audience: _____

4. **Topic:** Explaining the steps to your favorite dance

Purpose: _____

Audience: _____

Composition

Lesson 96
The Writing Process: Drafting

After the prewriting stage, begin **drafting**, or writing, your piece in paragraph form. From the topic and purpose, you can create the **theme**, the point the piece will try to make. State the theme in a **thesis statement** in the first paragraph. Each paragraph usually has a *topic sentence*, or a statement of the main idea, and several supporting sentences that relate details about the topic. While writing, consider your chosen audience. The audience, as well as the theme and purpose, determines the style or voice of your writing. The **style** or **voice** gives your writing its "feel."

▶ **Exercise 1** Create five thesis statements. For each thesis, use one topic and one purpose from the list below. You may repeat a topic to use with a different purpose.

PURPOSES	TOPICS		
to describe	horseback riding	the Navy	painting
to inform	oil	cats	comic books
to narrate	U.S. population	television	the moon
to persuade	*Star Trek*	fairy tales	cars
to instruct	the Civil War	baseball	poetry
to create a mood	coffee	popular music	watches
to entertain	swimming	Michigan	newspaper

Purpose: to describe   **Topic:** moon

To the naked eye, the moon looks like a large wedge of blue cheese.

1. _____

_____

2. _____

_____

3. _____

_____

4. _____

_____

5. _____

Composition

▶ **Exercise 2** Write a topic sentence and two supporting sentences for three of the following topics and purposes.

    Topic: computers **Purpose:** to instruct

    Computers are machines that process and store information.

    They consist of a monitor, a keyboard, and the computer itself, which does the processing.

    A computer disc stores the information for running the computer and operating programs.

1. Topic: your state **Purpose:** to persuade

_____

_____

_____

_____

_____

2. Topic: popular music **Purpose:** to inform

_____

_____

_____

_____

_____

3. Topic: cars **Purpose:** to describe

_____

_____

_____

_____

_____

_____

Composition

4. Topic: the night sky **Purpose:** to descibe

_____

_____

_____

_____

_____

_____

5. Topic: fads **Purpose:** to amuse

_____

_____

_____

_____

_____

_____

6. Topic: a friend **Purpose:** to narrate

_____

_____

_____

_____

_____

_____

7. Topic: etiquette **Purpose:** to inform

_____

_____

_____

_____

_____

_____

Composition

▶ **Exercise 3** Describe a voice or style that would be appropriate for the following audiences.

Type of writing and audience: letter to U.S. senator

Voice or style: formal and respectful _____

1. **Type of writing and audience:** a note to a friend

   Voice or style: _____

2. **Type of writing and audience:** a paper for the American Science Foundation

   Voice or style: _____

3. **Type of writing and audience:** editorial

   Voice or style: _____

4. **Type of writing and audience:** an article for a school newspaper on the gymnastics finals

   Voice or style: _____

5. **Type of writing and audience:** an apology to a teacher

   Voice or style: _____

▶ **Exercise 4** Write a paragraph about a specific change you would like to see in your community. Your audience is made up of political leaders from your community.

Students should focus on a specific area of concern. Paragraphs should be informative, somewhat

persuasive, and written in a formal style.

_____

_____

_____

_____

_____

_____

_____

_____

_____

_____

Composition

Lesson 97
The Writing Process: Revising

After you complete a first draft, you will want to **revise**, or improve, your writing. Revising allows you to improve the quality of your sentences and paragraphs. As you revise, check for three things. First, make sure that your paragraphs support your theme. Second, make sure that your organization is logical and that your details support your topic sentences. Third, check for clarity. Your sentences should be clear and logically linked.

▶ **Exercise 1** **Rewrite each paragraph, leaving in only the details that support the topic sentence.**

1. One of my favorite authors is Toni Morrison, an African American writer who was born in Ohio. Many famous writers were born in Ohio. My favorite book by Morrison is *The Bluest Eye*. It is about a girl who thinks that her horrible life will be better if she can change the color of her eyes. Another one of my favorite writers is Richard Wright. I just finished reading *Song of Solomon*, another of Morrison's award-winning novels.

_____

_____

_____

_____

_____

_____

_____

_____

_____

_____

2. Charles stood on the pitcher's mound, staring down at the batter. He fiddled with the ball in his glove, not sure what pitch to throw. The shortstop backed up to the outfield grass, anticipating the play. Charles knew that the outcome of the game could be decided by this one pitch. He couldn't believe that two of his teachers had given tests on the day of the big game. He wound up and fired toward home plate, pouring every ounce of energy into his right arm.

Composition

_____

_____

_____

_____

_____

_____

_____

_____

_____

_____

_____

3. Benjamin's backpack was full of practical camping gear. We got to our campsite and decided the first thing we had to do was build a fire. Sarah went to gather wood, while Benjamin pulled some old newspapers from his backpack and began tearing them into strips. Alicia and Ted cleared a spot on the ground and went searching for rocks to place around the fire. Colorado is known for its abundance of granite rocks. Sarah's mom joked that she had forgotten the matches, but she had just left them in the car. The last time we went camping, we didn't have a fire.

_____

_____

_____

_____

_____

_____

_____

_____

_____

_____

Composition

▶ **Exercise 2** **Revise the paragraphs so that each sentence is linked logically to the sentence before it. You may have to change the order of the sentences.**

1. Those two have known each other since the summer before first grade. Anila and Katie do almost everything together. Katie's family moved to another town when Katie was in the third grade. Six months later they moved back—right next door to Anila. In second grade, the girls made a pact that they would room together in college. They are closer than any other eighth-graders I know.

_____

_____

_____

_____

_____

_____

_____

_____

2. At seven o'clock I eat breakfast with my brother Chuck. I have a routine that I try to follow every morning. I arrive at the bus stop by 7:25, even though the bus doesn't get there until 7:35. I get up at 6:45 and make my bed before I get in the shower. That way, I'm not tempted to crawl back in for five more minutes of sleep. Chuck and I need those ten minutes at the bus stop to talk.

_____

_____

_____

_____

_____

_____

_____

_____

Composition

3. An example of the proper way to use *lie* is "I need to lie down because I'm not feeling well." I always need to look in a dictionary to see which word to use. An example of the proper way to use *lay* is "Do you want me to lay the clothes on top of the dryer?" I have trouble using the words *lie* and *lay*.

_____

_____

_____

_____

_____

▶ **Exercise 3** **Revise the paragraph below for order and clarity.**

Many animals can perform amazing leaps. Only one is the champion jumper of the animal world. If you guessed the kangaroo, you're wrong. It's not even the frog, or grasshopper either. A special elastic material in its rear legs lets the flea make vertical leaps. The distances are astounding. This elastic material is like a tiny spring. It stores energy. Then it is suddenly released when the flea jumps. This gives the flea its stupendous jumping ability. If humans could jump 130 times their own height, they could jump over the Eiffel Tower! The tiny flea, which can jump 130 times its own height, takes the prize.

_____

_____

_____

_____

_____

_____

_____

_____

_____

Composition

Lesson 98

The Writing Process: Editing

After revising your writing to make it clear, you need to edit your work. When you **edit**, you correct errors in grammar, usage, spelling, capitalization, and punctuation. Use the following proofreading marks.

TO:	USE THIS MARK:	EXAMPLES
insert	^ (caret)	corect
delete	ℰ (dele)	thex
insert a space	#	allright
close up a space	⌒	tele phone
capitalize	≡	georgia
lower case	/	Block
check spelling	sp	nucleer sp
switch order	⤸	the store local
indicate new paragraph	¶	...at the end. The winter...

▶ **Exercise 1** Edit each sentence for spelling, punctuation, and capitalization errors.

We won't be abel to make it to philadephia by five oclock.

1. mike asked Mary to go to a fourth of July picnick.

2. I looked around for her, but she wis not their.

3. The can oe capsized, making Cecil angri.

4. In the event of an emergincy, please exit the bilding?

5. In 1976, he attend ed the university of california.

6. I use A special racket when Im in a tournamint.

7. Hemade a small down payment with the Money he earned mowing mr kahn's yard.

Composition

8. My grandfather owns a store hardware in idaho.

9. Making speeches is the bestwayto refine yor communication skills.

10. I ansered the phone, but noone was there.

11. She gave me a note, which I didnt understan.

12. I remember whne he came to hour school.

13. this Summer I read the book *The Gathering* By Virginia Hamilton.

14. Sante fe, New mexico, is a beautiful spott.

15. Proofread you're sentences closely for spelling errers.

16. Raphaels closet was fillled with clothes that didnt fit.

17. Alishas' house is on Forest avenue.

18. Can you lend me some money to by Katherine a valentine's day present.

19. The subway was fourty mintes late on wendesday.

20. I need knew glasses.

▶ **Exercise 2 Edit each sentence for spelling, punctuation, capitalization, and grammar.**

The (fakt) that Julia cando this amaze me.

1. He past the ball in the knick of time.

2. after a while, the theif came back threw the window.

3. Sym phonic music filt the concert hall.

4. Willie spent thirteen dollors on his Girlfriend.

5. The Smiths bring plenty of of matches whenthey goes camping.

6. Josie and me are coming down this wekend.

7. i wander why he didnt' bring his sister.

Composition

8. John f kennedy was a popular presadent.

9. Did mary called from the university of austin observatory?

10. The secret passage led them too a hiddne room.

11. First pre heat the oven, than bake, for twenty minutes.

12. The countrys landfills are all most full.

13. We had grate time watching the Houston astros.

14. MS. ruiz and I has the same middle name.

15. Maria's Uncle an Aunt live near Mt. Rushmore.

16. There aren't no apples in the refrigerater.

17. After the Midnight movie, they took there time going home.

18. Kalyn and Luisa runs three miles everday.

19. Mr. franklin delivered the letter from mymom on tuesday.

20. Latoya and me explaind the accident to officer Kelton.

▶ **Exercise 3 Edit each paragraph.**

1.   One of the most exciting times to watch of these butter flies is in late Winter and early spring. They emerge from hibernation, and you can see them flew about, long before the leafs and flowers blooms. It is interesting to see them feed on the sap from recently cut trees and ranches. Later in spring, the caterpillars begin to hatch.

2.   Lamont arrived and I arrived in Baltimore on March 8. Aunt Glenda and uncle Leon were waiting fore us at the the airprot. They had tickets for a base ball game, so went strait their and then we all three went out to eat at an Jamaican restaurant called Mickey's. Its a day we'll never forget.

Composition

3.   My friend Kyle and me has decided to start a recycling program in our

nieghborhood. We've called a meeting on thursday and have invited allof the

neighbors. Were going to ask themto save there aluminum, plastic, and glass

containers. Every Saturady morning we'll go door-to-door andcollect them.

Then, with my stepFather's help, we'll load them into his van and then after

we have a full load, we'll thake them to the recycling bins at madisons grocery.

Composition

Lesson 99
The Writing Process: Presenting

After you have completed your writing, it's time to **present** it to your audience. Whether it is a teacher, a family member, or a judge, your audience is something you've been thinking about since the prewriting stage. Your audience has helped determine the style or voice of your writing.

You might present some pieces of writing by handing them to your teacher. You might present other pieces more publicly. For example, you could send a letter you've written to a local newspaper or to your governor, prepare a movie review for the school newspaper, or give a speech to the members of a club. Writers have many ways or places in which to present their work—including newsletters, newspapers, magazines, radio, television, and even the stage and concert hall!

▶ **Exercise 1** **Suggest a place in which to present each type of writing described below.**

review of an art show at your school _school newspaper or local art magazine_

1. letter complaining about a product that was faulty _____

   _____

2. poem about children _____

3. request for information about water pollution in your community _____

   _____

4. humorous song about people who play football _____

   _____

5. research report on the effects of loud music on listeners _____

6. family recipe for holiday cookies _____

7. public service announcement describing a car wash sponsored by your class

   _____

8. article describing teen-agers' opinions of a law that raises the driving age

   _____

9. biography of someone famous who lives in your city _____

10. review of a children's movie _____

Composition

11. campaign speech for student council _____

_____

12. request for donations to save a local endangered animal _____

_____

13. travel log and slides of your recent trip to Japan _____

_____

▶ **Exercise 2** **Choose a form of writing in Exercise 1 that interests you. Write a piece that fits into that category. Then describe your audience and list possible places in which to present your work.**

_____

_____

_____

_____

_____

_____

_____

_____

_____

_____

_____

_____

_____

Audience: _____

_____

Places to Present: _____

_____

Composition

Lesson 100
The Writing Process: Outlining

Outlining is a way to organize prewriting information before you begin your first draft. The information in an outline is ordered from general to specific. To write an outline, indicate your main topics with roman numerals. Indicate supporting details with capital letters. If you subdivide your supporting details, use regular numbers. If a main topic has subtopics, there must be at least two subtopics. If you divide a subtopic, there must be at least two divisions. An outline of an essay about how to plan a party might begin like this:

I. Things to do before the party
   A. Send invitations
   B. Buy food
      1. Pizza for ten
      2. Plenty of soft drinks
II. Things to do after the party
   A. Take friends home
   B. Clean up

▶ **Exercise 1 Reorganize the topics in the outline so that they are in the proper order.**

I. I want to develop better student/adult relations
   A. Why I am running for student council
      1. Redecorate cafeteria
      2. Student/teacher mentor program
   B. Put more student artwork in halls
      1. I want to make school more cheerful
      2. Student suggestion box in office

_____

_____

_____

_____

_____

_____

_____

_____

_____

▶ **Exercise 2 Organize the following topics and details into an outline about Antarctica.**

Rarely above 32° F (O° C)
World's lowest temperature
  recorded here in 1983
Size
Larger than either Europe
  or Australia

Plants and animals
Large enough to be considered a continent
Coastal waters have large numbers of penguins,
seals, and whales
Temperature
Interior has only a few small plants and insects

_____

_____

_____

_____

_____

_____

_____

_____

▶ **Exercise 3 Prewrite for 10 minutes about a place you have visited. Then construct an organized outline from your notes.**

_____

_____

_____

_____

_____

_____

_____

_____

_____

_____

_____

Composition

Lesson 101
Writing Effective Sentences

To capture and keep your reader's attention, you need to use a variety of sentence types in your writing. Vary the length of your sentences by making some long and some short. This helps to create a sound and a rhythm in your writing that will hold your reader's interest. Too many short sentences make your writing sound choppy. Too many long sentences make your writing harder to follow. Also, vary the order of words and phrases in sentences. Instead of always starting with the subject and verb, try starting with a phrase. You can also create variety by combining two sentences that express the same idea into one sentence.

Most of your sentences will be in the **active voice** with the subject performing the action. For example, **"Hal baked the cake"** is in the active voice. Sentences written in the **passive voice** have less direct action: **"The cake was baked by Hal."** Both examples give the same information, but the sentence written in the active voice is more direct and more interesting than the one written in the passive voice. Generally, use passive voice only when you do not know or do not want to state who or what is performing the action.

▶ **Exercise 1 Rewrite each sentence. Add details and use active voice to make each sentence more interesting.**

The present was given to me by my aunt. <u>Aunt Carlotta gave me a copy of my favorite book,</u>

<u>autographed by the author.</u>

1. Matt and his dad go on vacation together.

_____

_____

2. Principal Hoffman had been tricked.

_____

_____

3. The bulletin board fell down from the wall.

_____

_____

Composition

4. Alton works on computers.

_____

_____

5. The Beatles were a band that had many hit songs.

_____

_____

6. Janet is employed at a coffee house.

_____

_____

7. The house lights were turned on by Lucinda.

_____

_____

8. The new year was celebrated by all of us.

_____

_____

9. Gabriel plays guitar.

_____

_____

10. The pilot amused the passengers.

_____

_____

▶ **Exercise 2** **In each sentence determine whether the verb is in the active voice or in the passive voice. Rewrite the sentence to be in the opposite voice.**

Sixteen candles decorated the cake. _active; The cake was decorated with sixteen candles._

1. The letter was written by Yori. _____

2. The painting was stolen by the thief. _____

3. The car was driven by Frederick. _____

4. Anthony was hit by a car. _____

5. Jeanine worked on her paper. _____

6. The glasses were broken by the server. _____

7. He put the clothes there last week. _____

8. Mr. Hall teaches history. _____

9. The gift was accepted by Tricia. _____

10. Mike figured out the strategy. _____

11. The soldiers attacked the fort. _____

12. Alvin broke the compass. _____

13. Aretha paddled the canoe down the river. _____

_____

14. The radio was turned on by Veronica. _____

15. The kiln was fired by Mrs. Pei. _____

▶ **Exercise 3** **Combine each set of three sentences to make one sentence that is more effective.**

   a. All living things are made of cells.
   b. Protozoans are single-celled animals.
   c. Humans have millions of cells.

Living things can be single-celled, like protozoans, or they can have many millions of cells like humans.

1. a. Looking for fossils is fun.
   b. Fossils can be thousands of years old.
   c. Fossils are the remains of ancient animals and plants.

_____

_____

2. a. Newspapers are filled with information.
   b. Most newspapers cost less than a dollar.
   c. I like reading newspapers.

_____

_____

Composition

3. a. Cars are a convenient form of transportation.
   b. Cars emit exhaust.
   c. Exhaust from cars causes air pollution.

_____

_____

4. a. Twelve people volunteered.
   b. Six said they could work part time.
   c. Six said they could work full time.

_____

_____

5. a. I turn on the radio every day.
   b. There are many radio stations.
   c. I like to listen to rock music.

_____

6. a. I want to buy a yearbook.
   b. The yearbooks are ten dollars this year.
   c. I've been saving money.

_____

7. a. My friend's name is Roscoe.
   b. We're going to the concert.
   c. We were able to get front-row seats.

_____

8. a. On Saturday, I have to baby-sit for my brother.
   b. She invited me to the dance Saturday.
   c. How can I tell her?

_____

_____

9. a. My dog's name is Big Ben.
   b. He loves to swim.
   c. Big Ben is a golden retriever.

_____

10. a. Many people suffer from stress.
   b. Stress causes heart disease.
   c. High blood pressure can be a sign of stress.

_____

Composition

Lesson 102
Building Paragraphs

Sentences in a paragraph can be arranged in different ways. Chronological order places events in the order in which they happened. Spatial order is the way that objects appear and relate to each other, as in a room or on a street. Compare/contrast order shows similarities and differences between objects or ideas.

The following paragraphs use the same idea, but the first uses compare/contrast order, the second uses spatial order, and the third uses chronological order.

I had trouble deciding between the two shirts. I liked the first shirt because it was my favorite color and fit nicely. However, it was just too expensive. The second shirt was five dollars cheaper and almost as nice as the first, so I bought it instead.

The pullover shirt I bought has swirls of white and blue on a red background. It has a blue knitted collar and short sleeves with blue knitted cuffs. At the neckline are three white buttons.

Before I buy a new shirt, I follow a special routine. First, I look for at least three shirts I want to try on. Then I go back to the dressing room and put each one on in front of the mirror. After I've done that, I ask my friend to give me his opinion.

▶ **Exercise 1** **Identify the type of order used in each sentence. Write *CC* for compare/contrast order, *S* for spatial order, or *CH* for chronological order.**

___CH___ Sew the shoulder seams before the side seams.

_____ 1. Sports cars are better than luxury cars when it comes to performance.

_____ 2. While Mel's place was just next door, the only way to get there from here was down the stairs and around the fence.

_____ 3. The lake was covered with so many geese that we had trouble seeing the tiny rowboat.

_____ 4. On Tuesday, the council voted on the referendum, but it was not until Friday that they received the court order.

_____ 5. In the entrance to the museum sat a large marble statue surrounded by gilded paintings.

_____ 6. The offices of both Findlay and Brown are run like well-oiled machines.

_____ 7. He was born in 1922, which was before the Great Depression.

_____ 8. Evergreen trees stay green all year, but deciduous trees lose their leaves in winter.

Composition

_____ **9.** First, postal workers sort the letters by zip code according to state, and then they file them in the appropriate mail slots.

_____ **10.** Gale's upstairs apartment overlooked the park, and as you walk in, you get a breathtaking view through her picture window.

▶ Exercise 2 **Number the following sentences in chronological order.**

_____ Explain to her that you want the seats my brother reserved for us.

_____ Follow these steps when you call to order our concert tickets.

_____ When she comes to the phone, tell her that I told you to call.

_____ Call and let me know when we can pick them up.

_____ Ask to speak to Rachel.

_____ Call the first of the three numbers listed in the phone book.

▶ Exercise 3 **Use compare/contrast order to write a paragraph about one of the following topics: your favorite relative, your last year in school compared to this year in school; the effect of pollution on the area where you live.**

_____

_____

_____

_____

_____

_____

_____

_____

_____

_____

_____

_____

Composition

▶ **Exercise 4** Write three short paragraphs about your favorite store or restaurant. Use spatial order in your first paragraph, chronological order in your second paragraph, and compare/contrast order in your third paragraph.

_____

_____

_____

_____

_____

_____

_____

_____

_____

_____

_____

_____

_____

_____

_____

_____

_____

_____

_____

_____

_____

_____

Composition

▶ **Exercise 5 Arrange these sentencers in chronological order.**

_____ These chemicals stimulate the nerves, which, in turn, send messages to the brain.

_____ Your tongue is covered with tiny bumps, small ones toward the front, larger ones toward the back.

_____ When you eat something, chemicals in the food touch the tips of the nerve endings in the taste buds.

_____ The experience of flavor is created by the combination of taste and the smell of the food.

_____ Inside these approximately 9000 bumps are tiny bundles of nerves called taste buds.

Composition

Lesson 103
Paragraph Ordering

Revising a first draft includes checking the unity, or **coherence**, of paragraphs. Open each paragraph with a topic sentence that states the main idea. Follow it with supporting sentences that back up that idea. Connect the sentences in a clear and logical way. Use words and phrases called **transitions** to link the sentences so they flow naturally. The following are some common transition words: *and, also, but, however, next, after, then, finally, since, therefore.* Sometimes you can organize multiple points using words like *first, second,* or *on the other hand.* Paragraphs in a paper should be coherent in the same way sentences in a paragraph should be coherent. Use transitions to link paragraphs.

▶ **Exercise 1** Underline the sentence in each paragraph that should be the topic sentence.

1. First, ask your neighbors if they have any odd jobs you can do. You might be able to help a neighbor with a garden, baby-sit, or take care of someone's pet while he or she is on vacation. Another way to earn money is to have a yard sale. If you are short on cash during your summer vacation, here are some ways to earn money. You and your friends can gather old clothes or household items that are no longer needed and share the profits from the sale.

2. The first stage is infancy. The infancy stage is the first year of a child's life. In the second stage, the child is called a toddler. The toddler stage is from ages one to three. Between the ages of three and five, a child is called a preschooler. There are three stages of early childhood.

3. I have to decide whether to join the volleyball team or the basketball team. I can't play on both teams because the teams practice on the same days. I played on the volleyball team last year, so it might be fun to do something different this year. Before the end of the day, I have to make a tough decision. On the other hand, I know more people on the volleyball team.

Composition

Exercise 2 Write three cohesive and unified paragraphs, using the given facts. Add details to make each paragraph more interesting.

1. Jerome does volunteer work.
   He volunteers at the local children's hospital.
   He helps to plan play-time activities for the young children.
   Donnella is his favorite patient.

   _____

   _____

   _____

   _____

   _____

   _____

   _____

2. Teresa and I are planning a surprise party.
   Kira will be twelve this Saturday.
   Teresa is going to take her somewhere.
   We're going to decorate the house while she's gone.
   She'll be surprised when she walks through the door.
   Everyone will be hiding inside the house.

   _____

   _____

   _____

   _____

   _____

   _____

   _____

   _____

   _____

Composition

3. To find out what's happening in the world, I can read the newspaper or watch the news on television.

I can't decide whether I get more information from the newspaper or television.

On television, I can see what things look like.

News stories are shorter on television because the time is limited.

Newspapers give me more information because they don't have to worry about time.

I can read newspapers whenever I want to during the day.

_____

_____

_____

_____

_____

_____

_____

_____

_____

_____

_____

▶ **Exercise 3 Each sentence below represents the topic sentence of a paragraph about Martin's Lake. Check the sentence that best continues the story started in paragraph one.**

Paragraph One: Nothing cools me off better on a hot summer day than bobbing around in Martin's Lake. Let the sun burn off my pale shell, as long as there's cool refreshing pond water to rinse away the heat!

_____ In the winter, dozens of ice skaters glide across the lake or hover around the fire barrel.

_____ Citizens of Martinsville enjoy night fishing at the lake.

_____ My summer romance with Martin's Lake began when I was twelve.

_____ A gaggle of geese honk out their warnings to lake visitors.

Composition

▶ **Exercise 4** Write a two-paragraph announcement about an upcoming event at your school. Make sure details are presented in proper chronological order and that paragraphs one and two are clearly linked.

_____

_____

_____

_____

_____

_____

_____

_____

_____

_____

_____

_____

_____

_____

_____

_____

_____

_____

_____

_____

_____

_____

_____

_____

Lesson 104
Personal Letters: Formal

A **personal letter** is often a letter to a friend or relative, an invitation, or a thank-you note. Different situations call for different kinds of personal letters. A letter to an adult relative or an adult acquaintance will probably have a different tone and style of writing than a letter to a friend or someone your own age. A letter to an adult is usually more formal. Avoid slang when writing formal letters, and show respect for your reader. However, a formal letter does not have to be uninteresting. Use descriptive language in a formal letter, and include some personal information. If you are writing a thank-you note, include a detailed description of the gift and what you intend to do with it.

Dear Uncle Otis,

Thank you for your wonderful birthday present. The portable stereo you gave me is something I have been hoping for. I plan on taking it to my aerobics class to replace the old radio my instructor uses. I can also take it outside while I practice basketball.

I hope that you and Aunt Florence are doing well, and I hope that you can come see me play when the basketball season begins. I look forward to seeing you at Thanksgiving.

Again, thank you for the thoughtful present.

Love,
Rhonda

▶ **Exercise 1** **Revise the following letter to make its style more formal.**

Hey Grandma,

How's it going? Thanks for throwing me that awesome birthday party. It was a real blow-out! My friends thought you guys were really cool, even though you're older.

Man, that cake you made was so great, and even though I thought the games you and Mom made up were going to be really goofy, my friends were into them!

Thanks again, you're the greatest.

See ya,
Chris

Composition

_____

_____

_____

_____

_____

_____

▶ **Exercise 2** Write either a formal letter to a relative, inviting him or her to a school activity, or a formal letter to a teacher, counselor, or coach expressing thanks for something special she or he did.

_____

_____

_____

_____

_____

_____

_____

_____

_____

_____

_____

_____

_____

Composition

Lesson 105
Personal Letters: Informal

Informal letters are a good way to keep in touch with friends and relatives close to your own age. You might send an informal letter to a pen pal or write an informal letter on a postcard. In an informal letter, you can use slang and language that is more conversational in tone.

▶ **Exercise 1** Write a letter to a friend who has moved to another city or town. Explain what you have been doing while your friend has been away.

_____

_____

_____

_____

_____

_____

_____

_____

_____

_____

_____

_____

_____

_____

_____

_____

_____

Composition

▶ **Exercise 2** Write a postcard to a relative who is close to your age. Imagine that you are on vacation in the town, city, or area where you live. Describe what it looks like and what there is to do.

_____

_____

_____

_____

_____

_____

_____

_____

_____

▶ **Exercise 3** Write a postcard to a friend describing a place you have been to that your friend has not visited.

_____

_____

_____

_____

_____

_____

_____

_____

_____

Composition

Copyright © by Glencoe/McGraw-Hill

Lesson 106
Business Letters: Letters of Request or of Complaint

A **letter of request** is a letter asking for information or service. It is written in a formal style. When writing a letter of request, it is important to be clear and courteous. Explain what you need and why you need it. Be sure to provide the reader with enough information to answer your request.

▶ **Exercise 1** **Revise the following letter of request.**

Ms. Eckhart:

I need more information about that program of yours, the Youth Recycling Initiative. I'm real good with recycling stuff, I know alot about it. I'd like to do some work for you because maybe someday I'll get into recycling as a career. So please send me some information, and I hope we can work together.

Thanks,

Emmett Turner

_____

_____

_____

_____

_____

_____

_____

_____

_____

_____

_____

_____

_____

_____

Composition

A **letter of complaint** is a letter informing someone of a problem or a concern. It is sometimes a request for action. Even though you may be upset when writing such a letter, you do not want to offend your reader. The letter should be reasonable, clear, and concise. Explain the problem and how you wish the reader to respond to it.

▶ **Exercise 2** **Revise the following letter of complaint.**
Restaurant Manager
Torito's
531 Smith Rd.
Lexington, KY 40516

April 3, 1996
Restaurant Manager,
What's up with your price changes? Are you trying to keep kids out? We've been giving you all this business after school for two years, and this is the thanks we get? Boy, am I mad!
I tell you, you better lower your prices again! We're all going to go somewhere else if you don't, and then you'll be sorry when you go out of business and you're poor and broke.
With anger,
Jill and Billy

_____
_____
_____
_____
_____
_____
_____
_____

Composition

Lesson 107
Business Letters: Stating Your Opinion

An **opinion letter** states your view of a subject. Audiences for an opinion letter might include a newspaper's editors and readers, government officials, leaders of organizations, or business people. When writing an opinion letter, your tone should be formal. A good opinion letter also contains plenty of facts to support your opinion.

The following is an example of a brief, but effective, opinion letter:

Sports Editor
Daily Chronicle
1574 Clarence Dr.
Ion, WA 43125

July 16, 1996

Dear Editor:
Not only is Clarence Williams a football hero, but he is a hero in community service as well. One of your writers recently made the mistake of assuming that Clarence is not involved in making this community a better place. Just because Clarence won't blow his own horn, it doesn't mean he's not involved with the community.
Clarence established the Big Red Fund, which challenges 3,000 students in 7 junior high schools to stay in school and study hard. Clarence has visited the schools and donated money for computers and science laboratory equipment. Also, Clarence worked with a local food bank to deliver meals to 100 needy families at Christmas.
Although he receives no media attention for his deeds, Clarence Williams is indeed making a contribution to our community.

Sincerely,
Judy O'Rourke

▶ **Exercise 1 Revise the following opinion letter. Add details if necessary.**
Dear Congressman Riley,
I can't believe you voted against more funding for community parks! How ridiculous! We need more money here in your hometown for our local park. Maybe if you were here more often you would know that. Maybe you can still do something about it. Lots of people and especially kids are counting on you.
Local businesses won't donate money. They say there are more important things to spend

Composition

money on in this town. And they won't listen to kids anyway, and the adults here aren't doing anything!

Help!

Aminah Wilson

_____

_____

_____

_____

_____

_____

_____

_____

_____

_____

_____

_____

▶ **Exercise 2** Imagine that your school has suggested fining parents if their children skip school. Develop an opinion on this issue, weighing the good points and bad points. Then write an opinion letter to the principal of the school.

_____

_____

_____

_____

_____

_____

_____

Composition

*I*ndex

Index